Public and Private Responsibilities
in Long-Term Care

Recent and related titles in gerontology

Bringing the Hospital Home: Ethical and Social Implications of High-Tech Home Care
Edited by John D. Arras

The Future of Long-Term Care: Social and Policy Issues
Edited by Robert H. Binstock, Leighton E. Cluff, and Otto von Mering

Public Health and Aging
Edited by Tom Hickey, Marjorie A. Speers, and Thomas R. Prohaska

The Future of Age-Based Public Policy
Edited by Robert B. Hudson

Long-Term Care Decisions: Ethical and Conceptual Dimensions
Edited by Laurence B. McCullough and Nancy L. Wilson

Personal Assistance: The Future of Home Care
Robert Morris, Francis G. Caro, and John E. Hansan

Robert H. Binstock, Consulting Editor in Gerontology

Public and Private Responsibilities in Long-Term Care

Finding the Balance

EDITED BY

Leslie C. Walker
Elizabeth H. Bradley
and Terrie Wetle

THE JOHNS HOPKINS UNIVERSITY PRESS

Baltimore and London

The views expressed in this book do not necessarily
represent the views of the National Institute on Aging
or the U.S. Department of Health and Human Services.

© 1998 The Johns Hopkins University Press
All rights reserved. Published 1998
Printed in the United States of America on acid-free paper
9 8 7 6 5 4 3 2 1

The Johns Hopkins University Press
2715 North Charles Street
Baltimore, Maryland 21218-4363
The Johns Hopkins Press Ltd., London
www.jhu.press.edu

A catalog record for this book is available from the British Library.

Library of Congress Cataloging-in-Publication Data

Public and private responsibilities in long-term care : finding the
  balance / edited by Leslie C. Walker, Elizabeth H. Bradley, and
  Terrie Wetle.
      p.   cm.
  Includes bibliographical references and index.
  ISBN 0-8018-5901-8
      1. Long-term care of the sick—United States—Finance.   2. Long-
  term care of the sick—Government policy—United States.
  3. Insurance, Long-term care—United States.   I. Walker, Leslie C.,
  1962-   . II. Bradley, Elizabeth H., 1962-   . III. Wetle, Terrie
  Todd, 1946-   .
  RA644.6.P8   1998
  362.1'6'0973—dc21   98-3335
                                                                CIP

Contents

LIST OF CONTRIBUTORS   vii

PREFACE   xi

INTRODUCTION: The Financing and Organization of
Long-Term Care   1
ROBERT H. BINSTOCK

Part I
Public and Private Roles in Long-Term Care:
A Theoretical Context

CHAPTER 1
Deceptive Dichotomies: Political Reasoning and Government
Involvement in Long-Term Care   25
MARK SCHLESINGER

CHAPTER 2
Self-interested Behavior and Social Welfare: Perspectives
from Economic Theory   62
ELIZABETH H. BRADLEY

CHAPTER 3
Community Perceptions of Public and Private Responsibility
in the Context of Cultural Diversity   77
DONNA L. YEE

CHAPTER 4
Justice and Prudential Deliberation in Long-Term Care   93
NORMAN DANIELS

Part II
The Public-Private Dilemma in Long-Term Care:
Policy Responses

CHAPTER 5
Public-Private Partnerships in Long-Term Care 115
MARK R. MEINERS

CHAPTER 6
Jump Starting the Market: Public Subsidies for Private
Long-Term Care Insurance 134
JOSHUA M. WIENER

CHAPTER 7
Empowering the Community: Public Initiatives in
Consumer-directed Services 150
KEVIN J. MAHONEY, LORI SIMON-RUSINOWITZ,
MARK R. MEINERS, HUNTER L. McKAY,
AND KATHLEEN C. J. TREAT

CHAPTER 8
Access to Public Resources: Regulating Asset Transfers
for Long-Term Care 165
LESLIE C. WALKER AND BRIAN BURWELL

CONCLUSION: Integrating Theory and Practice in
Long-Term Care 181
LESLIE C. WALKER AND ELIZABETH H. BRADLEY

INDEX 197

Contributors

ROBERT H. BINSTOCK, Ph.D., is professor of aging, health, and society at Case Western Reserve University. A former president of the Gerontological Society of America, he has served as director of a White House Task Force on Older Americans for President Lyndon B. Johnson, and as chair and member of a number of advisory panels to the federal, state, and local governments as well as foundations. Professor Binstock is the author of more than 150 articles on the politics and policies affecting aging. His nineteen books include *The Future of Long-Term Care* (1996); *Dementia and Aging: Ethics, Values, and Policy Choices* (1992); and four editions of the *Handbook of Aging and the Social Sciences* (the most recent published in 1996).

ELIZABETH H. BRADLEY, Ph.D., is assistant professor in the Department of Epidemiology and Public Health at the Yale University School of Medicine. Dr. Bradley's research involves the use of economic theory in understanding individual decision-making in long-term care, with a focus on end-of-life treatment decisions. Before her academic career, Dr. Bradley served as a health care administrator at Massachusetts General Hospital.

BRIAN BURWELL is vice president for Medicaid Policy Research at the MEDSTAT Group, Cambridge, Massachusetts. His work has focused on Medicaid, long-term care, and disability policy, areas in which he has published extensively.

NORMAN DANIELS, Ph.D., is the Goldthwaite Professor and professor of medical ethics at Tufts Medical School. He has written widely in the philosophy of science, ethics, and political and social philosophy. He served as a member of the Ethics Working Group of the Clinton White House Health Care Task Force and most recently as a member of the Public

Health Expert Panel on Cost Effectiveness and Clinical Preventive Medicine. He is currently serving on the National Academy of Social Science Study panel on the social role of Medicare.

KEVIN J. MAHONEY, Ph.D., is a faculty member at the University of Maryland Center on Aging, where he serves as the national project director for the Cash and Counseling Demonstration and Evaluation funded by the Robert Wood Johnson Foundation and the Office of the Assistant Secretary for Planning and Evaluation at the U.S. Department of Health and Human Services. During his twenty-four-year career in gerontology and long-term care, Dr. Mahoney has served in a number of policymaking and administrative positions in state governments. An expert on long-term care innovation, he speaks and writes extensively on consumer direction, the roles of the public and private sectors in financing long-term care, long-term care insurance, and care management.

HUNTER L. MCKAY is deputy director of the national program office for four Robert Wood Johnson Foundation programs: the Partnership for Long-Term Care, State Initiatives in Long-Term Care, Service Credit Banking in Managed Care, and the Medicare-Medicaid Integration Care program.

MARK R. MEINERS, Ph.D., is associate professor and associate director for the University of Maryland Center on Aging in College Park. He is the originator of the Robert Wood Johnson Foundation Partnership for Long-Term Care and has served as the national program director for this initiative since its beginning in 1987. Dr. Meiners is nationally recognized as one of the leading experts on financing and program development in long-term care. His research on long-term care insurance has been a major catalyst to the current interest in this topic.

MARK SCHLESINGER, Ph.D., is associate professor of public health, head of the Division of Health Policy and Administration, and fellow of the Institution for Social and Policy Studies, Yale University. He is also a visiting associate professor at the Institute for Health, Health Care Policy, and Aging Research at Rutgers University. Dr. Schlesinger's research includes analyses of public attitudes toward health care reform, public perceptions and attitudes shaping intergenerational tensions and age-targeted social programs, and the comparative performance of private nonprofit, for-profit, and public agencies.

LORI SIMON-RUSINOWITZ is deputy director of the Cash and Counseling Demonstration and Evaluation Project at the University of Maryland Center on Aging. She has been interested in aging and disability issues for the past ten years. As part of the cash and counseling project, she is overseeing a study of consumers' preferences for consumer-directed personal care.

KATHLEEN C. J. TREAT is coordinator of the service credit program at the Center on Aging at the University of Maryland. She directs the design and implementation of volunteer programs based in health maintenance organizations to support frail elders living in the community under a national, multisite grant funded by the Robert Wood Johnson Foundation.

LESLIE C. WALKER, M.P.H., is director of the Braceland Center for Mental Health and Aging at the Institute of Living/Hartford Hospital. She holds a dual appointment as assistant professor in medicine and in community medicine and health care at the University of Connecticut School of Medicine. Her research has focused on long-term care financing, ethical issues, and health services for patients with dementia. Her interest in developing this edited volume grew from her recent work as principal investigator for the evaluation of the Robert Wood Johnson–funded Connecticut Partnership for Long-Term Care.

TERRIE WETLE, Ph.D., is deputy director of the National Institute on Aging of the National Institutes of Health. She was most recently the director of the Braceland Center for Mental Health and Aging at the Institute of Living/Hartford Hospital and associate professor of community medicine and health care, School of Medicine, University of Connecticut. She is the former associate director of the Division on Aging and assistant professor of medicine at Harvard Medical School and director of the Program in Long Term Care Administration at Yale University. Her research interests include social gerontology, the organization and finance of health care, and ethical issues in geriatric care. She has authored more than a hundred scientific publications and serves on the editorial boards of several journals.

JOSHUA M. WIENER, Ph.D., is a principal research associate at the Urban Institute, where he specializes in research on Medicaid and on long-term care. During 1993, Dr. Wiener worked for the White House Task Force on National Health Care Reform, where he formulated policy options on Medicare and on long-term care. He is the author or editor of seven books and over fifty articles on long-term care, Medicaid, health reform, health care rationing, and maternal and child health.

DONNA L. YEE, Ph.D., the director of policy and research at the National Asian Pacific Center on Aging, conducts numerous studies in the area of long-term care. Her previous experience includes positions as a clinician, supervisor, and administrator in community-based and institutional long-term care organizations.

Preface

With the growing interdependency of individual and social rights and responsibilities, the traditional distinction between public and private sectors in the U.S. economy and society at large is less clear than previously described in the academic and policy literature. The policy struggle that characterizes debates regarding long-term care financing illustrates collective uncertainty about where the boundary between public and private roles lies, and whether such a boundary can and should exist amid the evolving models of health reform. A central thesis of this volume is that the traditional juxtaposition of public and private responsibilities in long-term care may no longer be germane in framing policy discussions around long-term care financing. A second thesis is that successful social policy must be informed by theoretical perspectives from a number of academic disciplines. Similarly, the volume reflects a presumption that analysis of existing long-term care policies and programs can provide important insights regarding social norms and constructs, which in turn may refine social theories. This mutual relationship is represented in the structure of the volume, which contains both theory-based and programmatic components.

A number of excellent texts published in recent years address issues of the organization and financing of long-term care. Among the most directly relevant are two prior books from Johns Hopkins: *The Future of Long-Term Care: Social and Policy Issues* (edited by Binstock, Cluff, and von Mering) and *Caring for the Elderly: Reshaping Health Policy* (edited by Eisdorfer, Kessler, and Spector). These and other recent works provide essential insights into the political, social, and economic factors that influence the organization

This work was supported in part by the Braceland Endowment of the Braceland Center for Mental Health and Aging at the Institute of Living/Hartford Hospital's Mental Health Network, Hartford, Connecticut.

and financing of long-term care. However, explicit discussion and application of relevant theory have been limited. This volume is intended to complement the existing literature by developing and applying relevant theoretical frameworks to this issue. Multiple perspectives regarding individual and societal obligations to provide and finance long-term care are offered. The inclusion of theory facilitates a review of the defining characteristics of financing programs, rather than the programs themselves. In addition, this book attempts to stimulate continued policy discussions by reframing the traditional notion of private versus public responsibilities into a more integrated approach to social policy. A guiding principle of the text is that public and private responsibilities in the long-term care arena intersect and overlap, thereby blurring the line. The perspectives of different disciplines and programmatic stances illustrate the complexity and challenge in formulating policy for financing long-term care that will ultimately be acceptable to the broader society.

Part I of this edited volume presents relevant theoretical frameworks from the disciplines of political science, economics, sociology, and philosophy. Part II includes four chapters that describe policy and market efforts to integrate public and private sectors in financing long-term care. The conclusion highlights the value of cross-disciplinary perspectives in long-term care policymaking and draws on previous sections of the text to integrate theory, policy, and practice.

The introduction by Robert H. Binstock lays a critical foundation for the subsequent chapters by presenting an overview of contemporary organization and financing of long-term care. Dr. Binstock describes current and predicted demand for long-term care services and existing health care delivery systems. He also examines current financing mechanisms, including the role of managed care. Finally, Dr. Binstock offers a vision of the future of long-term care in the context of the political environment, with consideration of potentially changing perceptions of long-term care over the coming decades.

Part I presents relevant theory from a variety of disciplines. Those represented (political science, economics, sociology, and philosophy) were selected in order to provide the reader with conceptual tools with which to analyze specific long-term care programs. These perspectives are central to a comprehensive assessment of the relative merits of social policy in this arena. The authors identify major tenets of theory from their disciplines relevant to long-term care and apply these theoretical constructs to long-term care. Although highly diverse (as intended), the theoretical discussions offer three unifying themes: that there are multiple interpretations of "public" and "private," that there is theoretical support for the notion that responsibility for long-term care should not rest solely with the individual or family, and that incongruent policy objectives may impede development of efficient financing mechanisms.

The importance of examining social norms in a political context is highlighted by Mark Schlesinger in his chapter on allocation of responsibility for long-term care. He describes an approach to understanding allocation issues that relies on several policy metaphors to define respective public and private responsibilities. Dr. Schlesinger enumerates a number of problems with the public-private dichotomy, and suggests an alternative framework for viewing long-term care reform.

There are several tenets of economic theory that are relevant to understanding individual decision-making with respect to long-term care. In her chapter, Elizabeth H. Bradley describes fundamental principles of welfare economics that bear directly on long-term care financing policy, equity, and efficiency. Dr. Bradley discusses the challenges posed by these principles in the development of long-term care financing models. She also provides an analysis of the interrelationships between private behavior and public policy as they are manifested in the phenomenon known as "crowding out."

Observing that race, ethnicity, and cultural factors are central in the design of effective social policies, Donna L. Yee discusses three value areas that illustrate how race/ethnicity and culture define community perceptions of public and private responsibilities for long-term care financing. These value areas include concepts of self-reliance, traditional family-based paradigms, and health beliefs. Dr. Yee cautions that successful design and implementation of long-term care policies requires the inclusion of all groups in the moral and policy debate about public and private responsibilities in this arena.

In his chapter regarding issues of justice and prudential deliberation, Norman Daniels considers essential moral questions that are frequently overshadowed in policy debates by concerns of economic costs and political feasibility. Dr. Daniels discusses individual and societal obligations to make provision for long-term care. If there is a shared obligation between individuals and society, how is it divided? He suggests an approach based on a prudential lifespan perspective that recognizes the importance of providing an appropriate range of long-term care services for individuals in need.

The program-based section of the volume begins with a chapter by Mark R. Meiners describing a multiple-state initiative to create a model of long-term care financing that integrates both public and private roles.

Supported by the Robert Wood Johnson Foundation (RWJF), the Partnership for Long-Term Care program focuses on the potential role that private insurance might play in filling the need for long-term care within the nation's health care system. This chapter discusses the major elements of this Partnership program, as well as important insights regarding the linkage of public and private interests gained throughout the program's development and early implementation.

Noting the limitations of the current market for private long-term care insurance, in his chapter Joshua M. Wiener discusses three current approaches to public subsidies designed to promote its purchase. Dr. Wiener presents an analysis of the relative strengths and weaknesses of the following strategies: providing employers a tax subsidy for the purchase of long-term care insurance policies for their employees by allowing them to deduct insurance contributions as a business expense; providing a tax deduction or credit to individuals for purchase of private long-term care insurance; and waiving some or all of the Medicaid asset depletion requirements for purchasers of qualified private long-term care insurance policies.

There have been numerous public policy initiatives to support informal caregiving, including family leave and tax incentives for family caregiving, the purchase of long-term care insurance and respite care benefits, and even family responsibility laws. Kevin J. Mahoney and colleagues focus on two recent initiatives that blend public and private resources to cultivate informal provision of long-term care. The cash and counseling demonstration seeks to modify existing Medicaid programs to facilitate the provision of informal care. Service credit banking is intended to expand the availability of informal care through the development of a formal system to organize volunteer service. The chapter closes with a discussion of how the dynamic boundaries between formal and informal care affect the development of a rational overall approach for financing and delivering long-term care.

In their chapter on issues of defining access to Medicaid coverage for long-term care, Leslie C. Walker and Brian Burwell discuss Medicaid estate planning as a policy issue that illustrates the complexity of integrating public and private roles in long-term care financing as well as the consequences of inappropriate or ineffective policy responses to this phenomenon. After defining Medicaid estate planning, the authors summarize relevant federal legislation and regulations intended to address the perceived increase in the number of individuals transferring or protecting assets in order to become eligible for public coverage for nursing home care. Next, factors that may influence this behavior are described, ranging from individual perceptions and attitudes to long-term care financing policies. Walker and Burwell suggest that policies which attempt to define the relative responsibilities in this arena raise complex ethical and philosophical questions.

The volume concludes with a chapter by Walker and Bradley that synthesizes the preceding discussions and offers new insights into the design and implementation of politically feasible long-term care policies. First, the chapter identifies common themes of responsibility that emerge in the respective theory-based discussions, including definitions of public versus private, the allocation of responsibility for long-term care, and underlying objectives of long-term care financing policy. Next, the chapter discusses the integration of theory and practice in the context of the programs described in Part II. Finally, the chapter highlights future policy and management issues in long-term care, including the importance of multidisciplinary efforts in policy development, the need for improved understanding of public and private constructs for long-term care, and the significance of the role of community in the financing of long-term care.

The demographic revolution brings with it the challenge of caring for growing numbers of persons who will need long-term services for some portion of their lives. The changing health care system and budgetary concerns fuel a perceived crisis in long-term care, and encourage rethinking models and theoretical perspectives. It is our hope that this volume will encourage creative thinking about this crucial issue.

Public and Private Responsibilities
in Long-Term Care

The Financing and Organization of Long-Term Care

ROBERT H. BINSTOCK

To provide a foundation for the reader unfamiliar with the complex structure of long-term care, this chapter presents essential information regarding organization and financing characteristics. Additionally, the chapter explores the role of various managed care models in long-term care and discusses future directions for this component of the nation's health care system.

At the turn of the century, the financing and organization of long-term care is an issue of major importance in U.S. society. The impending aging of the baby boom augurs an enormous increase in the demand for long-term care services, even as other special populations—persons with developmental disabilities, the younger disabled, and persons with chronic diseases such as AIDS, emphysema, and diabetes—will have ongoing services needs. Private-pay prices for long-term care are very high and rising so rapidly that public subsidies may become essential for greater proportions of the populations needing care. Yet the goal of containing the growth of public expenditures for long-term care—especially in the Medicaid and Medicare programs—is high on the agenda of national and state policymakers, because such expenditures have been increasing rapidly in recent years. At the same time, the recent and rapid growth of managed care, in both the private and public sectors, portends many changes in the financing, organization, and delivery of long-term care. In the quickly shifting environment of these public and market forces, traditional long-term care provider systems and the incentives that shape their operations will inevitably change rapidly and substantially.

In short, the arena of long-term care is in turmoil. A number of major societal dynamics indicate that the need for long-term care services in the years immediately ahead will grow tremendously, even as the financing of such services—with appropriate quality—may become increasingly problematic.

The aim of this chapter is to present an overview of contemporary financing and organization of long-term care to serve as background for the discussions that follow in the remaining chapters. First, the chapter describes the need for long-term care and the various settings in which it is provided. Second, it examines the costs and financing of long-term care. Third, it discusses various managed care programs that attempt to integrate acute and long-term care. Finally, it considers the outlook for the future, given the contemporary political context for financing long-term care.

Need and Settings for Long-Term Care

Nearly 13 million U.S. citizens have long-term care needs (U.S. General Accounting Office, 1994). The common stereotype that most of this population is elderly and resides in nursing homes is inaccurate. People aged sixty-five and older represent 57 percent of those with long-term care needs, and only 22 percent of older persons with long-term care needs are in nursing homes. Working-age adults account for 40 percent of the long-term care population, and another 3 percent are children; together, about 15 percent of these two groups reside in institutions. This chapter focuses primarily on issues involving the long-term care of older people.

Need for long-term care is generally defined in terms of a person being functionally dependent on a long-term basis due to physical and/or mental limitations. Two broad categories of functional limitations are widely used by clinicians to assess need for care. One category is dependence in basic *activities of daily living* (ADLs)—getting in and out of bed, toileting, bathing, dressing, and eating (Katz et al., 1963). The other category is limitations in *instrumental activities of daily living* (IADLs)—taking medications reliably, preparing meals, managing finances, doing light housework and

Table I-1
Services That May Be Needed by Disabled Individuals and Their Families

Diagnosis	Nutrition counseling
Acute medical care	Protective services
Ongoing medical supervision	Supervision
Treatment of coexisting medical conditions	Home health aide
	Homemaker
Mental health services	Personal care
Medication and elimination of drugs that cause excess disability	Paid companion/sitter
	Shopping
Multidimensional assessment	Home-delivered meals
Skilled nursing	Chore services
Physical therapy	Telephone reassurance
Occupational therapy	Personal emergency response system
Speech therapy	Recreation/exercise
Vision care	Transportation
Audiology	Special equipment (ramps, hospital beds, etc.)
Dental care	
Adult day care	Escort service
Respite care[a]	Legal services
Family/caregiver education and training	Financial/benefits counseling
	Family support groups
Family/caregiver counseling	Hospice
Patient counseling	Autopsy

Source: Adapted from U.S. Congress, Office of Technology Assessment (1990, p. 16).
[a]"Respite care" includes any service intended to provide temporary relief for the primary caregiver. When used for that purpose, homemaker, paid companion/sitter, adult day care, temporary nursing home care, and other services included on the list constitute respite care.

other chores, being able to get in and out of the home, using the telephone, and so on (Rosow & Breslau, 1966). (Persons with mental illness and children are often assessed by other criteria, such as problems in behavior or the ability to attend school.) The range of services that may be needed by persons who have difficulties in carrying out their ADLs and IADLs, as well services needed by their primary caregivers, is extensive. A list of such services is presented in table I.1.

Long-term care services are delivered across a continuum of care that ranges from intensive institution-based care to supportive health and wellness programs. Major categories and settings of the continuum include extended (such as nursing homes), acute (inpatient hospitalization of various types), ambulatory (such as outpatient physician practices), and home care (such as homemakers and personal care attendants).

Services can be provided for individuals regardless of where they reside. A variety of "demedicalized" alternatives to the traditional nursing home and home care settings for long-term care have proliferated in recent years.

About a million persons aged sixty-five and older currently live in unsubsidized housing that provides supportive services (Lewin-VHI, Inc., 1992); this compares with 1.6 million who reside in nursing homes (U.S. Bureau of the Census, 1993). The supportive services offered in these settings vary considerably in physical design, residential and personal care services, the acuity of populations they serve, and overall quality of care (Pynoos & Golant, 1996). Unsubsidized residential settings that offer supportive services include assisted-living complexes (Kane & Wilson, 1993; Regnier, Hamilton, & Yabate, 1995), continuing care retirement communities (American Association of Homes for the Aging/Ernst & Young, 1993; U.S. General Accounting Office, 1997), board and care homes (Hawes, Wildfire, & Lux, 1993; Sirrocco, 1994), and congregate housing (Kaye & Monk, 1991). In addition, supportive services are provided in federally subsidized housing (Pynoos, 1992; Struyk et al., 1989). Each of these settings serves individuals whose need for services can also be met in other types of settings, including nursing homes and community residences.

Regardless of setting, it is clear that the overall demand for care will increase substantially in the twenty-first century. When much of the baby boom—a large cohort of 74 million people born in the United States between 1946 and 1964—reaches the ranks of old age in 2030, the absolute number of people aged 65 and older will have more than doubled (from 31 million in 1990 to about 70 million), and older people will constitute 20 percent of the U.S. population. Moreover, the number of persons in advanced old ages will also more than double. The population aged 75 and older will have grown from 13 million in 1990 to 32 million in 2030, and those aged 85 and older will have tripled from 3 million to 9 million (U.S. Bureau of the Census, 1996a). Rates of disability increase markedly at these advanced old ages. One reflection of this can be found in the present rates of nursing home use in different old age categories. About one percent of U.S. citizens aged 65 to 74 years are in nursing homes; this compares with 6.1 percent of persons aged 75 to 84, and 24 percent of persons age 85 and older (U.S. Bureau of the Census, 1993). Similarly, disability rates increase in older old age categories among older persons who do not live in nursing homes, from nearly 23 percent of those aged 65 to 74 who experience difficulty with ADLs to 45 percent of those aged 85 and older (Cassel, Rudberg, & Olshansky, 1992).

The tremendous growth expected in the older population, in itself, suggests that there will be millions more disabled elderly people in the decades ahead. Whether rates of disability in old age will increase or decline in the future, however, is a matter on which experts disagree, depending on their assumptions and measures (e.g., Fries, 1989; Manton, Corder, & Stallard, 1993, 1997; Schneider & Guralnik, 1990; Verbrugge, 1989). Assuming no changes in age-specific risks of disability, Cassel, Rudberg, and Olshansky (1992) calculate a 31 percent increase between 1990 and 2010 in the number of persons aged sixty-five and older experiencing difficulty with ADLs. Using the same assumption, the Congressional Budget Office (1991) projects that the nursing home population will increase 50 percent between 1990 and 2010, double by 2030, and triple by 2050. Even those researchers who report a decline in the prevalence of disability at older ages in recent years emphasize that there will be large absolute increases in the number of older U.S. citizens needing long-term care in the decades ahead (see, e.g., Manton, Corder, & Stallard, 1997).

The Costs of Financing and Care

Aggregate expenditures for long-term care are already sizable and likely to increase substantially in the decades immediately ahead. The total national long-term care bill in 1995 was $106.5 billion; 73 percent was spent on nursing home care and 27 percent on home and community-based care (Levit et al., 1996). Out-of-pocket payments by individuals and their families account for 32.5 percent of the total. Private insurance benefits pay for 5.5 percent. Other private funds account for 4.6 percent. The remaining 57.4 percent is financed by federal, state, and local governments.

The growth rate of long-term care expenditures is steep. Between 1985 and 1995, expenditures nearly tripled, increasing by 193 percent (Levit et al., 1996). According to one study (Mendelson & Schwartz, 1993), the phenomenon of population aging accounted for only 22 percent of the growth in long-term care expenditures between 1987 and 1990 (the other factors were increased intensity in the utilization rate of services, inflation in health-sector prices, and general inflation). Nonetheless, a consensus among experts is that population aging will contribute significantly to long-term care expenditures in the years ahead when the baby boom cohort needs such care. Accordingly, the Congressional Budget Office (1991), using 1990 as a baseline year, has projected that total national costs of long-term care will almost double by 2010 and more than triple by 2030.

Paying for care out of pocket

Paying the costs of long-term care out of pocket can be a catastrophic financial experience for patients and their families. The average annual cost of a year's care in a nursing home was more than $46,000 in 1995 (Levit et al., 1996), a sharp increase from $37,000 in 1993 (Wiener & Ill-ston, 1996). Although the use of a limited number of services in a home or other community-based setting is less expensive, noninstitutional care for patients who would otherwise be appropriately placed in a nursing home is not necessarily cheaper and is often more expensive (Weissert, 1990).

For a high percentage of older people, long-term care is simply un-affordable. Among persons aged sixty-five and older, 40 percent have a pretax income of less than 200 percent of the poverty threshold—under $14,618 for an individual and $18,440 for a married couple in which the man is aged sixty-five or older (U.S. Bureau of the Census, 1996b). Under one-tenth of older persons in nursing homes can finance a year of care from their income (Hanley, Wiener, & Harris, 1994).

Although dozens of governmental programs are sources of funding for long-term care services (U.S. General Accounting Office, 1995), each source regulates the availability of funds with frequently changing rules as to eligibility and breadth of service coverage. Thus, persons needing long-term care and their caregivers often find themselves ineligible for financial assistance from these programs, and unable to pay out of pocket for needed services. In one study about 75 percent of the informal, unpaid caregivers of patients with dementia reported that they did not use formal, paid services because they were unable to pay for them (Eckert & Smyth, 1988).

The cost of care will undoubtedly grow in the future. Price increases in nursing home and home- and community-based care have consistently exceeded the general rate of inflation. Trends in long-term care labor and overhead costs indicate that this pattern will continue.

In-kind, or informal, care

A number of researchers have estimated that about 80 percent to 85 percent of the long-term care provided to older persons outside nursing homes is presently provided on an in-kind basis by family members—spouses, siblings, adult children, and broader kin networks (Hanley et al., 1990).

About 74 percent of dependent community-based older persons receive all their care from family members or other unpaid sources, about 21 percent receive both formal and informal services, and only about 5 percent use just formal services (Liu, Manton, & Liu, 1985). The vast majority of family caregivers are women (Brody, 1990; Stone, Cafferata, & Sangl, 1987). The family also plays an important role in obtaining and managing services from paid service providers. It is important to note that caregiving by families does not tend to decline significantly even when they are able to supplement their caregiving with formal, paid services (Edelman & Hughes, 1990; Tennstedt, Crawford, & McKinlay, 1993).

The capacity and willingness of family members to care for disabled older persons, however, may decline when the baby boom cohort reaches old age because of broader social trends. The family, as a fundamental unit of social organization, has been undergoing profound transformations that will become more fully manifest over the next few decades as baby boomers reach old age. The striking growth of single-parent households, the growing participation of women in the labor force, the high incidence of divorce and remarriage (differentially higher for men), all entail complicated changes in the structure of household and kinship roles and relationships. There will be an increasing number of "blended families," reflecting many lines of descent through multiple marriages and the birth of children within complex family structures. This growth in the incidence of step- and half-relatives will make for a dramatic new turn in family structure in the coming decades. Already, such blended families constitute about half of all households with children (National Academy on Aging, 1994).

One possible implication of these changes is that kinship networks in the near future will become more complex, attenuated, and diffuse (Bengtson, Rosenthal, & Burton, 1990), perhaps with a weakened sense of filial obligation. If changes in the intensity of kinship relations significantly erode the capacity and sense of obligation to care for older family members when the baby boom cohort is in the ranks of old age and disability, demands for governmental support to pay for long-term care may increase accordingly.

The role of private insurance

Private insurance policies that cover long-term care—a relatively new product—are very expensive for the majority of older persons. Moreover, benefits are limited with respect to when they first become available and how long they will be paid. A typical good-quality policy will provide benefits of $100 a day for nursing home care and $50 a day for home or adult day care (at a program outside the home). From the time that eligibility for benefits is determined there is usually a ninety-day "waiting period" before benefits are paid; in effect, this is a deductible amounting to $9,000 for nursing home care and $4,500 for home and adult day care. There is also the problem of price inflation over time. Policies do offer inflation protection for an additional premium, but this additional coverage may not be enough to cover the full rate of inflation in long-term costs.

Only about 4 percent to 5 percent of older persons have any private long-term care insurance, and only about one percent of nursing home costs are paid by private insurance (Wiener, Illston, & Hanley, 1994). A number of analyses have suggested that even when the product becomes more refined, no more than 20 percent of older U.S. citizens will be able to afford private long-term care insurance (Crown, Capitman, & Leutz, 1992; Friedland, 1990; Rivlin & Wiener, 1988; Wiener, Illston, & Hanley, 1994). (For a fuller discussion of long-term care insurance, see Chapter 6 in this volume.)

A variation on the insurance policy approach to financing long-term care is continuing care retirement communities (CCRCs), which promise comprehensive health care services—including long-term care—to members should they be needed (Chellis & Grayson, 1990; Sherwood et al., 1997). According to a report issued by the U.S. General Accounting Office (1997), there are about 350,000 residents living in CCRCs. Only about one-third of these CCRCs, however, provide long-term care for their residents under lifetime contracts in which the CCRC assumes a resident's financial risks for long-term care services (including nursing home care). CCRC residents tend to be middle- and upper-income persons who are relatively healthy when they join the community; they pay a substantial entrance fee and monthly charge in return for a promise of "care for life." The U.S. General Accounting Office found, in eleven field visits to CCRCs that provide long-term care, that entry fees ranged from a low of $34,000 for a studio apartment for one individual to a high of $439,600 for a two-bedroom home for a couple. It has been estimated that about 10 percent of older people could afford to join such communities (Cohen, 1988).

Because most older people prefer to remain in their own homes rather than join age-segregated communities, an alternative product termed "life care at home" (LCAH) was developed in the late 1980s and marketed to middle-income customers with lower entry and monthly fees than those of CCRCs (Callahan & Somers, 1994; Tell, Cohen, & Wallack, 1987). There are, however, only about five hundred LCAH policies in effect (Williams & Temkin-Greener, 1996).

The role of public programs

Those who cannot pay for long-term care out of pocket or through various private insurance arrangements rely on public funds for their care. For persons who are not eligible for care through programs of the Department of Veterans Affairs, the available sources of payment include Medicaid, Medicare, and a variety of other federal, state, and local governmental programs.

The bulk of public financing for long-term care is through Medicaid, the federal-state program for the poor. The program paid $22.5 billion for nursing home and home care services in 1995, which was 37.9 percent of all expenditures for long-term care (Levit et al., 1996).

Medicaid finances the care—at least in part—of about three-fifths of nursing home patients (Wiener & Illston, 1996) and 28 percent of home- and community-based services (American Association of Retired Persons, 1994). Eligibility for Medicaid subsidy is determined by income and asset tests administered by state governments. In most states, the program's reimbursement rates to nursing homes are substantially lower than private-pay rates. Consequently, those homes that have a mixture of Medicaid and private-pay patients generally engage in "cost-shifting," setting their private-pay rates at a high enough level to offset the "losses" they incur on their Medicaid residents (although such practices are prohibited in some states).

Medicaid does not pay for the full range of home care services that are needed for most clients who are functionally dependent. Generally speaking, the program provides reimbursement only for the most "medicalized" services that are necessary to maintain a long-term care patient in a home environment. Services that are not reimbursed include essential IADL supports such as chore services, assistance with grocery shopping and meal preparation, transportation, companionship, periodic monitoring, and respite programs for family members and other unpaid caregivers.

Medicaid does include a special waiver program, however, which allows states to offer a wider range of nonmedical home care services, if limited to those patients whose services will be no more costly than Medicaid-financed nursing home care. But the volume of services in these waiver programs—which in some states combine Medicaid with funds from the Older Americans Act, the Social Services block-grant program, and other state and local government sources—is small in relation to the overall demand (Hudson, 1996).

Although many patients are poor enough to qualify for Medicaid when they enter a nursing home, a substantial number become poor after they are institutionalized (Adams, Meiners, & Burwell, 1993). Persons in this latter group deplete their assets to meet their long-term care bills, eventually "spending down" and becoming poor enough to qualify for Medicaid.

In the early 1990s, the Robert Wood Johnson Foundation began financing an experimental program in selected states, with the prime goal of reducing Medicaid spending by providing an asset-protection incentive for people to purchase private long-term care insurance. This Partnership for Long-Term Care program is designed to enable middle-class persons to avoid spending down and yet have Medicaid pay for some of their long-term care. At the same time, it has the purpose of reducing the period that Medicaid will pay for long-term care services needed by an individual. Through this program, state governments agree to exempt individuals who apply for Medicaid eligibility from having to spend down assets to qualify for the program, if they have previously had some long-term care paid for by a state-certified private insurance policy. (For a fuller discussion of these experiments, see Chapter 5 in this volume.)

An unknown number of individuals become eligible for Medicaid by sheltering their assets—illegally or legally with the assistance of attorneys who specialize in so-called Medicaid estate planning. Because sheltered assets are not counted in Medicaid eligibility determinations, such persons are able to take advantage of a program for the poor, without actually being poor themselves. Asset sheltering has become a source of considerable concern to the federal and state governments as Medicaid expenditures for nursing homes and home care have been increasing rapidly—nearly doubling from 1990 to 1995 (Levit et al., 1996).

The frequency of asset sheltering and the sums involved are, in the nature of the case, difficult to ascertain. A few studies have attempted to document the nature and extent of the phenomenon in selected states (Burwell, 1993; Burwell & Crown, 1995; Walker & Gruman, 1996). In 1996, Congress enacted a law that makes it a federal crime to shelter assets to become eligible for Medicaid. Yet the law is so vague that, practically speaking, it has been unenforceable. (For a fuller discussion of asset sheltering, see Chapter 8 in this volume.)

The federal Medicare insurance program, in which almost all older U.S. citizens participate, pays for some nursing home and home care, but only on a relatively short-term basis. Moreover, the services covered are for postacute or subacute care, not the broader range of long-term care services. Following a hospitalization of a few days or longer, Medicare pays for up to a hundred days of care in a skilled nursing facility as long as the care includes skilled nursing and/or rehabilitation on a daily basis. After the first twenty days, however, the patient is required to pay up to $95 a day. In 1995, Medicare paid $7.3 billion for nursing home care, which was 10 percent of all payments to nursing homes (Levit et al., 1996).

Medicare also reimburses fully for part-time or intermittent home care therapy or skilled health care if a physician continues to authorize the need for such care. In the early 1990s, the interpretation of "part-time" and "intermittent" became more lenient than previously, and the program's expenditures for home care grew substantially. Consequently, the program's outlays for home care increased by 176 percent from 1991 to 1995, from $4.2 billion to $11.6 billion. Medicare reimbursements in 1995 accounted for 44 percent of all home care payments (Levit et al., 1996).

A number of other public programs, with varied criteria for eligibility, paid only 1.7 percent of nursing home and home care expenditures in 1995 (Levit et al., 1996). The Department of Veterans Affairs (DVA) is the largest of these payers. The DVA provides both nursing home and domiciliary care to about 75,000 veterans in DVA facilities, although only low-income veterans are eligible for domiciliary care. It also provides home health services to about 5,000 persons, and will pay for up to six months in a DVA-authorized community nursing home for veterans whose disabilities are not service-connected (Wiener & Illston, 1996). Nursing home care is covered indefinitely for longer periods when the veteran requires care associated with a service-connected disability.

Managed Care and Long-Term Care

Until recently, the application of managed care with capitated financing to long-term care has been confined largely to a series of experimental and demonstration programs. Generally speaking, the goals of these programs have been to integrate access to acute and long-term care, maintain or enhance the quality of care, and reduce public subsidies for care (Newcomer & Wilkinson, 1996). Differences among these programs illustrate some of the issues and challenges generated by various sources of funding and different types of older patient populations.

A model initially tested at several sites in the 1980s is the social/health maintenance organization (S/HMO), financed by the federal government. The S/HMO offers enrollees a limited package of home- and community-based long-term care benefits on a capitated basis as a supplement to Medicare HMO benefits, and attempts to enroll primarily healthy older customers (Leutz, Greenberg, & Abrahams, 1985). Results from these early experiments were equivocal with respect to the viability of financing arrangements, particularly the costs of frail enrollees (Newcomer, Harrington, & Friedlob, 1990; Harrington, Newcomer, & Preston, 1993). Moreover, certain disabled groups of patients had higher mortality rates than a fee-for-service comparison group (Manton et al., 1993). Congress has established a second round of S/HMO demonstrations to test refinements such as heavy involvement of geriatricians and geriatric nurse practitioners; standard protocols for obtaining adequate medical and social histories and for diagnosing and managing conditions frequently found in older patients; increased attention to the effects of prescription drugs on patients; and outpatient alternatives to hospitalization and nursing home placement.

While the S/HMO attempts to enroll healthy older persons to demonstrate what is financially feasible with such a population, the On Lok model, developed at a San Francisco neighborhood center in the 1970s and early 1980s, is targeted to community-based older persons who are already sufficiently dependent in daily functioning to be appropriately placed in a nursing home (Ansak, 1990). In this capitated model, most patients are eligible for both Medicare and Medicaid. Services are organized around an adult day care program that not only serves as a social program and as a respite for caregivers, but also functions much like a geriatric outpatient clinic with substantial medical observation and supervision (Zawadski & Eng, 1988).

The On Lok model, replicated at ten demonstration sites as the Program for All-inclusive Care for the Elderly (PACE), appears to have integrated acute and long-term care fairly well under its managed care approach. Whether it can be extended beyond the very frail population it has served to date—patients who are already functionally dependent and dually eligible for Medicare and Medicaid—remains to be seen. To some extent, this is what is being explored in the second round of the S/HMO demonstrations. Early evaluations of the PACE demonstrations indicated that they were experiencing problems of financial viability, high staff turnover among physicians and adult day care center directors, and patient mix in terms of both acuity and dementia (Kane, Illston, & Miller, 1992). By 1997, however, Congress was sufficiently satisfied with results from the demonstrations to move beyond the demonstration phase and authorize the establishment of PACE programs by any suitable local sponsoring organization (Pub. L. No. 105-33, 1997).

The National Academy for State Health Policy reports that fifteen states are providing long-term care to older people through risk-based Medicaid managed care programs (Horvath & Kaye, 1995). One of these, for example, is the Minnesota Long-term Care Options Project (LTCOP), which attempts to integrate acute and long-term care, incorporating elements of both the S/HMO and On Lok models. In contrast to the S/HMO, LTCOP targets Medicaid-eligible enrollees and accordingly offers a benefit package that includes nursing home care as well as home- and community-based care. The program also includes a less functionally dependent population than the On Lok model. Hence, it provides an opportunity to test broader approaches to integrating acute and long-term care than have been tried to date (Johnson, 1996).

Similarly, the Arizona Long-Term Care System (ALTCS) provides long-term care services within a broader statewide demonstration project that finances health care for the Medicaid population on a capitated basis. ALTCS is limited to individuals whom the state certifies as at risk of institutionalization, and covers acute care services as well as long-term care. The program appears to save the state some money (largely because of how it provides services to the population with mental retardation and developmental disabilities). One study indicates, however, that the quality of nursing home care in this Arizona program is lower than in neighboring New Mexico, which has a conventional fee-for-service system (Wiener, 1996a).

The growth of Medicare managed care (primarily in the form of HMOs) also has important implications for long-term care. Even as Medicare's implementation of prospective hospital reimbursement on the basis of diagnostic-related groups led hospitals to discharge patients as quickly as possible, the incentive systems of Medicare HMOs lead them to transfer patients from acute care to subacute care expeditiously, at the lowest possible cost. As they compete for Medicare enrollees, those HMOs that do not own the appropriate long-term care services, for which Medicare's capitation payment makes them responsible, have made contractual arrangements with providers of such care—especially with large for-profit nursing home chains—shifting financial risk to the latter. Reportedly, HMO substitution of subacute care for hospital days enables them to reduce their costs by 50 percent or more (Shield, 1996). Consequently, the incentives for providers of long-term care shift from the traditional reimbursement-driven basis (which encourages more services) to a cost-control basis emphasizing less services (Mechanic, 1994). Although evaluations of Medicare HMOs generally indicate that they produce acute care outcomes that are roughly comparable to outcomes from fee-for-service providers (see Brown et al., 1993), outcomes may be worse in HMOs for elderly people with chronic illness and disabilities (Nelson et al., 1997; Shaughnessy, 1994; Ware et al., 1996).

In summary, a great many experiments, demonstrations, and models for integrating acute and long-term care for older people are being tried, and more will emerge in the years ahead. Research to date has provided some useful preliminary information on these programs (Wiener, 1996a). But a great deal more high-quality research will be needed to sort out the comparative effectiveness of managed care approaches with respect to the integration of care, quality of care, and cost-savings in public expenditures. As these issues are clarified, managed care may play a major role in shaping future directions for the financing and organization of long-term care.

Outlook for the Future

From the mid-1980s until the mid-1990s, a number of national policy-makers were sympathetic to the dilemmas confronting middle-income individuals who needed long-term care—their inability to pay out of pocket for services or for private insurance that provides adequate coverage, and the anxieties of spending down their modest assets in the process of becoming eligible for Medicaid. In the early 1990s, advocates for the elderly and younger disabled persons were optimistic that the federal government would establish a new program for funding long-term care that would not be means-tested as is Medicaid.

A number of legislative bills introduced between 1989 and 1994 included some version of such a program, including President Clinton's failed proposal for health care reform (Binstock, 1994). None of these proposals became law, the major reason being that any substantial version of such a program would cost tens of billions of dollars each year at the outset.

By the mid-1990s, optimism regarding expanded governmental funding for long-term care was quashed. A new Republican majority in Congress proposed to limit federal spending on Medicaid and Medicare as part of a broader agenda for balancing the annual federal budget and redistributing responsibilities of the federal government to the states. The budgetary concerns were substantial with respect to these two programs. From 1987 to 1994, combined Medicaid and Medicare outlays for long-term care of older people increased by 153 percent for nursing homes and 543 percent for home care (Health Care Financing Administration, 1996). For the 1995–2005 period, Burner and Waldo (1995) project that expenditures from the two programs will increase by 98 percent for nursing homes and 119 percent for home care.

In 1995, Congress initially proposed to cap the rate of growth in Medicaid expenditures to achieve projected savings of $182 billion by 2002, and then put forward versions that involved a smaller amount of savings. Such changes were vetoed by President Clinton. They resurfaced in 1996 with proposed reductions of $72 billion, but no legislation was enacted that year. After his reelection in 1996, however, President Clinton proposed containing the growth of federal Medicaid expenditures at an annual level equivalent to the nation's increase in per capita economic output for each year (Pear, 1997). This approach remains on the policy agenda, although governors oppose it because of the pressure it would place on state Medicaid budgets.

If federal expenditures on Medicaid are capped, many states are unlikely to make up the resulting gaps from their own funds. According to one analysis (Kassner, 1995), the 1995 congressional proposals for limiting Medicaid's growth would have trimmed long-term care funding by as much as 11.4 percent by the year 2000 and meant that 1.74 million Medicaid beneficiaries would have lost or been able unable to secure coverage. In addition, this analysis assumed that states would make their initial reductions in home- and community-based care services (because nursing home residents have nowhere else to go), and concluded that such services would be substantially reduced from current levels. Five states were projected to completely eliminate home- and community-based services by the end of the century and another nineteen to cut services by more than half. Whether such specific predictions might come true if Medicaid is capped, ongoing federal and state efforts to control Medicaid costs are likely to have adverse consequences for access to and the quality of Medicaid-financed care (Cohen & Spector, 1996; Holahan et al., 1995; Liebig, 1997; Wiener, 1996b).

Federal measures to limit Medicare funding of home care have already been undertaken. The Balanced Budget Act of 1997 (Pub. L. No. 105-33, 1997) required that prospective payment reimbursement for the program's home health care services be implemented by 1998, with rates set on the basis of the case-mix service requirements for individual service recipients.

At present, the challenges of financing long-term care in the twenty-first century seem enormous. The prospects of paying for long-term care for oneself or one's parents are daunting. Out-of-pocket payments for care are becoming larger and increasingly unaffordable for many; neither the projected income and asset status of members of the baby boom cohort nor the present dynamics of the market indicate that these trends will abate. Only a minority of older persons may be able to afford premiums for private long-term care insurance. Broad societal trends suggest that informal, unpaid care by family members may become less feasible in the future than it is today. It is possible that technological innovations in the provision of care could reduce costs while maintaining or enhancing the quality of care (Binstock & Spector, 1997; Cluff, 1996), but little effort has been invested to date in the development of such innovations.

When members of the baby boom reach the ranks of old age in the decades ahead, many of them and their families may look to government to subsidize their long-term care. Yet, even the safety net that government programs now provide by financing long-term care for the poor is seriously threatened by contemporary federal and state budgetary politics. The political context is such that public resources for long-term care are likely to be even less available in relation to the need for care than they have been to date. What is likely to happen as the demand for long-term care increases in the decades ahead?

Perhaps the entrance of the baby boom into the ranks of old age may precipitate a grassroots movement that will revitalize political awareness of the problem of long-term care financing as a major issue in U.S. society. Such a movement might well be joined by millions of younger disabled persons and their advocates, although the constituencies of the elderly and the disabled have a checkered history of working as allies because of differing philosophical and political concerns and models of care (Binstock, 1992).

The prospects of success for such a grassroots movement will probably depend on effective promulgation of the notion that long-term care is an essential part of health care (a notion that traditionally has been anathema to the younger disabled constituency). This would make it possible for long-term care to receive adequate attention in more general policy debates about the future of U.S. health care.

For most of the twentieth century, long-term care has been eclipsed by the glamour and prestige of hospital-based medical care that is inherently dramatic because it deals with acute episodes of illnesses and trauma, and their relatively "high-tech" and "quick-fix" dimensions of diagnosis and intervention. Long-term care, on the other hand, tends to be undramatic, low-tech, and drawn out over time, involving large numbers of unskilled workers; moreover, many of the costs are associated with board and care aspects rather than medical interventions. Long-term care has not even been covered through traditional health insurance mechanisms such as employee benefit plans. When concerns are expressed about the fact that 40 million U.S. citizens are not covered by health insurance, coverage for long-term care is not part of the discussion.

It is possible that long-term care will come to be perceived more widely as part of the continuum of health care needed by all. As the baby boom cohort begins to approach the ranks of old age, the importance of long-term care—a formidable volume of need for it, the difficulties of financing it, and the challenges of delivering it effectively—is likely to become increasingly accepted throughout U.S. society. Such acceptance could bring with it a widespread understanding that long-term care is health care by another name. This perception may transform long-term care into a shared understanding of justice in health care in which ensuring access to long-term care is as much of a public responsibility as ensuring access to other kinds of health care. If so, the political context may be more favorable for even a substantially greater public role in financing long-term care than there is today.

References

Adams, E. K., Meiners, M. R., & Burwell, B. O. (1993). Asset spend-down in nursing homes: Methods and insights. *Medical Care, 31*, 1–23.

American Association of Homes for the Aging/Ernst & Young. (1993). *Continuing care retirement communities: An industry in action* (Vol. 1). Washington, DC: American Association of Homes for the Aging.

American Association of Retired Persons, Public Policy Institute. (1994). *The costs of long-term care*. Washington, DC: American Association of Retired Persons.

Ansak, M. (1990). The On Lok model: Consolidating care and financing. *Generations, 14*(2), 73–74.

Bengtson, V. L., Rosenthal, C., & Burton, L. (1990). Families and aging: Diversity and heterogeneity. In R. H. Binstock & L. K. George (Eds.), *Handbook of aging and the social sciences* (3rd ed., pp. 263–287). San Diego, CA: Academic.

Binstock, R. H. (1992). Aging, disability, and long-term care: The politics of common ground. *Generations, 16*(2), 83–88.

Binstock, R. H. (1994). Older Americans and health care reform in the 1990s. In P. V. Rosenau (Ed.), *Health care reform in the nineties* (pp. 213–235). Thousand Oaks, CA: Sage.

Binstock, R. H., & Spector, W. D. (1997). Five priority areas for research on long-term care. *Health Services Research, 33*, 715–730.

Brody, E. M. (1990). *Women in the middle: Their parent-care years*. New York: Springer.

Brown, R. S., Bergeron, J. W., Clement, D. G., Hill, J. W., & Retchin, S. M. (1993). *Does managed care work for Medicare? An evaluation of the Medicare risk program for HMOs*. Princeton, NJ: Mathematica Policy Research.

Burner, S. T., & Waldo, D. R. (1995). Data view: National health expenditure projections, 1994–2005. *Health Care Financing Review, 16*(4), 221–242.

Burwell, B. (1993). *State responses to Medicaid estate planning*. Cambridge, MA: SysteMetrics.

Burwell, B., & Crown, W. H. (1995). *Medicaid estate planning in the aftermath of OBRA '93*. Cambridge, MA: The MEDSTAT Group.

Callahan, J. J., Jr., & Somers, S. A. (1994). Life care at home: The experience and the issues. *Compensation & Benefits Management, 10*(2), 49–60.

Cassel, C. K., Rudberg, M. A., & Olshansky, S. J. (1992). The price of success: Health care in an aging society. *Health Affairs, 11*(2), 87–99.

Chellis, R. D., & Grayson, P. J. (1990). *Life care: A long-term solution?* Lexington, MA: Lexington Books.

Cluff, L. E. (1996). The role of technology in long-term care. In R. H. Binstock, L. E. Cluff, & O. von Mering (Eds.), *The future of long-term care: Social and policy issues* (pp. 96–118). Baltimore, MD: Johns Hopkins University Press.

Cohen, J. W., & Spector, W. D. (1996). The effect of Medicaid reimbursement on quality of care in nursing homes. *Journal of Health Economics, 15*, 23–48.

Cohen, M. A. (1988). Life care: New options for financing and delivering long-term care. *Health Care Financing Review* (Ann. Suppl.), 139–143.

Congressional Budget Office, Congress of the United States. (1991). *Policy choices for long-term care.* Washington, DC: U.S. Government Printing Office.

Crown, W. H., Capitman, J., & Leutz, W. N. (1992). Economic rationality, the affordability of private long-term care insurance, and the role for public policy. *Gerontologist, 32*, 478–485.

Eckert, S. K., & Smyth, K. (1988). *A case study of methods of locating and arranging health and long-term care for persons with dementia.* Washington, DC: Office of Technology Assessment, Congress of the United States.

Edelman, P., & Hughes, S. (1990). The impact of community care on provision of informal care to homebound elderly persons. *Journals of Gerontology: Social Sciences, 45*, S874–S884.

Friedland, R. (1990). *Facing the costs of long-term care: An EBRI-ERF policy study.* Washington, DC: Employee Benefits Research Institute.

Fries, J. F. (1989). The compression of morbidity: Near or far? *Milbank Quarterly, 67*, 208–232.

Hanley, R. J., Alecxih, L. M. B., Wiener, J. M., & Kennel, D. L. (1990). Predicting elderly nursing home admissions: Results from the 1982–89 National Long-Term Care Survey. *Research on Aging, 12*, 199–228.

Hanley, R. J., Wiener, J. M., & Harris, K. M. (1994). *The economic status of nursing home users.* Washington, DC: The Brookings Institution.

Harrington, C., Newcomer, R., & Preston, S. (1993). A comparison of S/HMO enrollees and continuing members. *Inquiry, 30*, 429–440.

Hawes, C., Wildfire, J. B., & Lux, L. J. (1993). *The regulation of board and care homes: Results of a survey in the 50 states and the District of Columbia.* Washington, DC: American Association of Retired Persons.

Health Care Financing Administration. (1996). Medicare and Medicaid statistical supplement, 1996. *Health Care Financing Review* (Stat. Suppl.), 453.

Holahan, J., Coughlin, T., Liu, K., Ku, L., Kuntz, C., Wade, M., & Wall, S. (1995). *Cutting Medicaid spending in response to budget caps.* Washington, DC: Kaiser Commission on the Future of Medicaid.

Horvath, J., & Kaye, L. W. (Eds.) (1995). *Medicaid managed care: A guide for states.* Portland, ME: National Academy for State Health Policy.

Hudson, R. B. (1996). Social protection and services. In R. H. Binstock & L. K. George (Eds.), *Handbook of aging and the social sciences* (4th ed., pp. 446–466). San Diego, CA: Academic.

Johnson, J. R. (1996). State and local approaches to long-term care. In R. J. Newcomer & A. M. Wilkinson (Eds.), *Focus on managed care and quality assurance: Integrating acute and chronic care,* Annual Review of Gerontology and Geriatrics 16 (pp. 112–139). New York: Springer.

Kane, R. L., Illston, L., & Miller, N. (1992). Qualitative analysis of the Program of All-Inclusive Care for the Elderly (PACE). *Gerontologist, 32,* 771–780.

Kane, R. A., & Wilson, K. B. (1993). *Assisted living in the United States: A new paradigm for residential care for frail older persons?* Washington, DC: American Association of Retired Persons.

Kassner, E. (1995). *Long-term care: Measuring the impact of a Medicaid cap.* Washington, DC: Public Policy Institute, American Association of Retired Persons.

Katz, S., Ford, A., Moskowitz, R., Jackson, B., & Jaffe, M. (1963). Studies of illness in the aged: The Index of ADL. *Journal of the American Medical Association, 185,* 94–99.

Kaye, L. W., & Monk, A. (Eds.) (1991). *Congregate housing for the elderly: Theoretical, policy, and programmatic perspectives.* New York: Haworth.

Leutz, W., Greenberg, J., & Abrahams, R. (1985). *Changing health care for an aging society: Planning for the social health maintenance organization.* Lexington, MA: Lexington/Heath.

Levit, K. R., Lazenby, H. C., Braden, B. R., Cowan, C. A., McDonnell, P. A., Sivarajan, L., Stiller, J. M., Won, D. K., Donham, C. S., Long, A. M., & Stewart, M. W. (1996). National health expenditures, 1995. *Health Care Financing Review, 18*(1), 175–214.

Lewin-VHI, Inc. (1992). *Policy synthesis on assisted living for the frail elderly* (final report submitted to Office of the Assistant Secretary for Planning and Evaluation). Fairfax, VA: Lewin-VHI, Inc.

Liebig, P. S. (1997). Policy and political contexts of financing long-term care. In K. H. Wilber, E. L. Schneider, & D. Polisar (Eds.), *A secure old age: Approaches to long-term care financing* (pp. 147–177). New York: Springer.

Liu, K., Manton, K. M., & Liu, B. M. (1985). Home care expenses for the disabled elderly. *Health Care Financing Review, 7*(2), 51–58.

Manton, K. G., Corder, L. S., & Stallard, E. (1993). Estimates of change in chronic disability and institutional incidence and prevalence rates in the U.S. elderly population from the 1982, 1984, and 1989 National Long Term Care Survey. *Journals of Gerontology: Social Sciences, 48,* S153–S166.

Manton, K. G., Corder, L., & Stallard, E. (1997). Chronic disability trends in elderly United States populations: 1982–1994. *Proceedings of the National Academy of Sciences, USA, 94,* 2593–2598.

Manton, K. G., Newcomer, R. J., Lowrimore, G. R., Vertrees, J. C., & Harrington, C. (1993). Social/health maintenance organizations and fee-for-service health outcomes over time. *Health Care Financing Review, 15*(2), 173–202.

Mechanic, D. (1994). Managed care: Rhetoric and realities. *Inquiry, 31,* 124–128.

Mendelson, D. N., & Schwartz, W. B. (1993). The effects of aging and population growth on health care costs. *Health Affairs, 12*(1), 119–125.

National Academy on Aging. (1994). *Old age in the 21st century.* Washington, DC: Syracuse University.

Nelson, L., Brown, R., Gold, M., Ciemnecki, A., & Docteur, E. (1997). Access to care in Medicare HMOs, 1996. *Health Affairs, 16*(2), 148–156.

Newcomer, R. J., Harrington, C., & Friedlob, A. (1990). Social health maintenance organizations: Assessing their initial experience. *Health Services Research, 25,* 425–454.

Newcomer, R. J., & Wilkinson, A. M. (Eds.) (1996). *Focus on managed care and quality assurance: Integrating acute and chronic care,* Annual Review of Gerontology and Geriatrics 16. New York: Springer.

Pear, R. (1997, March 12, 16). Clinton's plan to curb Medicaid costs draws bipartisan fire. *New York Times.*

Public Law No. 105-33 (1997). The Balanced Budget Act of 1997.

Pynoos, J. (1992). Linking federally assisted housing with services for frail older people. *Journal of Aging and Social Policy, 4*(3–4), 157–177.

Pynoos, J., & Golant, S. (1996). Housing and living arrangements for the elderly. In R. H. Binstock & L. K. George (Eds.), *Handbook of aging and the social sciences* (4th ed., pp. 303–324). San Diego, CA: Academic.

Regnier, V., Hamilton, J., & Yabate, S. (1995). *Assisted living for the aged and frail: Innovations in design, management, and financing.* New York: Columbia University Press.

Rivlin, A. M., & Wiener, J. M. (1988). *Caring for the disabled elderly: Who will pay?* Washington, DC: The Brookings Institution.

Rosow, I., & Breslau, N. (1966). A Guttman Health Scale for the aged. *Journal of Gerontology, 21,* 556–559.

Schneider, E. L., & Guralnik, J. M. (1990). The aging of America: Impact on health care costs. *Journal of the American Medical Association, 263,* 2335–2340.

Shaugnessy, P. W., Schlenker, R. E., & Hittle, D. F. (1994). Home health care outcomes under capitated and fee-for-service payment. *Health Care Financing Review, 16*(1), 187–222.

Sherwood, S., Ruchlin, H. S., Sherwood, C. C., & Morris, S. A. (1997). *Continuing care retirement communities.* Baltimore, MD: Johns Hopkins University Press.

Shield, R. R. (1996). Managing the care of nursing home residents: The challenge of integration. In R. J. Newcomer & A. M. Wilkinson (Eds.), *Focus on managed care and quality assurance: Integrating acute and chronic care,* Annual Review of Gerontology and Geriatrics 16 (pp. 60–77). New York: Springer.

Sirrocco, A. (1994). *Nursing homes and board and care homes* (Advance Data, No. 244). Hyattsville, MD: National Center for Health Statistics.

Stone, R., Cafferata, G. L., & Sangl, J. (1987). Caregivers of the frail elderly: A national profile. *Gerontologist, 27,* 616–626.

Struyk, R. J., Page, D. B., Newman, S., Carroll, M., Makiko, V., Cohen, B., & Wright, P. (1989). *Providing supportive services to the frail elderly in federally assisted housing.* Washington, DC: U.S. Government Printing Office.

Tell, E. J., Cohen, M. A., & Wallack, S. S. (1987). New directions in lifecare: An industry in transition. *Milbank Quarterly, 65,* 551–574.

Tennstedt, S. L., Crawford, S. L., & McKinlay, J. B. (1993). Is family care on the decline? A longitudinal investigation of the substitution of formal long-term care services for informal care. *Milbank Quarterly, 71,* 601–624.

U.S. Bureau of the Census. (1993). *Nursing home population: 1990* (CPH-L-137). Washington, DC: U.S. Government Printing Office.

U.S. Bureau of the Census (1996a). *65+ in the United States* (Current Population Reports, Special Studies, P23-190). Washington, DC: U.S. Government Printing Office.

U.S. Bureau of the Census (1996b). *Poverty in the United States: 1995* (Current Population Reports, Consumer Income, P60-194). Washington, DC: U.S. Government Printing Office.

U.S. Congress, Office of Technology Assessment. (1990). *Confused minds, burdened families: Finding help for people with Alzheimer's and other dementias.* Washington, DC: U.S. Government Printing Office.

U.S. General Accounting Office (1994). *Long-term care: Diverse, growing population includes millions of Americans of all ages.* Washington, DC: U.S. Government Printing Office.

U.S. General Accounting Office. (1995). *Long-term care: Current issues and future directions.* Washington, DC: U.S. Government Printing Office.

U.S. General Accounting Office. (1997). *Health care services: How continuing care retirement communities manage services for the elderly.* Washington, DC: U.S. Government Printing Office.

Verbrugge, L. M. (1989). Recent, present, and future health of American adults. In L. Breslow, J. E. Fielding, & L. B. Lave (Eds.), *Annual review of public health* (Vol. 10, pp. 333–361). Palo Alto, CA: Annual Reviews.

Walker, L., & Gruman, C. (1996). *Medicaid estate planning for nursing home care in Connecticut: Policies, practices, and perceptions reported by Connecticut Medicaid eligibility workers.* Hartford, CT: Braceland Center for Mental Health and Aging, unpublished manuscript.

Ware, J. E., Bayliss, M. S., Rogers, W. H., Kosinski, M., & Tarlov, A. (1996). Differences in 4-year health outcomes for elderly and poor, chronically ill patients treated in HMO and fee-for-services systems: Results from the Medical Outcomes Study. *Journal of the American Medical Association, 276,* 1039–1047.

Weissert, W. G. (1990). Strategies for reducing home care expenditures. *Generations, 14*(2), 42–44.

Wiener, J. M. (1996a). Managed care and long-term care: The integration of financing and services. *Generations, 20*(2), 47–52.

Wiener, J. M. (1996b). Can Medicaid long-term care expenditures for the elderly be reduced? *Gerontologist, 36,* 800–810.

Wiener, J. M., & Illston, L. H. (1996). Health care financing and organization for the elderly. In R. H. Binstock & L. K. George (Eds.), *Handbook of aging and the social sciences* (4th ed., pp. 427–445). San Diego, CA: Academic.

Wiener, J. M., Illston, L. H., & Hanley, R. J. (1994). *Sharing the burden: Strategies for public and private long-term care insurance.* Washington, DC: The Brookings Institution.

Williams, T. F., & Temkin-Greener, H. (1996). Older people, dependency, and trends in supportive care. In R. H. Binstock, L. E. Cluff, & O. von Mering (Eds.), *The future of long-term care: Social and policy issues* (pp. 51–74). Baltimore, MD: Johns Hopkins University Press.

Zawadski, R. T., & Eng, C. (1988). Case management in capitated long-term care. *Health Care Financing Review* (Ann. Suppl.), 75–81.

PART I

Public and Private Roles in Long-Term Care

A Theoretical Context

CHAPTER 1

Deceptive Dichotomies

Political Reasoning and
Government Involvement
in Long-Term Care

MARK SCHLESINGER

This chapter draws on political science concepts. It provides
a framework for describing public opinion related to long-
term care financing alternatives. In addition, the chapter uses
empirical data to better understand the ways in which congres-
sional staffers and the public may vary in their framing of the
long-term care financing debate.

Background

The power of public ideas in the making
of long-term care policy

In the public arena, ideas matter. And the ideas that matter most are
those that shape in important ways our understanding of social problems
and possible solutions. To those who founded the United States, this statement would seem self-evident. John Adams wrote that "liberty cannot be
preserved without a general knowledge among the people" about public
affairs. Thomas Jefferson argued that "the basis of our government being
the opinion of the people, the very first object should be to keep that
right and were it left to me to decide whether we should have a govern-

ment without newspapers, or newspapers without government, I should not hesitate a moment to prefer the latter." This respect for public awareness did not presume that the average U.S. citizen could be made aware of the detailed workings of government institutions (Carmines & Kuklinski, 1990). The ideas thought to matter for a strong democracy involved broad conceptions about the appropriate role for government, framed in terms of metaphors and symbols that could be comprehended by a populace that was largely politically untutored. This concern for a shared conception and understanding of political issues extended to political theorists writing during these early days of U.S. government.

> These theorists sought to speak to men who were not students of politics and to do so without condescending to them. However skeptical they were of the ability of men to shape their political circumstances, they addressed their arguments to a public audience because they believed that their theories could make a difference in men's lives. . . . To communicate their vision to audiences who lacked theoretical sophistication required a language which was rich and multi-faceted; it had to reach beyond the conventional understanding yet be intelligible to men of conventional understanding. (Zashin & Chapman, 1974, pp. 291–292)

Later commentators ranging from de Tocqueville to Keynes remarked on the power of ideas to move the political agenda in democratic polities. When ideas matter to the formation of public policy, it becomes important to understand how those ideas are framed by political leaders and interpreted by the general public. Social theorists in this tradition thus sought to understand and shape the dissemination of ideas, a process that was felt to be as important as the development of new theories for guiding policy.

In more recent times, this tradition of applied social theory has been largely supplanted by more technocratic conceptions of policy analysis and political science. Study of the language of public issues has largely disappeared from contemporary analyses. This change reflects several factors: growing cynicism about the importance of public debate in an era dominated by corruption and political scandal, conceptions of modern democracy that place few demands on the reasoning capacity of citizens (Sandel, 1996), and assessments by most political scientists that average U.S. citizens are so ignorant of political institutions that they can exercise little effective judgment about policy concerns. In the words of one such scholar,

> Nothing strikes the student of public opinion and democracy more forcefully than the paucity of information most people possess about

politics. Decades of behavioral research have shown that most people know little about their elected officeholders, less about their opponents and virtually nothing about the public issues that occupy officials from Washington to city hall. Those attitudes they express to interviewers are usually ephemeral and transient. (Ferejohn, 1990, p. 3)

Research has revealed that public attitudes are rarely consistent with conventional ideologies held by policy elites, and that opinions typically vary considerably over time and across policy domains (Jones, 1994). Nonetheless, despite abundant evidence of political ignorance and inconsistent attitudes, a small group of social scientists has begun to accumulate evidence that much of the public is able to both reason sensibly (Iyengar, 1991) and communicate effectively about these issues (Gamson, 1992). Although most of the public lacks a detailed understanding of the political sphere, they have a much clearer sense of the ends toward which they believe policy should be directed (Mayer, 1992; Graber, 1984). And the historical record suggests that government policy responds, albeit imperfectly and inconsistently, to changes in the average U.S. citizen's understanding of social issues (Page & Shapiro, 1992; Stimson, 1991). The influence of public opinion on government policy appears to hold across a variety of policy domains and has been shown in particular to shape policies regarding the health care system (Jacobs, 1993). Public ideas have the most influence on policymaking when the political process is not dominated by concentrated political interests (Campbell, 1992). This is most likely to occur at early stages in the debate over an issue, before large interest groups and institutions have mobilized to affect the outcome (Parsons, 1995).

Renewed recognition of the importance of public ideas to the policymaking process has reawakened interest in understanding how the public reasons and communicates about policy issues (Stone, 1997; Jones, 1994; Schön & Rein, 1994). But to date, this interest has produced relatively limited empirical research on the nature of public thinking about policy matters (Gamson, 1992; Hilgartner & Bosk, 1988; Graber, 1984). We know little about how public understanding of social issues matches or deviates from the ways in which these issues are framed by policymakers and other political elites. The little that is known on this front does not add up to a consistent story. Some analysts have claimed that elite interests have a powerful influence on public attitudes—in the extreme, that the public simply mimics elite positions—with these positions transmitted to the masses through various media (Reeves & Campbell, 1994; Zaller, 1992; Iyengar, 1991). Others have suggested that liberal and conservative ideologies that seem to guide elite policy opinions have little discernible influence on public attitudes (Delli Carpini & Keeter, 1996).

To better understand how policy issues are framed and understood, we need to carefully consider the different ways in which people try to make sense of complex sets of social concerns. These models of reasoning need to reflect the different contexts in which the public and political elites confront policy issues—the public having limited knowledge of political institutions and the political elites having a greater base of political knowledge and a much richer array of information about each policy issue. This chapter describes two models of political reasoning. Each relies on a different decision-making heuristic—a different set of mental guidelines—for reducing a complex situation to a more comprehensible set of dimensions.

The first of these heuristics involves *bivalent reasoning*—framing policy proposals in terms of dichotomized criteria. From this perspective, a particular proposal can be best understood by placing it on a spectrum between two well-defined end points. The labeling of particular policy proposals as either "liberal" or "conservative" is perhaps the best-known example of this reasoning process. The second of these heuristics involves *multivalent reasoning*—framing policy proposals in terms of a set of conceptual templates. In contrast to the bivalent reasoning model, these templates are not necessarily viewed as mutually exclusive; indeed, a particular proposal can embody multiple templates.

After describing these two ways of framing policy issues in more detail, the models will be used to study the ways in which the U.S. general public and policymakers think about long-term care reform. We are at a stage in the politics of long-term care that ideas are likely to have a particularly important role in shaping the policymaking agenda. Since the 1988 presidential election and the Pepper Commission report that followed, there has been relatively little attention given to long-term care reform at the federal level. Consequently, organized interests have focused on other aspects of the reform of health and social policy. However, growing cost pressures on state governments from Medicaid spending ensure that long-term care will reemerge on the political agenda. The terms of this emerging debate are likely being shaped by the ways in which we currently think about long-term care issues and policies, which we can discern from careful study of the bases of contemporary public and elite opinion. This study is based on data collected in the summer of 1995 from a matched set of surveys, one of public opinion and one of the attitudes of congressional staff who specialize in health policy issues.

Theoretical Context

Life is complicated and time is short. There is never enough time for either policymakers or members of the public to make themselves experts on the pressing social problems of the day. The problems themselves are too complex; long before the necessary expertise can be acquired, some other problem will have made its way to the forefront of the political agenda. Although policymakers have more time and resources than the public to devote to these matters, they must deal with a wide range of domestic and foreign policy matters and must become acquainted with considerable institutional detail in each arena in order to assess what policies might be effective (Jones, 1994). Even for members of Congress, who have staff specializing in particular policy areas, the complexity of those areas and the competing demands on their time make acquiring expertise a daunting process.

Certainly this is true for long-term care policy. The complicated exigencies of estate planning, the challenges of defining and enforcing quality home health care, the questions of intergenerational equity in the allocation of costs for long-term care needs are each in themselves complex. Taken together, they create a daunting set of challenges for defining fair and effective public policy. Although many people have had encounters with the long-term care system when friends or relatives need nursing home or home health care, this experience is episodic and highly idiosyncratic. Despite such experiences, few individuals understand the full array of long-term care services available in their community, the variation across communities, the ways in which those services are financed, or the opportunities for changing these arrangements. Even when congressional staff specialize in health policy (and many have issues in addition to health care in their portfolio), long-term care remains only part of a broader array of needs, institutions, and programs. Because long-term care needs typically seem more mundane and prosaic than other health care needs, they are likely to be pushed onto the proverbial back burner by media attention to hospital closures, Medicare budget cuts, gag rules in HMOs, or "drive-by" deliveries and mastectomies.

One can expect both policymakers and the public to look for short-cuts to making decisions, rules of thumb, or other heuristics that can guide them when they lack information to make fully informed choices. Political psychologists have speculated about a wide range of decision heuristics (Carmines & Kuklinski, 1990; Lau, 1990). In this chapter, we focus on two ways of framing choices about public policies, each of which captures a

decision-making process that has been shown by researchers to be important in understanding political reasoning.

Models of bivalent reasoning

The culture of the United States is rife with dualities. The legal system seeks truth through an adversarial system that pits prosecution against
defense. The most influential religions portray spirituality as a contest
between good and evil, embodied as God versus the Devil. The political system has been embodied as a competition between Republicans and
Democrats for so long that it is difficult for most voters to even take seriously the notion of a third party. Movie plots are invariably simplified into
stories of black and white; children soon learn that the quickest way to
discern the flow of events is to find out whether a particular character is a
"good guy" or "bad guy."

These cultural norms expressed in bivalent, or dichotomous, terms inevitably shape the understanding of a variety of issues. Public policy matters are no exception. The dualities common to U.S. culture are reflected
in political reasoning as well. Consider, for example, the persistence of
poverty in the United States. For most citizens, the fundamental question
is whether poverty is the product of personal characteristics (e.g., sloth or
bad planning) or structural features of the economy (e.g., high unemploy-
ment, racial discrimination, or deindustrialization). If the former, there
is no collective responsibility to address the problem; if the latter, it is a
legitimate focus of government action (Iyengar, 1991).

Faced with the complexity of addressing long-term care needs, it is
natural that both the public and policymakers might look to simple dichotomies to help them sort through and judge the various options. Such
bivalent reasoning reduces the cognitive burdens of policy assessments by
allowing decision-makers to place proposals along a spectrum with well-
defined end points. The dichotomy most often invoked in political debates
involves the categorization of policies into those that are "liberal" and
those that are "conservative." Following this approach, one first decides
where his or her preferences are on a continuum between liberal and conservative (with the end points perhaps embodied by the positions of particular well-known political figures, such as Jesse Helms on the Right and
Jesse Jackson on the Left.) By determining where a particular policy fits
on this continuum (again, perhaps in part by learning the assessments of
the politicians who define the end points), one can decide whether or not

to endorse the policy, even without knowing anything about its substantive content (Carmines & Kuklinski, 1990). Researchers suggest that this sort of ideological categorization is used more frequently and with greater consistency by policy elites than by the general public (Delli Carpini & Keeter, 1996). However, the most informed and politically active members of the public appear to behave more like elites in their reasoning processes (Sniderman, Glaser, & Griffin, 1990; Neuman, 1986).

A second dichotomy appears in a variety of social policy contexts and has become a particularly important theme in writing about long-term care reform: the distinction between public and private spheres of responsibility. This dichotomy appears consistently in the literature on long-term care policy, particularly in books written on this topic and government reports related to long-term care policy (Congressional Budget Office, 1991; Rivlin & Wiener, 1988). The distinction is particularly central to policy discussions in the United States; in most other Organization for Economic Cooperation and Development (OECD) countries, the balance sought in long-term care is more often between institutional and community services than between public and private responsibility (Organization for Economic Cooperation and Development, 1996).

The public-private categorization simplifies decision-making in much the same way as liberal-conservative positioning. Decision-makers establish their position on the appropriate allocation of responsibility for long-term care between public and private sectors. They then assess each proposed policy in terms of its balance between public and private, supporting those policies that come closest to their preferred mix. Because the determination of public versus private has more to do with the broad allocation of responsibilities for long-term care than with the details of the proposed programs, such bivalent reasoning makes it much easier to assess proposals than it is to carefully study how the programs might actually work.

Researchers suggest that the distinction between liberal and conservative ideologies has greater influence on the reasoning of political elites than the general public (Delli Carpini & Keeter, 1996). One might therefore expect that the public-private dichotomy also will be more salient for elite decision-makers than for the general public. Nonetheless, because elites play a primary role in framing the terms of much of the public debate, notions of public and private responsibility may well diffuse to the broader public understanding of long-term care (Zaller, 1992). How widely this framework has actually been adopted by those thinking about long-term care issues is not well known.

The limitations of bivalent policy assessments in long-term care

Although bivalent reasoning is embedded in much of contemporary U.S. culture, there are several reasons to suspect that neither the liberal-conservative nor the public-private categorization provides a particularly clear or comprehensive way of thinking about policymaking in the long-term care arena. Most U.S. citizens are able to place their own political beliefs somewhere on the spectrum between liberal and conservative. However, it is much more challenging to categorize most long-term care policies in this way. Consider the issue of family responsibility for long-term care needs. What would be the conservative position here? Conventionally, we think of conservative ideologies favoring continuity with past allocations of responsibility. To the extent that the literature invokes family caregiving and multigenerational shared households as the norm in the golden past before the corrupting influences of government intervention (Longman, 1986), one would expect that conservatives would favor family responsibility over government responsibility for long-term care.

But other readings of history suggest that in this golden age many families felt little sense of responsibility in providing for long-term care. For example, in a national survey conducted in 1957 (nine years before Medicaid began to pay for nursing home and home health care), less than half the public reported that they felt any responsibility to care for an elder parent (Crystal, 1982). Hence, the only way to ensure family responsibility for long-term care was to enact laws that mandated that responsibility, as many states felt compelled to do in the early twentieth century (Achenbaum, 1978). But this makes the "conservative" position one that favors government intervention into private relationships within a family—exactly the opposite of the conventional conservative ideology that protects the sanctity of the private sphere from government intrusion (Steiner, 1981).

Faced with such inconsistencies, it is often difficult to define with any certainty when particular long-term care policies might be considered liberal or conservative. The distinction between public and private is equally problematic, albeit for different reasons. Perhaps the most fundamental problem stems from the ambiguous definitions of these terms when they are applied to long-term care.

The terms *public* and *private* have been given a variety of interpretations in the literature on long-term care policy. Policies defined as private in one sense may be viewed as public in another. Some authors assert that the distinction between public and private is most appropriately made based on who pays for services, with governmental mechanisms defined as public and all other arrangements (including insurance) classified as private (Chen, 1996; Kane & Kane, 1995; Leutz, 1986). Other authors argue that the key contrast involves the provision of services, distinguishing government-owned service providers from their private counterparts (Courtney, 1996; Coleman, 1995). But *private* is an ambiguous term. Some authors reserve it for services provided by individuals or family members; others, for formal services as long as they are provided through nongovernmental agencies (Poole, 1995). Nor is it clear how one should classify voluntary nonprofit agencies, which play an important role in the provision of nursing homes, home health care, and residential care facilities (Marmor, Schlesinger, & Smithey, 1986). These are sometimes referred to as third-sector organizations, reflecting their purported positioning between public and private spheres.

A slightly different distinction is sometimes made related to the form that the services take. From this perspective, an important aspect of the term *private* involves the tailoring of care to the idiosyncratic needs of individual elders, juxtaposed against the more standardized or institutionalized approach of public settings (Kane, 1995). Still other authors argue that the appropriate distinction between public and private involves authority over decision-making. In this case, the public sector involves all those resource allocations that are determined by governmental rulemaking, and the private sector all decisions that are made outside the bounds of public regulation (Coleman, 1995; Fraser, Koontz, & Moran, 1986; Kutza, 1981). From this perspective, some authors draw a further distinction in terms of the role of the market, with private long-term care referring to all services that are allocated in accord with market forces (Wiener, 1994).

Given these diverse meanings, what government policies would qualify as public or private? Almost by definition, no action taken by government could be labeled completely private—even if the policy relied entirely on the nongovernmental provision of services, individual selection of providers, and financing by elders or their families—since the policy would have been invoked under the auspices of government authority. The only policy that would meet all these criteria for being public would be a uniform national program, fully financed by tax dollars and administered under government auspices, which gave recipients no individual choice among service providers. Since virtually all policies fall somewhere between these extremes, and since different observers read different meanings into the terms *public* and *private*, this supposedly clarifying framework may easily introduce substantial ambiguity and confusion into policy debates.[1]

The ambiguity arises not only because the terms *public* and *private* are inconsistently applied to long-term care services. Many of the societal institutions that are at the core of the existing service system for long-term care are simply difficult to classify in terms of a public and private dichotomy. Consider two examples. Virtually all long-term care, whether purchased with public or private dollars, is actually administered at the level of the local community. The substantial resources provided by the Older Americans Act, for example, are administered locally through Area Agencies on Aging, often through an array of private nonprofit service providers (Newcomer, Benjamin, & Estes, 1983). From the standpoint of service provision, will this be viewed by the average U.S. citizen as a public program because it operates under the auspices of federal legislation? Or will the local character of services mask this federal framework, much as the use of private insurers to administer the Medicare program has masked its governmental origins?

Policies that require employers to provide long-term care as a fringe benefit of employment—analogous to health insurance provision in the Clinton administration's Health Security Act—represent another case that is difficult to classify in terms of the public-private dichotomy. Certainly employers are private institutions. But a mandate from government that requires employers to act in particular ways essentially deputizes employers to act for a public purpose. Would most observers consider this a public or a private initiative?

For all these reasons, the duality between public and private, like the duality between liberal and conservative, may be a poor predictor of whether particular policies are viewed as appropriate for meeting the long-term care needs of U.S. citizens with chronic illnesses and impairments. This does not mean that bivalent reasoning has no value in understanding support for long-term care policies. Because the distinction between public and private action has appeared so frequently in the literature, arguably it has become an influential intellectual frame for those who have been exposed to these writings. Consequently, one would expect that policymakers

---

1. In this regard, it may be helpful to compare the use of the public-private distinction in long-term care to its application to welfare reform involving cash assistance programs. Because these welfare programs involve simply allocating money, all the aspects of the term *private* related to the nature of services, their standardization, or their responsiveness to market forces that complicate the analysis for long-term care are not relevant to the assessment of welfare policies.

who are familiar with long-term care and the associated literature would be more likely to make use of this dichotomy for assessing policy than would the general public. In addition, because policy elites are more likely than the general public to adopt consistent positions across policy domains (Delli Carpini & Keeter, 1996), the relevance of liberal-conservative or public-private distinctions found in other policy areas will likely spill over to indirectly shape attitudes toward long-term care as well.

If the above analysis is correct, bivalent reasoning based on these dichotomies may not be adequate for understanding attitudes toward particular long-term care policies. Other forms of reasoning are likely to come into play. Further, these alternative heuristics are likely to be particularly important in shaping the opinion of the general public.

A model of multivalent reasoning: Using policy metaphors

As an alternative approach to reasoning about policy, the multivalent model relies on a richer array of comparisons than suggested by bivalent reasoning.[2] Like conventional dichotomies, this alternative framework is predicated on the notion that few decision-makers, either policymakers or the general public, have the opportunity to gain great expertise about most complicated policy issues. Consequently, when a new issue reaches the policy agenda, people do not attempt to become experts in the matter (Jones, 1994). The model of policy metaphors predicts that they instead look for other situations, social institutions, or policy arrangements with which they have greater familiarity. By comparing this new issue to the domains in which they have greater experience, they begin to identify the range of policies that might be applied to the problem. Based on their experiences in these other domains, decision-makers can make some predictions about which of these alternatives is likely to work best when applied to the newly emerging social problem.

The importance of reasoning by analogy was succinctly captured in an example described by Stone (1988). In discussing the emerging policy issues raised by surrogate mothers, she observes that

the question of paramount importance is whether a surrogate motherhood contract is a contract for the sale of a baby or for a socially useful service. On the one hand, Mrs. Whitehead [the surrogate mother] could

2. The model of policy metaphors and its application to health care policy in general is described in greater detail in Schlesinger and Lau (1997).

be seen as "renting her womb." Like any professional service provider, she agreed to observe high standards of practice—in this case, prenatal care. Like any physical laborer, she was selling the use of her body for a productive purpose. On the other hand, Mrs. Whitehead could be seen as "producing and selling a baby." She underwent artificial insemination in anticipation of a fee—no fee, no baby. . . . She agreed to accept a lower fee if the baby were born with any mental or physical handicaps—low-value baby, low price. Is a surrogate motherhood contract for a service or for a baby? (pp. 1–2)

In this example, the comparison is made between two conceptions of surrogate motherhood, making this seemingly another form of bivalent reasoning. But some additional thought reveals the differences between metaphorical comparisons and the dichotomies described earlier. In the bivalent framework, if a particular policy is seen as more like one extreme (e.g., liberal, public) it is necessarily *less* like the alternative (e.g., conservative, private). The two end points are thus viewed as mutually exclusive in bivalent reasoning. In contrast, metaphors can be simultaneously true and false; a surrogate mother arrangement can be made more like a contract for services without making it any less the sale of a baby. And it can be simultaneously viewed as a business transaction and a social interaction, such as family obligation that depends on norms of reciprocation. Each metaphorical comparison illuminates certain aspects of the behavior in question; our understanding of the behavior is developed from the interpretation of a variety of these comparisons. For this reason, I refer to this approach to framing issues as "multivalent reasoning."

Previous writings have revealed a variety of instances in which metaphorical reasoning has powerfully shaped the ways in which political elites address social problems (Gamson & Modigliani, 1989; Lipsky & Smith, 1989; Schön & Rein, 1994; Stone, 1988). But we know very little about the relative importance of metaphorical reasoning compared to other decision-making heuristics in guiding policymakers' judgments and virtually nothing about how any heuristics shape public opinion about long-term care.[3]

How might metaphorical reasoning shape public opinion about social

3. Edelman (1971, 1993) has written extensively about the role of metaphors and other political symbols in shaping public opinion. From his perspective, symbolic arguments are for the most part manipulated by political elites to mislead the public by masking the absence of substantive action taken to deal with pressing social problems. Though exposure to any political campaign provides some validation for this claim, Edelman fails to recognize that metaphorical reasoning may also play a constructive role when used independently by the public to make sense of complicated policy issues.

policy? Every society has a set of commonly understood ways of arranging social institutions and judging their performance. Each of these arrangements is a sort of archetype, an ideal against which people compare the consequences of actual policies or project the expected outcomes of proposed policy reforms. It is the process of comparison that makes these archetypes function as metaphors.

Which archetypes represent the alternatives against which policymakers or the public assess arrangements for long-term care? As a result of the incorporation of nursing homes and home health agencies into Medicare and Medicaid, arguably long-term care has become sufficiently "medicalized" that policy in this area will be judged against the dominant institutional templates that have emerged for health care more generally (Caplan, 1988). Elsewhere I describe in more detail the historical development of different arrangements that provide the core metaphors for U.S. health policy (Schlesinger & Lau, 1997). Here I simply sketch the content and evolution of five primary metaphors:

- *Health Care as a Societal Right,* available to all citizens of the country under roughly equal terms, with these terms determined collectively for the nation as a whole through the political process at the federal level.
- *Health Care as a Community Obligation,* also reflecting a collective obligation, though in this case defined at the local level, with each community taking responsibility only for illnesses that befall those in their geographic area, with the standards of appropriate treatment defined independently by each locality.
- *Health Care as an Employer Responsibility,* a variant on the community metaphor, in which the community is defined in terms of relationships in the workplace, requiring each employer to assume responsibility for all workers and their dependents, and allowing the terms of appropriate care to be defined through negotiations between workers and management in each firm.
- *Health Care as a Marketable Commodity,* distributed according to each person's ability to pay for medical services, with standards of care determined through individual choice and market forces.
- *Health Care as a Professional Service,* with the terms of appropriate treatment determined through scientific definitions of need, shaped through professional training, and distributed according to a combination of the client's ability to pay and some professional obligations to offer services on a pro bono basis.

Each of these metaphors can be traced to their emergence in a particular historic era. Notions of community obligation are the oldest, rooted in colonial applications of British poor laws (Light, 1997). Policies related to health care as a marketable commodity can be traced to the late nineteenth century, with professionalization of medical care playing a larger role in policymaking after the turn of the century (Starr, 1982). Support for health care as a societal right was first enunciated in the United States and internationally in the mid-1900s, embodied in the enactment of national health service and health insurance programs in many countries, but with more limited applications within the United States (Beauchamp, 1988). Notions of employer responsibility also have historic roots stretching back to the nineteenth century, but were reflected in public policy only after 1980 (Silow-Carroll et al., 1995).

These general ways of arranging responsibility for health care can serve as templates for thinking about long-term care, even though there has been little direct discussion of most of these metaphors in the context of long-term care. Consider the claim that a socially valued good or service ought to be considered a societal right (Glendon, 1991; Scheingold, 1974). Advocates of this position recognize that nothing in the U.S. Constitution establishes a right to most goods or services. But they argue that the service in question ought to be treated as if it were in fact a right. In other words, access to the service should have the same moral salience, applied with the same degrees of universality and enforced with the same vigor by national authorities (Stone, 1988).

Reasoning of this sort is metaphorical in two senses. First, it compares policies in the problem area to a set of ideals (in this instance, to the image of what rights mean in the U.S. ethos). Second, metaphorical reasoning creates a framework for identifying other concrete goods and services that are distributed according to a chosen principle (in this instance, a principle of societal rights). When Harris Wofford successfully campaigned for a Senate seat in Pennsylvania in 1991, he appealed to public sentiment in favor of universal health care by arguing that if the United States could guarantee every criminal a lawyer, it ought to be able to guarantee every citizen access to a physician (Hacker, 1996).

When the public or policy elites are confronted by an emerging societal problem, they may both assess the problem and evaluate potential solutions by comparing it to the portfolio of relevant metaphors. The combined meanings of the metaphors establish the parameters against which the performance of existing arrangements may be judged. It seems likely that there will be a shared public understanding about the metaphors that are potentially relevant to each policy problem, based on collective perceptions about the nature of that problem. But the *desirability* of following a particular metaphor may depend more on each person's individual experience with the institutions invoked by that metaphor. Hence, we may all agree that long-term care might be viewed in part as a community obligation, in part as a marketable commodity, but our support for reforming long-term care to match either of those two templates will depend on how close each of us feels to the community in which we live or how effective the market is in meeting our needs.

Reasoning by policy metaphors thus invokes a set of comparisons, bounded by the number of metaphors deemed relevant to any particular social problem. To the extent that the five metaphors for health policy are relevant to long-term care, such comparisons allow for a more multivalent response than do the dichotomies reflected in the liberal-conservative or public-private paradigms. The comparisons invoked by these metaphors may be more meaningful than the more conventional dichotomies for long-term care. For example, the desirability of a system of locally administered services, such as those provided under the Older Americans Act, may be more accurately understood in terms of its compatibility with the community obligations metaphor, rather than by classifying such services as either public or private. The actual relevance of these different forms of policy reasoning can only be assessed by empirically exploring the determinants of support for particular long-term care reform strategies among the U.S. public and policymakers.

An Application to Long-Term Care: Empirical Evidence

The objective of this empirical study was to assess the role of these different conceptual frameworks for predicting support for long-term care policies. If my premise is accurate, support for the policy metaphors should be associated with support for particular long-term care reform strategies. Further, data on individuals' support for various metaphors should add significantly to the prediction of their support for various reforms, even after controlling for their preferred allocation of responsibility on the public-private spectrum or their liberal-conservative predisposition. In other words, multivalent framing should add to our information concerning long-term care policy support, beyond what is understood by the traditional bivalent framing of reforms as either public or private, or liberal or conservative.

Sources of data

To explore these questions, data were drawn from two surveys fielded during the summer and fall of 1995. One survey collected information from the U.S. public, the other from congressional staffers who oversaw health issues for members of the Senate and House of Representatives. Both surveys were designed to assess the prevalence of support for different strategies of reform applied to a variety of health and human services.

Public attitudes: The public opinion survey was based on a random sample of households containing at least one adult over the age of eighteen. The survey was fielded using random digit dialing from July 6, 1995, through August 1, 1995. After taking into account ineligible telephone numbers (e.g., business or inactive numbers), the survey had an overall response rate of 69.1 percent, yielding 1,527 interviews. Item nonresponse ranged from 0.5 percent to 3.9 percent.

Interviews required on average thirty-five minutes to complete. They covered attitudes on the salience of problems and preferred policy responses in a number of different policy domains, including medical care, long-term care, treatment of substance abuse, public education, and homelessness. The alternative policy approaches that respondents were asked to assess included uniform national programs such as Social Security, market models relying on vouchers, and professionally mediated interventions (equivalent to managed care plans in medical care). Information was also collected on respondents' political ideology, their favored allocation of responsibility for social problems between public (e.g., federal government) and private (e.g., individuals and their families), the perceived complexity of various societal problems, and a variety of sociodemographic characteristics.

To keep the survey a manageable length, certain questions were presented to subsets of respondents. All respondents were asked about the appropriate policy responses for medical care and basic needs. The sample was split, on a random basis, with half of the respondents asked about policy reforms in long-term care, half about reforms associated with the treatment of substance abuse. A similar random assignment was used for education and homelessness. To ensure that question ordering did not affect choices among policy alternatives, these were presented in a randomly determined order for each respondent.

Sociodemographic characteristics of survey respondents generally matched those of the adult U.S. population in terms of education, marital status, gender, and household size. The proportion of low-income African

American and Latino respondents was about a third lower than what one would expect from a representative sample. Controlling statistically for race, ethnicity, and income do not, however, significantly alter the results presented below.

Elite attitudes: Congressional staff who were responsible for health care were identified using published directories. They were subsequently contacted by telephone and asked to participate in the study. Surveys were completed between June and October of 1995. Taking into account respondents who were ineligible because they were participating in other aspects of this study, the overall participation rate was approximately 35 percent, yielding a total of 172 completed interviews. Similar to the survey of the general public, half of the congressional staff sample were asked questions about long-term care. Of those who did not participate in the survey, slightly more than half reported that they could not as a result of office policy. Subsequent analysis of respondents and nonrespondents suggested that there were no statistically significant differences between the two groups in terms of the ideological position of the member for whom they worked,[4] the proportion of their constituents who voted for Clinton or Bush in 1992, the length of time their member had been in Congress, or the member's margin of victory in his or her last election.

The survey for congressional staff was structured to replicate much of the survey of public opinion, including the subsetting of the sample for certain policy domains and the randomly ordered presentation of policy alternatives within each domain. In addition to the questions asked of the general public, staffers were asked about the importance of particular policy concerns for their constituents, the impact of those issues on the electoral prospects for their member, and the challenges of communicating with constituents about those issues. Item nonresponse ranged from 0.6 percent to 6.5 percent.

Measures

Support for particular long-term care policies: The surveys included measures of support for four approaches to long-term care reform that received attention from policymakers and the media during the mid-1990s: (1) incorporating long-term care coverage into the Medicare program; (2) pro-

---

4. This measure was assessed using both the published Americans for Democratic Action ratings of overall liberalism in voting and the National Journal ratings of liberalism for domestic and international affairs.

viding vouchers that could be used to purchase long-term care services through the market; (3) making long-term care coverage a fringe benefit of employment; and (4) incorporating long-term care into professionally run organizations, analogous to the social/health maintenance organizations. The question about support for each of these reforms was introduced to respondents with an initial statement: "People talk about a number of ways of changing how we provide long-term care to the disabled and elderly. I am going to describe different options. For each, I'd like you to tell me whether you support or oppose the policy." Responses were placed on a four-point scale, ranging from "strongly support" to "strongly oppose." [5]

Bivalent reasoning: Bivalent reasoning, or dichotomous framing of issues, was measured in two ways. The first measure of bivalent framing was based on respondents' preferred allocation of responsibility for addressing social problems between public and private spheres, using question formats from the General Social Survey (Davis & Smith, 1994). Respondents were asked to decide between two statements, one favoring individual responsibility, the other assigning responsibility to the federal government. (Respondents could agree exclusively with either statement, favor one more than the other, or favor both equally.) For example, in the long-term care domain, respondents were asked to consider these statements: "Some people think that it is the responsibility of government in Washington to help people pay for nursing homes and home health care for the elderly" and "Others think that this is not the responsibility of the federal government and that people should take care of these things themselves." This item measured allocations of public (federal government) and private (individual) responsibility for long-term care. Although this question captured only one aspect of the public-private dichotomy, because allocations of responsibility are very important in shaping public assessments of government policy (Skitka & Tetlock, 1993; Iyengar, 1991), this was deemed the most salient dimension to measure in the survey.

The second measure of bivalent reasoning captured one's ideological predisposition, which was assessed through conventional measures used in political science. Respondents were asked to place themselves on a continuum with "liberal" and "conservative" as the two end points and "moderate or middle of the road" as the midpoint. For some analyses, this measure was dichotomized as conservative or nonconservative. Nonconservative included those who reported themselves as politically liberal or moderate.

5. Congressional staff were asked an identically worded question. On this survey, however, the response scale was given a "neutral" midpoint.

Multivalent reasoning—policy metaphors: To assess metaphorical reasoning, respondents were asked about their support for the five templates identified earlier: societal rights, community obligation, employer responsibility, marketable commodity, and professional service. To capture their general support for each approach, respondents were asked about its desirability when applied to "basic needs," defined as "food, housing, education, and health care." The descriptions of the five approaches are provided in Table 1.1. The statements were derived from a set of intensive interviews conducted prior to the development of the survey instrument, suggesting that the wording used here both captured the most salient features of the five archetypical strategies and invoked concepts that could be understood by a broad cross-section of the U.S. public. Notice that the wording of each describes an allocation of responsibility, a sense of emotional response (comfort) with the social institutions associated with this approach, and a concrete comparison that grounds the assessment in some other widely known policy.

Data analysis

Standard frequency analyses were used to describe respondents' support for various long-term care policy reforms as well as support for bivalent and multivalent modes of framing policy issues. Differences in levels of support for various reforms among those who prefer public versus private allocation of responsibility in long-term care were compared using *t*-statistics. Similar analyses were conducted for comparisons by ideological predisposition. The added contribution of individuals' support for various policy metaphors was assessed by comparing three regression models, each modeling respondents' support for the various long-term care reforms. The first model included respondents' support for public versus private allocation of responsibility as an independent variable. The second model included the public-private allocation measure as well as individuals' ideological predisposition (nonconservative or conservative). The third model included both these bivalent frames of reasoning and added the respondents' support for the policy metaphors.[6] The impact of each of these

6. Note that this is a conservative estimate of the marginal contribution of the metaphors. Because support for the metaphors is somewhat correlated with ideology or allocations of responsibility, examining the added variance explained by the metaphors understates their full contribution. However, support for the metaphors is not that closely correlated with either political ideology or allocations of responsibility, so this approach offers a reasonably accurate portrayal of the marginal importance of multivalent measures in explaining policy support.

Table 1.1
Wording for Survey Questions about Policy Metaphors

Metaphor	Description
Societal Right	Some people talk about meeting basic needs as a "societal right." You need national solutions to adequately address the full range of people's basic needs and ensure that the needs of *all* people are met. You can rely on the federal government to be fair and responsive in administering these programs. One way to better meet basic needs would be to design more federal programs to be like Social Security.
Community Obligation	Basic needs can be defined as a community responsibility. Community organizations are best able to understand and provide for the basic needs of people who live in their city or town. People feel most comfortable getting help from those who live in the same area they do. For these reasons, programs to help meet people's basic needs are best run at the local level, like public schools are now run.
Employer Responsibility	Basic needs can be made the responsibility of employers. A good way to help people meet their basic needs is to let workers and managers freely bargain with each other to decide upon benefit packages that cover services like day care, health, or school scholarships in addition to wages. Companies can be relied upon to help their workers deal with these problems, although they may need some government subsidies to help pay the costs of these benefits.
Marketable Commodity	Market forces can determine how best to meet basic needs. Individuals are best able to decide for themselves which of their needs are most vital and how they should be met. Most people don't want others to make decisions about their families' needs. The best solution is a program like food stamps, giving people coupons of a certain value for housing, food, or education and allowing each family to determine what they will buy.
Professional Service	We can let professionals decide how best to meet basic needs. To really understand people's needs, you must have advice from experts who study education, housing and nutrition. The only people you can trust to make these decisions are people who can find scientifically correct answers. We should develop a program like the space program that could give specialists money to develop and administer new programs to improve housing, education, and health care.

measures was assessed in terms of the added percentage of variance in support, which is explained by the variables in question. Models were compared using the partial *F*-test to address whether the policy metaphors add significantly to the explanatory power of the models without the metaphor measures.

Results

Support for various long-term care reform strategies: The extent of support among public and elite respondents for each of these four reform strategies is presented in Table 1.2. The results indicate that respondents from the general public were considerably more supportive of Medicare-based reforms than were congressional staff. Staff were also less supportive of policies that would require that long-term care be provided as a fringe benefit of employment; indeed, this was the option that evoked the most opposition from staffers. Support for a professionally mediated model was also much lower among elite respondents, largely because there was a much greater "neutral" response than for the other two strategies. Both groups were about equally supportive of vouchers (though there were more strong opponents to this strategy among the general public). These findings suggest that the assessment of policy options for long-term care differs for public and elite respondents. However, the findings in Table 1.2 do not document that the *process* of policy assessment, including the terms in which long-term care reforms are framed, differs between the two groups.

Allocation of responsibility for long-term care and ideology: Preferred allocations for public versus private responsibility in long-term care as compared to other policy areas are shown in Table 1.3. Staffers reported being somewhat more oriented toward private responsibility than the general public: 42 percent of congressional staff assigned primary responsibility to the individual for meeting long-term care needs, while 31 percent of the public did so. For all the policy domains studied in this survey, the public favored more sharing of responsibility than did congressional staff in the sense that many respondents preferred arrangements that gave equal responsibilities to individuals and the federal government (see Table 1.3). For both sets of respondents, long-term care fell roughly in the middle of the public-private dichotomy compared to other policy areas. In terms of ideological dichotomy between liberal and conservative, 37 percent of the public and 43 percent of congressional staff consider themselves to be conservatives by this measure.

Support for metaphors: The levels of support for the different meta-

Table 1.2
Support for Four Long-Term Care Reforms

Reform Strategy	Extent of Support (%)				
	Strongly Oppose	Somewhat Oppose	Neutral	Somewhat Support	Strongly Support
General Public					
Medicare	17.7	15.0	NA	39.0	28.3
Fringe Benefit	18.8	15.4	NA	31.7	34.1
Vouchers	25.6	24.1	NA	33.5	16.8
S/HMO	27.5	25.1	NA	32.5	14.8
Congressional Staff					
Medicare	22.6	11.9	20.2	31.0	14.3
Fringe Benefit	35.1	18.2	11.7	27.3	7.8
Vouchers	8.3	32.1	10.7	32.1	16.7
S/HMO	15.7	25.3	33.7	21.7	3.6

phors among the two samples are reported in Table 1.4. Although there is considerable support from both groups for community-based obligations, there are substantial differences in support for the other four metaphors. Perhaps reflecting the somewhat more conservative predisposition of the elite respondents, staff were more supportive of the market metaphor than was the general public. But although staffers were less supportive than the public of the other three metaphors, the biggest difference was not for the societal rights metaphor—as one might suspect if the differences were driven by ideology—but for the professional service metaphor, which received scanty support among staffers.

The role of bivalent distinctions in predicting support for various reforms: Results in Table 1.5 examine the claim that distinctions between public and private approaches are meaningful for assessing support for long-term care policy interventions. One might have anticipated that the distinction between public and private would most differentiate support for the strategy involving Medicare, since this is the most distinctly "public" of the reforms (if respondents recognize Medicare as a government-run program). As evidenced in Table 1.5, members of the public who favored private responsibility were less supportive of this approach. Nonetheless, the substantive differences are quite small. Almost two-thirds of those who favored private responsibility were still supportive of the Medicare approach. A similar

Table 1.3
Preferred Allocations of Responsibility among General Public and Congressional Staff across Five Policy Domains

Policy Domain	Distribution of Preferences (%)				
	Entirely Private Responsibility	⟷	Responsibility Shared Equally	⟷	Entirely Public Responsibility
General Public					
Long-Term Care	13.8	17.6	32.6	18.0	18.0
Acute Medical Care	17.3	14.7	38.6	17.4	12.0
Treatment of Substance Abuse	21.4	17.2	34.2	15.5	11.7
Programs for the Homeless	19.3	19.5	29.4	16.1	15.7
Congressional Staff					
Long-Term Care	15.6	26.0	13.0	28.6	16.9
Acute Medical Care	32.5	13.8	11.9	19.4	22.5
Treatment of Substance Abuse	22.2	26.4	6.9	25.0	19.4
Programs for the Homeless	17.6	17.6	11.8	29.4	23.5

Table 1.4
Support for Particular Metaphors among General Public and Congressional Staff

Metaphor	Percentage Strongly or Somewhat Agreeing	
	General Public	Congressional Staff
Societal Right	39.1	26.3
Community Obligation	78.4	74.3
Employer Responsibility	68.9	47.1
Marketable Commodity	41.6	58.2
Professional Service	47.7	16.5

Table 1.5
Support for Long-Term Care Reforms by Preferred Allocation of Responsibility

Reform Strategy	Percentage Support among Those Favoring	
	Public Responsibility	Private Responsibility
General Public		
Include LTC within Medicare	72.9	64.0[a]
LTC as a Fringe Benefit	72.0	62.3[a]
Vouchers for LTC Services	53.1	48.6
Professionally Allocated Services (S/HMO)	50.4	45.7
Congressional Staff[b]		
Include LTC within Medicare	68.5	44.1[a]
LTC as a Fringe Benefit	62.8	22.6[a]
Vouchers for LTC Services	42.9	66.7[a]
Professionally Allocated Services (S/HMO)	48.5	36.6

[a]Difference statistically significant at a 5 percent confidence level.

[b]Neutral responses allocated to neighboring categories to make comparable to public respondents.

pattern occurred for mandated employer benefits. And for the other two reform strategies, knowing whether a respondent favors public responsibility has no meaningful predictive power at all.

The findings are strikingly different for congressional staff. For staffers, allocations of responsibility are strongly associated with their support for particular policy proposals. This is particularly true for reforms that make long-term care a fringe benefit of employment. Almost three times as many staffers who viewed long-term care as a public responsibility favored this approach compared to staffers who assigned responsibility to individuals. The voucher approach, on the other hand, is preferred by congressional staff who favored private allocations of responsibility. Interestingly, even for this group the reform that seems like the prototypical public programs —incorporating long-term care coverage into Medicare—was nonetheless endorsed by a substantial number of staffers. Support for long-term care models that rely on professionally allocated services appears to have less relationship to preferences about allocations of responsibility than do the other three strategies of reform.

Table 1.6
**Support for Long-Term Care Reforms by Preferred Allocation
of Responsibility**

	Percentage Support among Those Favoring	
Reform Strategy	Nonconservative Ideology	Conservative Ideology
General Public		
Include LTC within Medicare	69.9	63.3[a]
LTC as a Fringe Benefit	65.5	65.7
Vouchers for LTC Services	53.6	45.5
Professionally Allocated Services (S/HMO)	50.2	41.8[a]
Congressional Staff[b]		
Include LTC within Medicare	60.5	34.1[a]
LTC as a Fringe Benefit	55.3	17.1[a]
Vouchers for LTC Services	18.4	80.5[a]
Professionally Allocated Services (S/HMO)	18.3	32.5

[a] Difference statistically significant at a 5 percent confidence level.

[b] Neutral responses allocated to neighboring categories to make comparable to public respondents.

What about more ideological distinctions? If we separate respondents between those reporting themselves as conservatives (i.e., those who scored higher than 3 on our five-point scale) and those who reported being non-conservative (i.e., liberal or neutral), we observe a pattern very much like that shown for allocation of responsibility (Table 1.6). Among the general public, there were small, though statistically significant, ideological differences in support for including long-term care in Medicare. Conservatives were also less supportive of the professionally controlled model of long-term care reform. But there were no significant ideological differences in support for long-term care vouchers or employment-based benefits (see Table 1.6). And once again, even where there were statistically significant differences, the substantive gaps in preferences were not large. Though conservatives were less supportive of a Medicare-modeled reform of long-term care, this option was still supported by more than 63 percent of conservative respondents. Although conservatives were more negative than other respondents toward the professionally controlled model, even non-conservatives were not very supportive of this approach.

Ideological differences were more striking among congressional staff. Conservative staffers were more likely to reject the Medicare approach and mandated benefits approach than were conservatives in the general public. And ideology strongly predicted the propensity of congressional staff to embrace the voucher model, with conservative staffers being extremely supportive; liberals and moderates, strongly opposed. This contrasted with public attitudes toward vouchers, which were relatively neutral overall and unrelated to ideology. Interestingly, the professionally based model appeared to be favored more by conservative elites than moderate or liberal elites (though the differences reported in Table 1.6 are not statistically significant)—exactly the reverse pattern that holds among the general public.

These analyses suggest that dichotomous categorizations of public-private or liberal-conservative were only marginally useful in predicting public support for or opposition to long-term care reforms. However, the dichotomous categorizations were much more revealing of the policy positions taken by political elites.

The role of metaphors in predicting support for various long-term care reforms: To what extent does an understanding of policy metaphors improve our ability to predict attitudes toward particular long-term care reforms? Table 1.7 reveals several findings.

First, the added contribution of the policy metaphors to explaining support for various long-term care reforms was statistically significant for several long-term care reforms, but only moderate in magnitude. Second, support for the metaphors explained a greater proportion of the predicted variation in program support among the general public than among staffers. This was largely because the dichotomous measures explained so little among the general public. Among the general public, the metaphors explained on average about three times as much variance in program support as did ideology and preferred allocation of responsibility taken together. Since ideology and preferred allocation of responsibility explained more about staff support for policies, proportionally the metaphors added less to the understanding among elites than among the general public. Among the staffers, the metaphors increased the explained variation in support for particular programs by about a third across the four strategies of reform.

Finally, the usefulness of the various approaches to policy framing varied by different long-term care policies. For instance, allocations of responsibility (i.e., public versus private) were the most salient predictor of staff support for either the Medicare or fringe benefit approach to reforming long-term care. In contrast, ideological predisposition (i.e., nonconserva-

Table 1.7
Predicting Support for Specific Long-Term Care Reforms

Model for Long-Term Care Reform	Percentage Variation among Respondents Predicted by		
	Public-Private Allocation of Only	Ideology and Public-Private Responsibility	With Metaphors
General Public			
Include LTC within Medicare	2.4	2.6	6.1[a]
LTC as a Fringe Benefit	3.6	3.7	15.0[b]
Vouchers for Long-Term Care	0.3	0.6	3.0
Professionally Allocated Services (S/HMO)	0.4	1.6	7.7[b]
Congressional Staff			
Include LTC within Medicare	19.1	21.4	26.2
LTC as a Fringe Benefit	32.0	37.8	54.5[b]
Vouchers for Long-Term Care	12.1	36.3[b]	41.0
Professionally Allocated Services (S/HMO)	4.8	10.9	20.6[b]

[a] p-value < 0.10
[b] p-value < 0.05

tive versus conservative) was a more powerful predictor of staff support for the voucher model. Neither form of bivalent reasoning offered much insight into staff support for professionally allocated models of long-term care. For both congressional staff and the general public, multivalent framing (i.e., the policy metaphors) was most helpful in understanding support for treating long-term care as a fringe benefit or having long-term care be professionally allocated.

Discussion

Public policy is shaped by a variety of influences. The circumstances under which long-term care reform currently is being discussed make it likely that ideas will play an important role in shaping the course of the debate. Nevertheless, the most common conceptual framework in the policy literature for thinking about long-term care, the distinction between public and private responsibility, seems to have relatively little salience for the general public. The public-private distinction is more helpful in predicting the attitudes of political elites, but tells us less than either liberal-conservative ideology or the policy metaphors about support for at least two of the most common proposals for reform.

This limited salience of the public-private distinction is not all that surprising, given the ambiguities about the meaning of the terms *public* and *private* in the context of long-term care. For the public, neither of the dichotomous frameworks has much salience in predicting support for particular public policies. For congressional staff, ideological distinctions between liberal and conservative are in some cases important in identifying which proposals will be supported. But for both groups, notions of policy metaphors appear to add substantially to our ability to understand support for particular reform strategies.

To help us explore their implications more fully, it is useful to group our findings into two categories: (1) those reflecting similarities in the reasoning process between congressional staff and the general public; and (2) those reflecting differences between the two groups. From each set we can derive some insights into both patterns of political reasoning and the political prospects for future reform of the financing and delivery of long-term care services in the United States.

Both the general public and political elites report the appropriate allocation of responsibility for long-term care as a balance between individuals and society as a whole. For both groups, one would expect that preferences related to this allocation would be influenced in part by considerations of self-interest, in part by notions of societal justice, and in part by perceptions about the equity of the policymaking process. The attitudes and perceptions that predicted preferred allocations of responsibility were explored empirically in analyses not reported in detail here. The results suggested that the factors that shape elite and public opinion about the appropriate allocation of responsibility were most similar when they involve perceptions about the policymaking process. In particular, both congressional staff and the public were less willing to assign responsibility for long-term care to the federal government when they believed that elder interest groups exerted an unfair amount of influence on the policymaking process. This perception was relatively rare among the public, but quite common in Congress.

Among both public and elite respondents, allocation of responsibility was most influential in explaining support for treating long-term care as a fringe benefit of employment. For the congressional staff, this one consideration predicted a substantial portion of the variance in the acceptability of this proposal. Somewhat surprisingly, allocations of responsibility had only a modest relationship with support for those reforms that were the most "public" in nature, such as incorporating long-term care more completely under the Medicare program. (In the case of the public, one might suspect that this reflected their failure to understand that Medicare *is* a public program, but this explanation surely cannot apply to congressional staff.) For both groups, policy metaphors explained some of the variation in support, particularly for programs involving the use of fringe benefits or professionally mediated services.

Despite these similar findings, the two groups of respondents also displayed some important differences in political reasoning. Although congressional staff and the public were evenly divided in terms of allocating responsibility for long-term care, the former were considerably more polarized than the latter. Staffers generally preferred to assign responsibility to either individuals or the federal government, but not often to both equally (see Table 1.3). A larger portion of the public viewed responsibility as being appropriately shared between public and private actors. There were also some important differences in the reasons that the two groups favored a particular allocation of responsibility. In analyses not shown, members of the public who reported themselves as more egalitarian leaned toward a larger role for the federal government, while egalitarian members of Congress preferred more individual responsibility. Some factors that undermined congressional support for a federal role (e.g., ideology) had little influence on public opinion, while other considerations that mattered to the public (e.g., concerns about fraud and abuse in government health programs) had little salience for staff attitudes.

Clearly the sharpest distinction between elite and public opinion involves the relative importance of bivalent reasoning in determining support for reform strategies. For congressional staff, allocations of responsibility and ideological predispositions powerfully predicted attitudes toward a number of policy options, particularly those that involve treating long-term care as either a fringe benefit of employment or making long-term care services available through a voucher program. This is consistent with research on the difference between elite and public opinion on policy issues (Delli Carpini & Keeter, 1996).

Interestingly, the greater importance of bivalent reasoning among policy elites did not translate into a smaller role for metaphors in explaining policy support among this group. In fact, the policy option most completely predicted by ideology and preferred allocations of responsibility—

the proposal to treat long-term care as a fringe benefit—was also the one for which the metaphors added the most to explaining variance in support. Although bivalent reasoning explains much more of the variance in support among staff for the professionally allocated model than it does for the public, metaphors are still more predictive for staffers than for the public in explaining support for this strategy of reform.

Implications

Understanding political reasoning

These findings offer insights into broader patterns of political reasoning as well as the prospects for future long-term care reform. Compared to political elites, the U.S. public is clearly less likely to think about long-term care issues in dichotomous terms, whether liberal versus conservative or public versus private. It is less clear *why* these differences exist. For many years, political scientists have explained the apparent ideological naiveté of the public in terms of their inability to comprehend the sophisticated reasoning necessary to apply an abstract framework to concrete policy situations (Neuman, 1986). And yet we have evidence from our analyses of policy metaphors that the public can use certain conceptual categories to make sense of policy options. Why should it be easier for the public to use the multiple categories represented by the metaphors than the simpler dichotomous categories of prevailing ideological frameworks? Put differently, why should the supposedly more sophisticated political elites rely on simpler schemas for guiding their policy choices?

Neither this study nor previous research allows us to answer these questions conclusively. But we can speculate, guided in part by the findings presented here. It may be the case that the use of dichotomous conceptual frames is less an indication of sophisticated reasoning than of the need to signal a consistent position to voters and others who pay attention to elite political preferences. If one is running for election, it would be easier to describe oneself as "moderate conservative" (with a clear placement along a broadly understood ideological spectrum) than someone who favors a blending of societal rights with community responsibility. And consistency of position is clearly more important for most politicians than for the general public, who appear content to adopt quite inconsistent stances toward policy issues over time (Neuman, 1986).

If this explanation is correct, then one ought to see dichotomous reasoning displayed most powerfully for reform options that have the greatest political salience. In 1995, when this survey was conducted, two of the four reform options that respondents considered had been given the most recent political play—employer mandates and vouchers. Employer mandates were a central feature of the Clinton administration's health care reforms that were debated in 1993 and 1994 (Hacker & Skocpol, 1997). Vouchers were at the core of the Republican Party's proposals for reforming the Medicare program, proposals that received active consideration during 1995 (Pauly, 1996). In contrast, single-payer programs modeled on Medicare or professionally allocated services had been accorded less political attention. If our signaling hypothesis is correct, one ought to see the dichotomous measures of reasoning predicting more of the variation in staff support for mandated benefit and voucher reforms than for the other two.

As shown in Table 1.7, one observes this exact pattern. The dichotomous distinctions between public-private and liberal-conservative explain on average 37 percent of the variation in staff support for the two high-profile reform strategies, while accounting for only 16 percent of the variance for the other two approaches. This is true despite the fact that the public-private distinctions ought to be clearest for a federal program like Medicare, certainly more so than for a program that mandates employer actions, since this latter approach combines a role for public and private actors. Further, it is noteworthy that the same pattern does not hold among the general public. Vouchers represent the option least well predicted by ideology and assignments of responsibility for this group of respondents.

The prospects for future long-term care reform

Perhaps the most evident implications involving the prospects for future reforms are captured by the findings presented in Table 1.2. The general public and policy elites reach distinctly different assessments of potential reform strategies. The two options that have the greatest public support—incorporating long-term care benefits into Medicare or requiring them as fringe benefits of employment—are viewed with considerable disfavor among congressional staff. And while support for these two reforms cuts across liberal and conservative segments of the public, staffer attitudes are distinctly polarized by ideology. Conservative congressional staff, though recognizing the need to address long-term care, line up almost exclusively behind a voucher strategy, an approach that has little prospect for bipartisan support in Congress and only modest backing from the U.S. public (see Table 1.2).

The prospects for successfully reforming long-term care are further undercut by three additional factors. The first involves the challenges of communicating about potential reforms. As noted earlier, congressional staff rank long-term care second only to medical care reform in terms of their inability to communicate effectively with constituents. This is not terribly surprising in light of the results presented above. The language used to discuss long-term care reform in the academic literature—which relies on the distinction between public and private responsibilities—carries little meaning for the public. Equally important, the factors that encourage congressional staff to favor greater federal responsibility for long-term care are for the most part different from those that encourage the public to favor that allocation of responsibility. Casting reforms in terms of ideology—the language most salient in the political world—does not facilitate communication with the public. The language of policy metaphors might, although the analyses presented here suggest that it may add only moderately to efforts to increase public understanding.

The second barrier to effective reform rests in perceptions about the role of elder interest groups in the policymaking process. The survey revealed that 69 percent of the congressional staff respondents believed that elder interest groups had too much influence on federal policymaking. In contrast, only 11 percent of the public believed elder interest groups had too much influence. It is striking how many congressional staff believe that these groups have excessive influence on the creation of federal health policy, despite their relatively modest role in the debate about the Clinton health care reform proposal. Data from the surveys demonstrated that negative perception of elder interest groups' influence on the policymaking process significantly reduced elite support for federal responsibility in long-term care. This perception has substantially less support for a federal role in long-term care. Why congressional staff have such antagonistic impressions and why they are so much more negative than the general public cannot be determined from this survey, but it is likely to have substantial implications for the long-term prospects for reform.

The third challenge involves the influence of broader efforts at medical care reform. Since 1988, there has been little discussion in Congress of long-term care reform in its own right. But long-term care has been made a part of larger health care reform proposals, most notably that developed by the Clinton administration in 1993. What are the implications of combining the two types of services for the prospects of building support for a reform proposal? That depends largely on whether reforms favored for medical care are viewed as consistent with those favored for long-term care.

Table 1.8
**Consistency of Support between Congressional Staff and General
Public, Comparing Long-Term Care and Medical Care**

	Correlations between Medical and Long-Term Care Domains for	
Consistency Measured for:	Congressional Staff	General Public
Allocating Responsibility to Federal Government	0.72	0.38
Favoring Uniform National Program	0.34	0.29
Favoring Employer-mandated Benefits	0.62	0.37
Favoring Vouchers	0.30	0.20
Favoring Professionally Allocated Services	0.17	0.30

The results displayed in Table 1.8 suggest that the extent of compatibility depends on both the group involved and the policy they are considering. Among congressional staff, allocations of responsibility between individuals and society are made very similarly whether one is considering long-term care or medical care. Similarly, those who favor employer mandates for medical care are also disposed toward an employer role in long-term care. Consequently, a reform proposal that combines long-term care and acute medical care in a common model may seem sensible to staff if cast in terms of employer responsibility.

The public seems to view long-term care and medical care less consistently. The correlations in support for reforms across these two domains are relatively low. This makes combined policy approaches considerably more difficult. Interestingly, the data demonstrate a pattern that contradicts the general claims that elite attitudes are always more consistent than public opinion across policy domains (Neuman, 1986). Staffers' attitudes toward professionally allocated services are considerably less consistent than those of the public. The explanations for this curious pattern require additional study.

Changing demographics ensure that long-term care will remain on the public agenda for much of the next half century. However, if we are to be able to convert this continued public attention into effective public action, it is essential that we understand how to better communicate about these issues. The data presented here suggest that there are substantial gaps in terms of the strategies of reform favored by the public and political elites as well as the reasoning that the two groups use for assessing these alternative approaches.

For proposed reforms to garner public support and gain legitimacy, they must be reasonably consistent with public preferences and reasonably comprehensible by the public. To encourage this sort of matching, we need to develop a vocabulary of reform that is meaningful to both the public and policymakers. Given the rather skimpy base that currently exists, this will be a substantial challenge. Nevertheless, it is a challenge that must be met to ensure that the actions that government takes are perceived as legitimate by those whom they are intended to benefit.

References

Achenbaum, W. (1978). *Old age in the new land: The American experience since 1790.* Baltimore, MD: Johns Hopkins University Press.

Barone, M., & Ujifusa, G. (1995). *Almanac of American politics.* Washington, DC: The National Journal.

Beauchamp, D. (1988). *The health of the Republic.* Philadelphia, PA: Temple University Press.

Campbell, J. (1992). *How policies change.* Princeton, NJ: Princeton University Press.

Caplan, A. (1988). Is medical care the right prescription for chronic illness? In S. Sullivan & M. Ein Lewin (Eds.), *The economics and ethics of long-term care and disability* (pp. 73–89). Washington, DC: American Enterprise Institute.

Carmines, E., & Kuklinski, J. (1990). Incentives, opportunities and the logic of public opinion in American political representation. In J. Ferejohn & J. Kuklinski (Eds.), *Information and democratic processes* (pp. 240–268). Urbana: University of Illinois Press.

Chen, Y. (1996). A "three-legged stool" for financing long-term care in the United States. *Ageing International, 23*(2), 53–65.

Coleman, B. (1995). European models of long-term care in the home and community. *International Journal of Health Services, 25*(3), 455–474.

Congressional Budget Office, Congress of the United States. (1991). *Policy choices for long-term care.* Washington, DC: Congressional Budget Office.

Cook, F. L., & Barret, E. (1992). *Support for the American welfare state.* New York: Columbia University Press.

Courtney, M. (1996). Long-term prospects. *Nursing Times, 92*(27), 31–32.

Crystal, S. (1982). *America's old age crisis: Public policy and the two worlds of aging.* New York: Basic Books.

Davis, J., & Smith, T. (1994). *General social survey, 1972–1994: Cumulative codebook.* Chicago, IL: National Opinion Research Corporation.

Delli Carpini, M., & Keeter, S. (1996). *What Americans know about politics and why it matters.* New Haven, CT: Yale University Press.

Edelman, M. (1971). *Politics as symbolic action.* New York: Academic.

Edelman, M. (1993). Contestable categories and public opinion. *Political Communication, 10,* 231–242.

Ferejohn, J. (1990). Information and the electoral process. In J. Ferejohn & J. Kuklinski (Eds.), *Information and democratic processes* (pp. 3–19). Urbana: University of Illinois Press.

Fraser, I., Koontz, T., & Moran, W. (1986). Medicare reimbursement for hospice care: An approach for analyzing cost consequences. *Inquiry, 23*(3), 141–153.

Gamson, W. (1992). *Talking politics.* New York: Cambridge University Press.

Gamson, W., & Modigliani, A. (1989). Media discourse and public opinion on nuclear power: A constructionist approach. *American Journal of Sociology, 95*(1), 1–37.

Glendon, M. (1991). *Rights talk: The impoverishment of political discourse.* New York: The Free Press.

Graber, D. (1984). *Processing the news: How people tame the information tide.* New York: Longman.

Hacker, J. (1996). National health care reform: An idea whose time came and went. *Journal of Health Politics, Policy and Law, 21*(4), 647–696.

Hacker, J., & Skocpol, T. (1997). The new politics of U.S. health policy. *Journal of Health Politics, Policy and Law, 22*(2), 315–339.

Hilgartner, S., & Bosk, C. (1988). The rise and fall of social problems: A public arenas model. *American Journal of Sociology, 94*(1), 53–78.

Iyengar, S. (1991). *Is anyone responsible? How television frames political issues.* Chicago, IL: University of Chicago Press.

Jacobs, L. (1993). Health reform impasse: The politics of American ambivalence toward government. *Journal of Health Politics, Policy and Law, 18*(3), 629–655.

Jones, B. (1994). *Reconceiving decision-making in democratic politics.* Chicago, IL: University of Chicago Press.

Kane, R. (1995). Expanding the home care concept: Blurring distinctions among home care, institutional care, and other LTC services. *Milbank Quarterly, 73*(2), 161–186.

Kane, R., & Kane, R. (1995). Long-term care. *Journal of the American Medical Association, 273*(21), 1690–1691.

Kinder, D., & Sears, D. (1985). Public opinion and political action. In G. Lindsay & E. Aronson (Eds.), *The handbook of social psychology* (Vol. 7, 3rd ed., pp. 659–741). New York: Random House.

Kluegel, J., & Smith, E. (1986). *Beliefs about inequality: Americans' views of what is and what ought to be.* New York: Aldine de Gruyter.

Kutza, E. (1981). *The benefits of old age: Social welfare policy for the elderly.* Chicago, IL: University of Chicago Press.

Lau, R. (1990). Political motivation and political cognition. In E. Higgins & R. Sorrentino (Eds.), *Handbook of motivation and cognition* (Vol. 2, pp. 297–329). New York: Guilford.

Leutz, W. (1986). Long-term care for the elderly: Public dreams and private realities. *Inquiry, 23*(3), 132–139.

Light, D. (1997). The rhetorics and realities of community health care: The limits of countervailing powers to meet the health care needs of the twenty-first century. *Journal of Health Politics, Policy and Law, 22*(1), 105–146.

Lipsky, M., & Smith, S. Rathgeb. (1989). When social problems are treated as emergencies. *Social Service Review, 63*(1), 5–25.

Longman, P. (1986). *Born to pay: The new politics of aging in America.* Boston, MA: Houghton Mifflin.

Marmor, T., Schlesinger, M., & Smithey, R. (1987). Nonprofit organizations and health care. In W. Powell (Ed.), *Between the public and private: The nonprofit sector* (pp. 221–239). New Haven, CT: Yale University Press.

Mayer, W. (1992). *The changing American mind.* Ann Arbor: University of Michigan Press.

Neuman, W. (1986). *The paradox of mass politics: Knowledge and opinion in the American electorate.* Cambridge, MA: Harvard University Press.

Newcomer, R., Benjamin, A. E., & Estes, C. (1983). The Older Americans Act. In C. Estes & R. Newcomer (Eds.), *Fiscal austerity and aging: Shifting government responsibility for the elderly* (pp. 187–206). Beverly Hills, CA: Sage.

Organization for Economic Cooperation and Development. (1996). *Caring for frail elderly people: Policies in evolution,* Social Policy Studies No. 19. Paris: OECD.

Page, B., & Shapiro, R. (1992). *The rational public.* Chicago, IL: University of Chicago Press.

Parsons, W. (1995). *Public policy.* Aldershot, UK: Edward Elgar.

Pauly, M. (1996). Will Medicare reforms increase managed care enrollment? *Health Affairs, 15*(3), 182–191.

Poole, D. (1995). Shaking the kaleidoscope. *Health and Social Work, 20*(3), 163–166.

Reeves, J., & Campbell, R. (1994). *Cracked coverage: Television news, the anti-cocaine crusade and the Reagan legacy.* Durham, NC: Duke University Press.

Rivlin, A., & Wiener, J. (1988). *Caring for the disabled elderly: Who will pay?* Washington, DC: The Brookings Institution.

Sandel, M. (1996). *Democracy's discontent: America in search of a public philosophy.* Cambridge, MA: Harvard University Press.

Scheingold, S. (1974). *The politics of rights: Lawyers, public policy and political change.* New Haven, CT: Yale University Press.

Schlesinger, M., & Kronebusch, K. (1994). Intergenerational tensions and conflict: Attitudes and perceptions about social justice and age-related needs. In V. Bengtson & R. Harootyan (Eds.), *Intergenerational linkages: Hidden connections in American society* (pp. 152–184). New York: Springer.

Schlesinger, M., & Lau, R. (1997). Imaginative political rationality: Policy metaphors and the public understanding of health care reform. *Journal of Health Politics, Policy and Law.* Forthcoming.

Schlesinger M., & Lee, T. (1993). Is health care different? Popular support for federal health and social policies. *Journal of Health Politics, Policy and Law, 18*(3), 551–628.

Schön, D., & Rein, M. (1994). *Frame reflection: Toward the resolution of intractable policy controversies.* New York: Basic Books.

Sears, D., & Citrin, J. (1985). *Tax revolt: Something for nothing in California.* Cambridge, MA: Harvard University Press.

Silow-Carroll, S., Meyer, J., Regenstein, M., & Babgy, N. (1995). *In sickness and health? The marriage between employers and health care.* Washington, DC: The Economic Research Institute.

Skitka, L., & Tetlock, P. (1993). Of ants and grasshoppers: The political psychology of allocating public assistance. In B. Mellers & J. Baron (Eds.), *Psychological perspectives on justice* (pp. 205–233). New York: Cambridge University Press.

Sniderman, P. , Glaser, J., & Griffin, R. (1990). Information and electoral choice. In J. Ferejohn & J. Kuklinski (Eds.), *Information and democratic processes* (pp. 117–135). Urbana: University of Illinois Press.

Starr, P. (1982). *The social transformation of American medicine.* New York: Basic Books.

Steiner, G. (1981). *The futility of family policy.* Washington, DC: The Brookings Institution.

Stimson, J. (1991). *Public opinion in America: Moods, cycles and swings.* Boulder, CO: Westview.

Stone, D. (1988). *Policy paradox and political reason.* Glenview, IL: Scott, Foresman.

Stone, D. (1997). *Policy paradox: The art of political decision making.* New York: Norton.

Tetlock, P., & Mitchell, G. (1993). Liberal and conservative approaches to justice: Conflicting psychological portraits. In B. Mellors & J. Baron (Eds.), *Psychological perspectives on justice: Theory and applications* (pp. 234–255). New York: Cambridge University Press.

Wiener, J. (1994). *Sharing the burden: Strategies for public and private long-term care insurance.* Washington, DC: The Brookings Institution.

Yankelovich, D. (1995). The debate that wasn't: The public and the Clinton health care plan. *Brookings Review, 13*(3), 36–42.

Zaller, J. (1992). *The nature and origins of mass opinion.* Cambridge: Cambridge University Press.

Zashin, E., & Chapman, P. (1974). The uses of metaphor and analogy: Toward a renewal of political language. *Journal of Politics, 36,* 291–326.

CHAPTER 2

Self-interested Behavior and Social Welfare

Perspectives from Economic Theory

ELIZABETH H. BRADLEY

This chapter discusses central concepts from economics as they apply to long-term care financing. The principle of economic efficiency is described, and illustrations of market failure as well as several market interventions to enhance economic efficiency are presented.

The purpose of this chapter is to discuss major tenets of welfare economics in the context of long-term care policy. The chapter examines conditions under which one would expect individual behavior to support or detract from the welfare of the larger society. The roles and implications of imperfect information, externalities, and public goods associated with long-term care financing are explored. Finally, the chapter discusses areas in which cross-disciplinary efforts might be fruitful for long-term care policymaking.

The chapter is organized into three sections. The first section provides background concerning the principles of efficiency and introduces the conditions under which self-interested behavior maximizes social welfare. The second section offers a theoretical context that focuses on two of these conditions most pertinent to long-term care: the condition of perfect information and the condition of no externalities or public goods. The third section discusses the application of the theoretical context to long-term care. The chapter concludes with a summary of major points as well as a brief discussion of areas for collaboration with other disciplines in the design and analysis of long-term care policy.

Background

Welfare economics: Equity and efficiency

Two principles are central to long-term care financing policy in the United States: equity and efficiency. The principle of equity, though fundamental to social programs and policymaking, is an elusive one. What constitutes an equitable solution or policy is generally a normative question and depends on the interpretation of shared values, norms, and goals of a group or society. As Stone (1996) demonstrates in her treatise on "splitting the pie," there is substantial diversity in the criteria one might use to define equity in the allocation of scarce resources. As a result, different policy alternatives may be deemed equitable, depending on one's values and perspective.

In contrast to normative judgments concerning the principle of equity, the principle of efficiency is generally understood by economists as involving positive tools of analysis. Market and policy solutions to the problem of resource allocation are compared and contrasted, based on the solution's ability to effect improvements in technical and allocative efficiency. Technical efficiency occurs when the economy produces the maximum sustainable output from a given set of inputs. Allocative efficiency is the situation in which either inputs or outputs are utilized in such a way that no one can be made better off without making someone else worse off. Within this framework, policy proposals can be ranked based on the degree to which they promote technical and allocative efficiency, without regard for the distribution of the gains from the policies, that is, without equity judgments. Typically, economic analyses of alternative policies focus on technical and allocative efficiency, leaving considerations of equity to other disciplines such as political science, sociology, and law.

Welfare economics is the branch of economics concerned with the social desirability of alternative economic states. Welfare economics is founded on the fundamental theorem that individuals' pursuit of self-interest can result in the maximization of social welfare if certain conditions are met. The theorem is a powerful one, demonstrating that unregulated self-interested behavior can result in efficient allocation of societal resources. Importantly, the discipline of economics has identified a number of general conditions under which the pursuit of self-interest is expected to maximize social welfare. If such conditions are not met or are only partially met, the unregulated pursuit of self-interest (by firms and individuals) results in less than maximized social welfare.

The general conditions under which self-interested behavior maximizes social welfare pertain both to the organization of providers of goods and services and to the product or service itself. First, markets must either have numerous buyers and sellers or must be "contestable," meaning they must have free market entry and exit of producers and consumers. Second, markets must be characterized by perfect information. Finally, the product or service must not generate externalities or be characterized as a public good.

Because markets for both long-term care provision and financing are generally characterized as having numerous buyers and sellers, the theoretical context of this chapter explores in greater detail the two conditions that are more problematic for long-term care markets: perfect information and no externalities or public goods.

Theoretical Context

Asymmetric and imperfect information

The condition of perfect information pertains to both the buyers' and sellers' information concerning the nature and value of the product being bought or sold. Two distinct aspects of the perfect information condition are particularly relevant to the market for long-term care. The first is the problem of asymmetric information, in which the sellers (or buyers) have more information than the buyers (or sellers). This problem, first described in the context of the used car market, has become known as the "Lemons Principle" (Akerlof, 1970). When the potential buyers know only the average quality of used cars, yet the sellers know the actual quality of the cars they are selling, market prices will be lower than the true value of the highest-quality cars. Potential sellers of the higher-quality cars will withhold their cars from the market, given the low price. The higher-quality cars are hence driven out of the market by the lemon cars. In the end, the bad drives out the good until, in some cases, no market is left.

A parallel to the Lemons Principle exists for some forms of insurance, when the sellers know only the average risk associated with the insurance policy buyers. Buyers, however, may know their actual risk. Market prices will be higher than the true value of the insurance for the lowest-risk buyers. Thus, only higher-risk buyers purchase the insurance. This phenomenon, in which higher-risk individuals are able to purchase insurance at less than the actuarially fair price due to asymmetric information, is called "adverse selection." In time, adverse selection results in higher prices, further limiting the purchasing of insurance by lower- or average-risk individuals. Ultimately, high-risk individuals drive out lower-risk individuals, until, in some cases, no market exists.

In addition to the problem of asymmetric information, a second aspect of imperfect information is deficient consumer information. In the context of long-term care, the condition of perfect information requires that potential buyers of long-term care insurance understand alternative products and can accurately assess the value of alternative financing choices. Embedded in the perfect information condition is the requirement that potential buyers can also assess their future long-term care needs, including the likelihood of requiring long-term care and the nature and value of that care. While it is likely that only a subset of buyers (or those acting in their behalf) need to have perfect information to discipline the market, substantial deficiencies in consumer information may compromise efficiency and reduce the likelihood that self-interested behavior will promote social welfare.

The traditional modeling of consumer decision-making, consistent with the condition of perfect information, is based on expected utility theory. First explicated by Von Neumann and Morgenstern (1947), expected utility theory is founded on the assumptions that individuals have well-defined utility functions based on consistent and ordered preferences and that individuals behave in ways that maximize their expected utility. Utility represents the individual's level of satisfaction or welfare. This theory suggests that individuals assess the expected utility associated with their possible choices (or purchases) and choose the option that generates the greatest expected utility. Inherent in this theory is the premise that consumers have and can assess information not only about the possible "payoffs" associated with each purchase but also the objective probability of each payoff occurring. For complex problems, such informational needs may be substantial.

Since the original expected utility theory, a second generation of utility models has evolved that suggests that decision-makers weigh the utility of possible outcomes by their subjective, rather than objective, probability of occurring. These models are termed *subjective utility models* (Savage, 1954; Edwards 1955, 1962). While subjective probability theory relaxes the assumption requiring that individuals accurately assess and use objective probabilities, the theory retains the fundamental components of the original expected utility theory: (1) there exists a well-defined utility function that allows individuals to assign cardinal ranking as a measure of one's utility (or liking) of particular outcomes; (2) decision-makers have well-defined sets of alternatives; (3) decision-makers can assign consistent joint probabilities to all future events; and (4) decision-makers will choose the alternative that maximizes the expected value of the events that follow their choice.

Over the past thirty years, a large body of empirical research has demonstrated that individuals systematically make choices that are inconsistent with expected utility models of behavior (Cohen & March, 1974; Hogarth, 1975; Simon et al., 1992; Kahneman, Slovic, & Tversky, 1988). Although several descriptive theories of decision-making under uncertainty have grown out of this empirical work (Edwards, 1992; Bell, Raiffa, & Tversky, 1988; Simon, 1983; Simon, Edigi, & Marris, 1992), both prospect theory (Kahneman & Tversky, 1979) and the behaviorist (Simon, 1983, 1992) models of decision-making have been particularly influential.

The authors of prospect theory, Kahneman and Tversky (1979, 1988), demonstrated through repeated experiments that most individuals violate the implications of subjective utility theory even in simple choice situations where probabilities are fully identified. Based on their empirical research, the authors note several discrepancies between their empirical findings and expected or subjective utility theory and suggest a theory that better fits the empirical evidence. Their descriptive theory, prospect theory, diverges from subjective utility theory in three significant aspects. First, prospect theory suggests that individuals think in increments concerning their current wealth or endowments and are particularly averse to changing from the status quo. In essence, losses from the status quo generate larger changes (decrements) in utility than equal gains from the status quo. Second, individuals do not distinguish between large numbers accurately. Potential gains of $100,000 are not adequately distinguished from gains of $110,000. Finally, individuals make systematic errors in estimating the probabilities of events occurring, often giving greater probabilities to rare events and smaller probabilities to more common events. A host of heuristics, or rules of thumb, have been described (Kahneman, Slovic, & Tversky, 1988) to account for some of this systematic divergence of observed behavior from expected utility models.

Behaviorist models of decision-making, like the descriptive models such as prospect theory, are based in empirical realities of decision-making under uncertainty. As described by Simon (1983), the behaviorist alternative to expected utility models posits that human beings are unable to apply the rules of expected utility theory due to limited knowledge of facts, inconsistent value structures, and inadequate reasoning power. Instead, the behaviorist approach argues that individuals operate with "bounded rationality" (Simon et al., 1992). The bounded rationality approach suggests that individuals have only a general picture of their lifestyle and future prospects, are able to contemplate changes in their lives with only a minimal number of contingencies, and can focus their attention on only a few things at a time. Simon (1983) argues that the typical decision-maker is concerned with fairly specific matters rather than comprehensive choices over large areas of his or her life. In fact, the complex calculus assumed by expected utility theory does not occur. Rather, one merely adapts to the complex array of choices by focusing one's attention on a limited set of alternatives and decisions. Individuals do not develop detailed scenarios.

These models of decision-making are important background when assessing the nature of imperfect or deficient information and its impact on individual choice. Both prospect theory and the behaviorist model of decision-making are especially pertinent for complex decisions that require substantial information, often involve events far in the future, and are accompanied by strong emotion. Such characteristics are central to many long-term care decisions.

Externalities and public goods

Externalities are defined as cases in which a consumer (or producer) affects the utility of another consumer (or producer) through actions that lie outside the price system. In these cases, purchasers (or producers) affect each other in ways outside the market. The classic example of an externality is pollution produced by automobile use. A consumer purchases an automobile (theoretically at a price equal to or greater than the purchaser's benefit of having that automobile) but may not pay the added price for the right to produce the pollution associated with driving the automobile. Thus, although the purchaser is likely to have adversely impacted the well-being of the larger society by increasing the level of pollution, the costs related to the added pollution are not borne by the purchaser; they remain outside the market. Pollution, a negative externality, demonstrates how the pursuit of individual self-interest does not result in the maximization of public or social welfare when externalities are present. For products with negative externalities, self-interested behavior results in overconsumption of the product or service (relative to a social optimum). In the case of positive externalities, self-interested behavior results in the underconsumption of the product or service.

A related but distinct type of good or service is that described in economic theory as a public good. Public goods are defined as those goods, such as national defense, which no one can be prevented from consuming (i.e., that is nonexcludable) and which can be consumed by one person without depleting it for another (i.e., is nonrival). Like goods and services associated with positive externalities, public goods are expected to be underprovided in an unregulated market. A central challenge of policy regarding these types of goods and services is how to incorporate external costs and benefits into private decision-making. When large numbers of individuals are involved, as in the extreme example of nonexcludable (public) goods, it is difficult to make voluntary arrangements that are satisfactory to all concerned (Feldstein, 1988).

Common solutions for enhancing adequate provision of public goods are twofold. First, as first suggested by Weisbrod (1988), the nonprofit organizational form has developed to fill the unmet needs related to public goods. Driven not by profit but by organizational mission, nonprofit organizations were instruments that could overcome the market failures related to public goods. The degree to which nonprofit are more likely than for-profit organizations to provide public goods in health care remains an empirical question and varies by industry sector (Schlesinger, Marmor, & Smithey, 1987; Schlesinger, Gray, & Bradley, 1996).

The second commonly embraced solution to the problem of public goods is to establish some form of collective decision-making to take the place of individual decision-making. Thus, the existence of public goods is a rationale for government intervention in the private market. To maximize social welfare, public goods or services should be produced until the marginal benefit of the last unit produced equals the summation of individuals' marginal benefits related to that unit. Although this is theoretically clear, the practical challenge of eliciting individuals' preferences and benefits for such goods is daunting. If individuals are to be taxed an amount reflecting their desire for the public good, they have an incentive to underestimate their desire for the good, allowing them to "free ride," that is, obtain benefits without sharing the cost of those benefits.

Related to the concept of free riding, in which individuals benefit from the provision of a public good without paying for that public good, economists have formalized what is known as the "crowding out" hypothesis. This hypothesis argues that the existence of public programs reduces private expenditures. Although the theoretical basis for the phenomenon is well accepted, the practical importance of crowding out is an empirical issue. Several econometric studies have focused on the crowding out of charitable contributions and, again, have demonstrated modest, though measurable, crowding out effects. Abrams and Schmitz (1978, 1984) find that government grants reduce charitable contributions by 28 percent. Clotfelter (1985) and Kingma (1989) find more limited crowding out effects of 5 percent and 12 percent, respectively. Experimental studies using hypothetical scenarios to demonstrate subjects' choices (Adreoni, 1993) report substantially larger, though still incomplete, crowding out effects.

Application to Long-Term Care

Private long-term care insurance and imperfect information

The limited role of private insurance in long-term care financing is notable. Although reasons for this limited role include the availability of Medicaid, high prices, and limited benefits (Pauly, 1990), information asymmetries and deficiencies may offer partial explanations.

Many insurance markets face some degree of adverse selection. However, the market for long-term care insurance is particularly vulnerable to adverse selection—the buyer of the insurance policy knows more about his or her future risk than the seller (Garber, 1995). The phenomenon is exacerbated in this market because a significant predictor of future institutionalization for long-term care is the nature and availability of social support. Unlike medical data, information on social support is not easily obtained by third-party insurers. However, one's level of social support is generally well known to the potential purchaser of long-term care insurance. Furthermore, if the price of insurance was reduced for those with greater social support to reflect their lower risk of nursing home use, both purchasers and their families might have an incentive to overestimate available social support. The asymmetry of information regarding risk factors for long-term care use and the barriers to overcoming that asymmetry may result in substantial adverse selection in this market. As in other markets characterized by adverse selection, the high risks drive out the average and lower risks, until the market fails to exist in any meaningful way.

A potential solution for addressing the problem of adverse selection is mandatory universal long-term care insurance. Under mandatory universal insurance, the market would include all individuals, not just those who are likely to use long-term care services. Such a policy would obviate the problem of adverse selection. However, in addition to the numerous political barriers to such a scheme, universal insurance might add to the problem of moral hazard. Moral hazard, a phenomenon relevant to health care insurance in general, is the price effect (Garber, 1995) in which the demand for (and utilization of) health care services increases due to the reduction in net price attributable to insurance. The more responsive demand for long-term care insurance is to price changes, the greater the potential for moral hazard. If formal care is a close substitute for informal care, one might predict that moral hazard may be substantial in this market. Thus, while adverse selection arising from asymmetric information limits the market for private long-term care insurance, the likely solution to this problem creates additional dilemmas of its own.

Less studied than the problem of adverse selection is the degree to which deficient information about alternative financing mechanisms on the part of potential buyers explains the limited demand for long-term care insurance by individuals. A fundamental assumption in expected utility theory is that consumers have perfect information. Relaxing this assumption leads to less than efficient markets and less than optimal individual decision-making. The implications of deficient consumer information are that the pursuit of self-interest may not result in the maximization of social welfare and, on an individual level, decisions may be made that will later be regretted or that will lead to reduced personal utility.

In the context of long-term care, specific efforts to correct imperfect information might include government interventions to enhance consumer awareness regarding choices in long-term care insurance, including the quality and cost of long-term care facilities. Government interventions may enhance the quantity and quality of information available in the market for long-term care and promote greater consumer awareness; however, such tactics do not address the more fundamental issues of information suggested by prospect and behavioral theorists. The prospect theory and behaviorist models of decision-making argue that overcoming the problem of deficient consumer information may involve more than merely disseminating information to consumers.

Alternative models of individual decision-making seem particularly relevant to long-term care decisions. Within this market, individuals may have cognitive and physical disabilities that make information processing more difficult. Further, the frequency with which multiple parties may be involved in long-term care decision-making for the recipient adds complexity to the decision-making process and may or may not enhance the assessment and processing of needed information.

In addition to factors affecting the processing of information by potential purchasers, there may be particular difficulties in disseminating information effectively in this market. Significant portions of elderly and other long-term care recipients may be socially isolated, resulting in limited access to information. Further, the degree to which individuals incorporate new information into decisions may be limited. The difficulty with which elderly persons and their families understand and incorporate private insurance options into their long-term planning remains substantial, despite educational efforts to overcome deficiencies in information (Walker et al., 1995). Because such information can be complex and requires the purchasers to consider future disability and death, effective educational efforts remain difficult to design.

Finally, information concerning quality of long-term care is difficult to articulate and measure. Standards for quality are particularly problematic in the market for long-term care services, where the focus is on care rather than cure. Even the fundamental goals for care may vary substantially among patients, their families, and clinicians (Bogardus, Bradley, & Jeung, 1997). In such a market, meaningful data on quality of care are difficult to articulate and disseminate in a credible, comprehensible way. Nevertheless, as the theory suggests, such information remains critical for optimal individual decision-making and the efficient allocation of resources by the private market.

Intergenerational allocation and externalities

Like the problem of imperfect information, the existence of externalities related to long-term care limits the likelihood that self-interested behavior will result in the maximization of social welfare. Externalities in the market for long-term care are twofold: those borne by family members and those borne by the larger society. Unlike the example of pollution, externalities associated with long-term care are positive. For example, the purchasing of long-term care insurance may produce benefits (to family members or the local community and the larger society) that are outside the market system. The existence of positive externalities suggests that, in an unregulated market in which individuals pursue their self-interest, there will be less than the optimal amount of long-term care insurance purchased.

The positive externalities that may accrue to family members or the local community are the benefits of not having to provide or finance long-term care for their loved one as well as not enduring the emotional burden of not adequately caring for their family member in need. The degree to which individuals consider benefits and burdens of future generations in decision-making is an empirical question. Evidence from econometric studies of alcohol and smoking behavior (Manning et al., 1991) suggest that positive externalities borne by remaining family members may not be fully accounted for by individual decision-making; however, such empirical evidence is not available concerning long-term care choices. From the theory, the less such externalities are incorporated in individual decision-making, the more problematic private decision-making is from the viewpoint of maximizing social welfare.

A caring society and public goods

The positive externalities that may accrue to the larger society have been identified as a major efficiency rationale for public hospitals and social insurance programs for infectious disease services (Feldstein, 1988). Although many of the patients cared for in long-term facilities do not have infectious diseases, communities and the larger society benefit from having elderly and disabled individuals cared for appropriately. However, the benefit may be more subtle than personal protection from an infectious disease. The benefit of living in a caring society that provides appropriately for its elderly and disabled is an example of a public good. The positive feeling associated with being part of an altruistic community is both nonexcludable and nonrival. Such public goods are likely to be underprovided when determined by private, rather than collective, decision-making processes. Inherent difficulties associated with eliciting preferences for such a society and taxing individuals appropriately to support this public good will challenge any comprehensive and collective program for long-term care.

Conclusions

Important conclusions can be drawn from a review of the economic theory related to self-interested behavior and social welfare. First, economic theory suggests that the pursuit of individual self-interest can maximize social welfare. This maxim is a cornerstone of reliance in the United States on a private, free market system, relatively unhindered by government intervention and regulation, despite knowledge of market failures. In addition, the unconstrained pursuit of self-interest is consistent with deeply held values in the United States, those of autonomy, individualism, and self-determination. Thus, in both economic and social contexts, the embracing of self-interested behavior is, to some degree, consistent with norms of organization and social objectives.

At the same time, economic theory identifies characteristics of either markets or products that cause a divergence between private and public incentives, and the related divergence between self-interested behavior and social welfare. These characteristics that are most pertinent to the provision and financing of long-term care include asymmetries and deficiencies in information as well as the existence of externalities and public goods. A full understanding of these characteristics can suggest areas in which public policy in long-term care can best augment or temper self-interested behavior to enhance the welfare of the larger society.

Despite the useful insights from economic theory, there are important areas in which the theory can benefit from the input of additional disciplines. One such area is the interaction of the individual, the family, and the community in terms of decision-making and future planning. Traditional economic models of decision-making view the individual as an independent, autonomous decision-maker, acting to maximize personal utility. While these models are robust enough to include the welfare of others as part of the personal utility function, the complex interactions within a family are generally left to other disciplines. With notable exceptions (Becker, 1991; McElroy & Horney, 1981), the study of economics views the family as a black box, focusing on market and policy interventions as they affect individuals within the family. Due to both the involvement of family members in long-term care provision and planning as well as the typical level of physical and social dependence of long-term care recipients, the paradigm of the independent, autonomous decision-maker may be less relevant in long-term care than in other areas of economic inquiry. Because family members are intimately involved in long-term care planning and because the ramifications of long-term care choices are substantial for the family unit, other disciplines, including psychology, anthropology, and sociology, are central to long-term care policy design and analysis.

Finally, a critical area in which economic analyses of long-term care policies should be augmented by other disciplines is the incorporation of equity concerns into policy analysis. Judgments of equity and distributive justice are generally not part of economic analyses, which focus more on efficiency of alternative policies. Although this may be appropriate for the discipline, issues of equity and distributive justice are central to the design and implementation of long-term care policy. Traditional economic analyses should be complemented by frameworks from other disciplines to ensure that the dual objectives of equity and efficiency, as well as the interaction of the two, are adequately reflected in the design and implementation of long-term care financing policies.

Acknowledgments

I am grateful to Jody Sindelar, Ph.D., John Rizzo, Ph.D., and Mark Schelsinger, Ph.D., for their comments on this chapter and related work. Research for this essay was supported in part by a training grant (No. 1T32HS00052) from the Agency for Health Policy and Research.

References

Abrams, B., & Schmitz, M. (1978). The crowding out effect of government transfers on private charitable contributions. *Public Choice, 33*(1), 29–39.

Abrams, B., & Schmitz, M. (1984). The crowding out effect of government transfers on private charitable contributions: Cross-sectional evidence. *National Tax Journal, 37*, 563–568.

Adreoni, J. (1993). An experimental test of the public goods crowding-out hypothesis. *American Economic Review, 83*(5), 1317–1327.

Akerlof, G. (1970). The market for "lemons": Qualitative uncertainty and the market mechanism. *Quarterly Journal of Economics, 84*, 488–500.

Arnott, R., & Stiglitz, M. (1991). Moral hazard and nonmarket institutions: Dysfunctional crowding out or peer monitoring? *American Economic Review, 81*(1), 179–190.

Becker, G. (1991). *A treatise on the family.* Cambridge, MA: Harvard University Press.

Bell, D., Raiffa, H., & Tversky, A. (Eds.) (1988). *Decision making: Descriptive, normative, and prescriptive interactions.* New York: Cambridge University Press.

Bergstrom, T., Blume, E., & Varian, H. (1986). On the private provision of public goods. *Journal of Public Economics, 29*, 25–49.

Bogardus, S., Bradley, E., & Jeung, M. (1997). *Goal-setting for dementia: The varying perspectives of patients, families, case managers, and physicians. Gerontologist, 37*, 26.

Bradley, E., Walker, L., Blechner, B., & Wetle, T. (1997). Assessing capacity to participate in discussions of advance directives: A study of the Patient Self-Determination Act. *Journal of American Geriatrics Society,* 95–101.

Clotfelter, C. (1985). *Federal tax policy and charitable giving.* Chicago, IL: University of Chicago Press.

Cohen, M., & March, J. (1974). *Leadership and ambiguity.* New York: McGraw Hill.

Edwards, W. (1955). The prediction of decision among bets. *Journal of Experimental Psychology, 50*, 201–214.

Edwards, W. (1962). Subjective probabilities inferred from decisions. *Psychological Review, 69*, 109–135.

Edwards, W. (Ed.) (1992). *Utility theories: Measures and applications.* Boston, MA: Kluwer Academy Press.

Feldstein, P. (1988). *Health care economics.* New York: Wiley.

Garber, A. (1995). To comfort always: The prospects of expanded social responsibility in long term care. In V. Fuchs (Ed.), *Individual and social responsibility: Child care, education, medical care, and long term care in America.* Chicago, IL: University of Chicago Press.

Hogarth, R. (1975). Cognitive processes and the assessment of subjective probability distribution. *Journal of American Statistical Association, 70,* 271–289.

Kahneman, D., Slovic, P., & Tversky, A. (Eds.). (1988). *Judgment under uncertainty: Heuristics and biases.* New York: Cambridge University Press.

Kahneman, D., & Tversky, A. (1979). Prospect theory: An analysis of decision under risk. *Econometrica, 47*(2), 263–291.

Kahneman, D., & Tversky, A. (1988). Subjective probability: A judgment of representativeness. In D. Kahneman, P. Slovic, & A. Tversky (Eds.), *Judgment under uncertainty: Heuristics and biases.* New York: Cambridge University Press.

Keller, L. R. (1996). Properties of utility theories and related empirical phenomena. In W. Edwards (Ed.), *Utility theories: Measures and applications* (pp. 3–23). New York: Kluwer Academy Press.

Kingma, B. (1989). An accurate measure of the crowd-out effect, income effect, and price effect for charitable contributions. *Journal of Political Economy, 97,* 1197–1207.

Manning, W., Keeler, E., Newhouse, J., Sloss, E., & Wasserman, J. (1991). *The costs of poor health habits.* Cambridge, MA: Harvard University Press.

McElroy, M., & Horney, M. (1981). Nash-bargained household decisions: Toward a generalization of the theory of demand. *International Economic Review, 22,* 333–349.

Pauly, M. (1990). The rational non-purchase of long term care insurance. *Journal of Political Economy, 98,* 153–168.

Savage, L. (1954). *The foundations of statistics.* New York: Wiley.

Schlesinger, M., Gray, B., & Bradley, E. (1996). Charity and community: The role of nonprofit ownership in a managed health care system. *Journal of Health Politics, Policy and Law, 21,* 697–751.

Schlesinger, M., Marmor, T., & Smithey, R. (1987). Nonprofit and for-profit medical care: Shifting roles and responsibilities. *Journal of Health Politics, Policy and Law, 12,* 427–457.

Simon, H. (1983). *Reasoning in human affairs.* Stanford, CA: Stanford University Press.

Simon, H., Edigi, M., Marris, R., et al. (1992). *Economics, bounded rationality, and the cognitive revolution.* Aldershot, UK: Edward Elgar.

Stone, D. (1996). *Policy paradox: The art of political decision making.* New York: Norton.

Walker, L., Gruman, C., Kyzivat, L., et al. (1995). The Connecticut Partnership for Long-Term Care: Current results of ongoing evaluation studies. *Gerontologist, 35,* 220.

Weisbrod, B. (1988). *The nonprofit economy.* Cambridge, MA: Harvard University Press.

Von Neumann, J., & Morgenstern, O. (1947). *Games and economic behavior.* Princeton, NJ: Princeton University Press.

CHAPTER 3

Community Perceptions of Public and Private Responsibility in the Context of Cultural Diversity

DONNA L. YEE

This chapter presents concepts from a sociological perspective, focusing on the role of community and the importance of social diversity in policy planning and implementation. The centrality of culture and race/ethnicity to health beliefs, health behavior, and health care service utilization is discussed. The relevance of these perspectives to long-term care financing policy is explored.

Race/ethnicity and culture are commonly viewed, in social policy discussions, as indicators of position within social and economic structures. Social scientists and health service researchers have often conceded that these characteristics underlie social factors that affect both interpersonal relationships and how individuals experience social exchanges, particularly in the United States (Bell, 1994; West, 1994; Woloshin et al., 1995). Despite this awareness, race/ethnicity and cultural factors are not always incorporated into efforts to design or assess the effectiveness of programs that implement social policies (Miranda & Kitano, 1986; Wilson, 1996).

Race and ethnicity are social constructs. The term *race* is sometimes used to identify persons of color; a single race may include one or several ethnicities. Ethnicity is often used to group people according to common traits or customs; one ethnicity may include both white people and people of color, as is the case of the Hispanic ethnicity. For the purposes of this chapter, race/ethnicity is used as a conjoint concept to reflect ascribed status of persons of color and ethnicity in the United States. This terminology reflects the intent to be inclusive while setting meaningful boundaries.

This chapter discusses three value areas to illustrate how race/ethnicity and culture influence community perceptions of public and private responsibilities for long-term care financing, including perceptions of self-reliance, traditional family-based paradigms, and health beliefs. These value areas will be considered in the context of community-based efforts to identify public and private roles in long-term care and to support autonomy among care receivers and their family members. The chapter emphasizes the need to consider race/ethnicity and culture as factors in developing and testing policies and programs targeted for vulnerable, chronically ill persons who are most likely to rely on public programs. Further, if cultural factors are to be incorporated into the conceptualization, design, and implementation of long-term care policies, then all groups must be included in the moral and policy debate about public and private responsibilities for long-term care.

Background

By the year 2050, demographers estimate that less than half of U.S. residents will be non-Hispanic whites. The mainstream United States will become more diverse racially and culturally. In the past decade, efforts to understand racial/ethnic and cultural effects in programs that finance the delivery of long-term care have sometimes resulted in comments by embattled white U.S. citizens about the disappearance of their mainstream culture (Capitman, Hernandez, & Yee, 1990; Leutz et al., 1992). Examples such as Indian, Mexican, and Chinese foods becoming common everyday fare on suburban dinner tables across the United States are cited as indicators of how the mainstream United States now includes and accepts all cultures. These and other examples are often cited as evidence of successful colorblind policies and the emergence of national values that decry oppressive relationships between minority and nonminority people, products, and lifestyles.

Despite the apparent success of assimilating foods, holidays, and other cultural artifacts of minority cultures into the mass culture, colorblind policies deny the important social, historical, political, and economic significance of cultural groupings within the larger society. Colorblindness assumes that no differences exist among people by asserting that "everyone is alike," "everyone should be treated the same," and "every person is human." Such policies suggest that differences are unimportant variations among people, and can be attributed to personal likes and dislikes. Colorblind policies posit a society where there is no social, political, or economic significance in how groups of people are ascribed social status, are afforded opportunities, or experience life.

The lack of acceptance of and appreciation for the diverse cultural threads that are the fabric of U.S. society is vividly demonstrated by current campaigns to establish English as the official language. Such nativist and anti-immigrant efforts have been successful in twenty-three states and forty cities (Epstein, 1996; Wu, 1996). Organized responses to the increased use of other languages in commerce, government, and even street names in several states (such as California, Hawaii, Florida, and Illinois) have included campaigns targeting public schools, government functions, and voter ballots as places where English should not be displaced. These organized responses, along with a broad range of federal, state, and local policy initiatives, represent a view that acceptance of diversity has gone too far, that diversity engenders conflict and divisiveness rather than consensus and unity in solving community problems.

Because diverse populations (particularly immigrants and people of color) represent cultural enrichment of communities and a ready supply of cheap labor to support the profit-maximizing objectives of entrepreneurs, approaches to the development of social policy that rely on centrally accepted values and norms are being challenged. Community values and norms appear transitory, not because old ones are wrong, but because more people are bringing different perspectives and life experiences to bear on the validity of mainstream norms in their lives.

Demographers have cited an alarming change in household composition across the United States. For each decade between 1960 and 1990, comparisons of cohorts of children who lived at any point with fewer than two parents by age seventeen show dramatic increases (from 13 percent in 1960 to 28 percent in 1990). Among whites, the percentage of children who had at any point by age seventeen lived with fewer than two parents increased from 34 percent in 1960, to 41 percent in 1970, to 46 percent in 1980. Among African Americans, the percentage was double that of whites in 1960 (66%), increasing to 75 percent in 1970 and 80 percent in 1980

(Hernandez, 1993). As these children become adults, patterns of informal care for parents are not likely to reflect past norms, but will represent a tidal change in how and whether private family resources are available to meet the long-term care needs of the frail and disabled.

Further, empirical evidence from this decade suggests that nearly 83 percent of persons under age sixty-five with chronic disabilities and 73 percent of disabled persons over age sixty-five rely exclusively on informal caregivers (Hoffman & Rice, 1996). Social science literature argues that most care of the chronically ill is provided by family members and other unpaid caregivers because cultural norms built on exchange and interdependence between generations make such care a private rather than public responsibility. However, traditional resources built on interdependent exchanges over a lifetime of mutual assistance are disappearing.

Finally, within the mainstream, middle-age and older adults find it challenging to respond to the needs not only of in-laws and birth parents but also of stepparents, aunts, half brothers, stepsisters, and longtime friends or fictive kin without family ties. Similarly, for Russian, Chinese, Vietnamese, and other refugees, the estrangement and segregation of generations reveal other pathways to a decline in the number of family members available as private resources for those afflicted with chronic conditions and disability. Individuals will be left to define for themselves a community where valued care and caring in old age can be reinvented.

In this context, will old age recoup its image as "golden"? How will differences among various groups of people be understood and incorporated into a changing United States? Will the differences matter in terms of public and private responsibilities and roles in the context of long-term care needs?

Theoretical Context

The challenge for long-term care policy in the twenty-first century will be to understand the ways in which diversity may shift assumptions about values that underlie public and private responsibilities to make long-term care available, to share or distribute the costs and burdens of caring among community members, and to assure access to acceptable and appropriate formal service systems. Three value areas (self-reliance, traditional family-based paradigms, and health beliefs) illustrate ways in which racial/ethnic community values may differ from the traditional Eurocentric constructs that underlie social policy in the United States. Variations in these values help explain existing tensions regarding public and private responsibilities in long-term care financing and policy.

Self-reliance

The dominant, mainstream Eurocentric view in the United States of public and private responsibility for long-term care is largely related to traditions of self-reliance, individual merit, and rugged individualism. Unlike social solidarity and communitarian, value-driven policies in European countries like Denmark and Germany or in Asian countries like Japan and China, the United States gives highest value to individual rights. Conflict between individual and family rights, such as who and in what order family members can provide substituted judgment for medical care, reveals the strong U.S. inclination to protect individual autonomy and fairly limited instances when the community can intrude upon an individual's liberty.

Norms of self-reliance and personal autonomy discount the extent to which social, political, and economic forces can compromise individual effort and life chances (Batts, 1989). For some, identification with a subpopulation presents added hurdles or barriers that can limit economic and social opportunity and truncate independence among marginal populations in society. The media seldom highlight everyday role models among the poor and communities of color. Overcoming seemingly overwhelming odds to promote neighborhood safety, the well-being of children and elders, or a community's financial viability is more often attributed to individual rather than community efforts. This absence of models of communitarian achievements is a missed opportunity to value interdependence, and shared roles and responsibilities. In the face of these challenges, how do co-located individuals and nuclear families become communities, particularly in multicultural settings where "minding your own business" and "not getting involved" are taught as essential survival skills?

In setting community standards for health, individual responsibility continues to be at the core of social policy, as evidenced by the federal government's Healthy People 2000 campaign (U.S. Department of Health and Human Services, 1990, 1994). Increasingly, longevity gains in the United States are attributed to individual efforts to observe healthy lifestyles that forgo cigarette smoking and support smoke-free environments, make it socially acceptable to drink alcohol only in moderation, and make seat belt use a social norm. Together with technological advances in medicine and mechanical aids to offset disability, individuals are viewed as increasingly empowered to contribute to and be personally responsible for their health status.

Nevertheless, there are places where ideas about individual (private) and communal or environmental (public) responsibility for health are in conflict. In their work on disease causality, Tesh (1995) and Hamlin (1995) provide examples of how efforts to improve community health were historically driven by theories of individual failings or disease agents, rather than by the idea that social and environmental issues such as poverty, unsafe working conditions, and overcrowding were the major contributing factors to poor health. Current public health campaigns to educate older persons about their risks for falls, cancer, and heart disease are substantially driven by constructs that empower individuals to take actions that improve and sustain health, as well as infer blame for individual improvidence and personal failings that cause or contribute to having such conditions. In related work, Skolbekken (1995) states that the increasing focus in the health literature on risk as a "result of developments in science and technology has changed our beliefs about the locus of control from factors outside human control to factors inside our control" (p. 291). He suggests that the selection of risks reported in the literature is a social construction that limits our understanding of the multifaceted causality of disease and risks. Increasingly, health service research has demonstrated that, just as risk of disease is not limited to personal failings or genetic predisposition, outcomes of care are not limited to the access of technology or how care is organized or financed (Diehr et al., 1989; Greenfield et al., 1987; Reed et al., 1992; Wenneker & Epstein, 1989).

The recent rise of tuberculosis cases in the past decade provides a current illustration of how values like self-reliance can conflict with ideas of public and private responsibility in the context of ethnicity, culture, and age. The specter of tuberculosis reopens sad and painful memories for many "newer" populations in the United States as well as for elders (Council on Scientific Affairs, 1991; Frieden et al., 1995; U.S. Department of Health and Human Services, 1986; Yip, 1996). The following example illustrates these points.

Mr. Vasquez's coughing had worsened over several months. Coughed blood could have been due to a chronic ulcer condition. At age seventy-six, he refused to stop smoking unfiltered cigarettes; his daily six-pack of beer was already a compromise to age and a limited income. He had pills that eased the stomach pain and controlled the discomfort. Three weeks previously, his regular doctor's tests suggested that an allergy of some kind was the problem. The last thing he wanted was some doctor telling him how to live his life. He thought he was too old to change set habits; he had already curbed his "bad" habits as far as he was willing. His wife, though, worried. At age seventy, she rarely drove, was aware of her own increasing forgetfulness, and depended entirely on her husband to get groceries, cash their checks, and manage their affairs. Her concern for him included a concern for their ability to continue managing independently. Their home was a haven. They had escaped to the rural South from New York City. After fifteen years, local residents were cordial; they tolerated these Yankee Puerto Ricans. Although born in the United States, they were still considered foreigners. The uncontrolled coughing, blood, shortness of breath, and sleeplessness were bad enough, but when his lips and finger tips turned blue, the Vasquezes called the public health nurse they knew from his last hospital discharge.

Although they lived thirty miles away, getting to the emergency room wasn't that bad. It was the waiting and not knowing why others were taken first. Then, after Mr. Vasquez was diagnosed, he was put in isolation. Everyone wore masks and gloves when they came near. He had a serious case of active TB. That was the start. The combination of seven different pills, some of them too big to swallow, to be taken at different times and days was bad enough. In addition, there was the drowsiness, having to wear a mask himself, and telling everyone to stay away. It made Mr. Vasquez feel he was under house arrest. After his release from the hospital, it took two hours to drive the fifty miles each way to the doctor's office, longer when he had to pull over to rest. It was hard on him, but better than being in the hospital. He wasn't sure, though, why the doctor only gave him appointments after office hours when there was no one else in the waiting room. There was no more Friday night poker. He didn't want any of his friends to blame him if they got TB. Everyone in the county knew. He was the only reportable case in the area. "Guess that's why the doctor didn't diagnose it sooner," he said. "They don't see tuberculosis around here much."

After three months the sputum tests were supposed to be negative. Mr. Vasquez anticipated being noninfectious and not having to wear a mask whenever he went out. The doctor, however, said it was getting serious. He was still infectious and could be getting resistant, even though he couldn't give him drugs that were any stronger. More pills were ordered in different combinations. Mr. Vasquez felt unfairly accused of not taking the pills, drinking and smoking beyond the amounts he had negotiated with the doctor, and blamed for not getting better. The doctor threatened, "Now, you know you can always find another doctor to take care of you." Of course they both knew he was the only pulmonologist in the five-county area. They argued: Mr. Vasquez, the doctor, Mrs. Vasquez, and the public health nurse, who gave him "strep" shots. The doctor insisted that the nurse watch Mr. Vasquez take his pills when she was there. They didn't trust him. Didn't they think he wanted to get better, to stop feeling so lousy?

It took twelve months before he was no longer infectious. If it wasn't for his supplemental insurance, he would not have been able to pay for all of those pills, shots, and nurse visits. Mrs. Vasquez continued to show negative results to TB tests. It was spring before he ventured out, knowing he might not be welcomed back to the poker game. He understood when the gas station attendant backed away and lowered his head when he talked. How much of it was the TB? Sure, rural folks may not be as educated as city people, but it was unclear how much of their behavior was because Mr. Vasquez was one of the only nonwhites in the area. He didn't ask for any favors. He was appreciative and upset that a neighbor brought some groceries; he neither wanted to put anyone out nor to be considered a charity case. Mrs. Vasquez was proud of her husband for beating the disease and grateful the bad year was over. They looked forward to getting back to normal.

To Mr. Vasquez, having an infectious disease had several meanings: a shadow from earlier years in the barrio, where almost everyone had or was exposed to TB and where he could do nothing about it; a personal affliction from which he tried to protect others; and the stigma of being from a poor immigrant community. Still, he didn't understand how he got TB many years and miles away from the barrio. He also realized he would always be an outsider to his neighbors; they would always keep him at a distance. On the one hand, he had done nothing personally to cause his illness and become a danger to others. He also had no part in his body's resistance to treatment; he followed the doctor's orders as best he could. He prized his self-reliance, but it also affected his wife and their ability to get along. His stubbornness and suspected "noncompliance" might have elicited the same response from the doctor even if he was white, but Mr. Vasquez may never be convinced of it. The doctor's comments and behavior over the year suggested that he was treating a rare and foreign disease and that his patient was uneducated and had little money. In fact, for Mr. Vasquez, this was not the story. Even after more than twenty office and hospital contacts, neither man ever talked about how he might have gotten sick, what the particular disease meant to either of them, or whether there had been any miscommunication because of assumptions about their public and private responsibilities as practitioner and patient, whether it would be different if he went to another doctor, or even about the costs of lengthy, complicated treatments.

In this example, the patient's behavior and understanding of his treatment did not mesh with the self-reliance norms of the U.S. health care system. In this case the doctor had the health system behind him, a system that defined the cause of the disease and a one-size-fits-all best treatment protocol. The willingness of the physician and patient to discover how their values differed might have resulted in less blaming, shaming, and distrust.

Traditional family-based paradigms

As the United States becomes increasingly multicultural, constructs like a societal melting pot of all cultures and incentives for immigrants and target populations to assimilate into a broader mainstream (i.e., adopt the dominant culture) could result in selectively held ideas about health, old age, disability, and help-seeking in unique ways that represent old culture and U.S. norms. For example, Confucianism prescribes a social order or hierarchy in families and society that results in harmony and fairness among competing interests. Filial responsibility as a private responsibility and public expectation define care patterns for dependent family members, particularly elders. Children are obliged to go to great extremes to respond to parental needs for care, safety, and security. In the next example, a family tries to accommodate differing values across generations and between private and public expectations in making care arrangements for an elder in need of long-term care. The story asks us to consider the extent to which children can be expected to forgo, or parents can demand that children forgo, their own economic well-being in order to support the comfort of a parent, assure care according to a parent's preferences, and make treatment or placement decisions.

> Mrs. Lee was not confused, although the discharge planner thought she was that, and forgetful too. She remembered having arrived in the United States from Hong Kong thirty years before, and working at a sewing factory most of that time. She had her green card to show she was a legal immigrant and her Medicare card. She wouldn't, however, answer many questions about her deceased husband, who had brought her to the United States. She might be eligible for widow benefits, since he had worked for the government, but it was hard to understand why there seemed to be so many versions of his name. Documents were inconsistent, showing names that differed or parts of a name in different order.
>
> Discussions of the doctor's order for home care were held with the daughter, Mabel, because Mrs. Lee spoke little English and needed a

translator. Mabel had described a close-knit extended family that kept in touch, and while wanting to, were not financially able to help one another. Mrs. Lee had many visitors who seemed solicitous and concerned about her. The discharge planner was anxious to quickly expedite the case, but could not decipher if family members who visited would be very reliable in terms of helping with shopping, cooking, cleaning, personal care, laundry, and taking Mrs. Lee to the doctor's office—tasks with which Mrs. Lee would need help.

The first challenge was to determine Mrs. Lee's eligibility for financial assistance and community long-term care services. Mrs. Lee certainly qualified for help now that she had finished the initial course of physical therapy after her stroke. Medicare would pay for some help, but only for limited tasks for a short time. In one interview Mrs. Lee said there was no money to pay someone to come in to help her. And Mabel later said her own recent separation from her husband meant she needed to keep her full-time office job to support her young children. They were at an impasse. Services and eligibility had been described and brochures about programs were given to Mabel, but they seemed unwilling to take steps to apply to get needed services. Why weren't they more cooperative? Surely Mabel knew that she only had to answer a few questions to get the help her mother needed, and she was scheduled to return home soon.

The discharge planner, though, was unaware of the talks Mrs. Lee was having with her daughter—to bring her home as soon as possible and to take care of her. Hospital food was inedible and hard to digest. Even though they seemed nice, she didn't like strangers taking care of her and could not understand them. She even offered to stay at her daughter's place until she was stronger. She was afraid her daughter would put her in a home. Young people were getting more like those in the United States; they were less willing to take care of their parents and often tried to get someone else to do all of the work. Mabel had been struggling with how to care for her children and her mother and continue working. Her mother didn't seem to understand how hard it would be to get her up and down the stairs, and coordinate all of the children's needs and her mother's too. Yet if she arranged for her mother to get home care services, it would require answering many questions about the family's papers and perhaps endangering the cousin's legal status. About seventy years earlier, Mabel's grandfather had bought a name to get to the United States, then successfully sponsored his brother's family in the ensuing decades. The family had always been able to take care of each other, but now everyone was overburdened. Mrs. Lee had nowhere to turn.

This story illustrates two key dilemmas in how private and public responsibilities for long-term care are considered in a context of culture and race/ethnicity. First, the discharge planner was unaware of the ways in which Mrs. Lee expected her daughter to take care of her when she returned home, as well as Mrs. Lee's fear that she could not rely on Mabel to fulfill her filial responsibilities, because she was a U.S. citizen. Second, the discharge planner was unfamiliar with the pressures and issues surrounding entitlement, program eligibility, and immigration status and their influence on the family's decisions about care. These issues were less about the family's need for education about services or how they might help, and more about the family's struggle with public and private roles and expectations in the context of Mrs. Lee's long-term care needs. Generational and cultural gaps involving Mrs. Lee, her daughter, and the service system needed discussion. The discharge planner was ill prepared to identify and negotiate the challenges presented by these gaps.

Health beliefs

Unlike the growing trend in the United States to make health care a mass-marketed commodity, health is not a commodity among many subpopulations. Health is seen as the absence of disease, a state of being that individuals seek to sustain. Health is viewed as a lifestyle and personal discipline rather than a state of minimized pain and functionality. Traditional (or "alternative") medicine and Western medicine can be viewed as competing or complementary means to an end (i.e., health). Western medicine aims to attack and overcome disease. Diagnoses are focused on the locus of discomfort or dysfunction. Alternatively, Traditional Chinese Medicine (TCM), for example, aims to facilitate *qi*, the vital energy that supports health. Its interventions focus on how channels support the flow of vital energy in the body overall. As a result, TCM interventions are often aimed at long-range regaining of health rather than immediate resolution of a complaint (Kaptchuk, 1983).

Recent studies in countries with Western health care systems indicate that growing numbers of individuals use alternative medicine to either complement or substitute for Western medicine (Eisenberg et al., 1993; Furnham & Forey, 1994; Murray & Shepherd, 1993; Murray & Rubel, 1992). Personal expenditures for these interventions do not preclude spending for Western medicine by the same individuals for the same conditions. From a market perspective, the sustained and growing demand for alternative medicine could indicate a strong level of consumer satisfaction and confidence in the efficacy of these products or practices. It could also indicate dissatisfaction with the Western medical model of care. However, the general exclusion of alternative medicine approaches from U.S. health plan coverage and medical training leads to misunderstandings about alternative modes of care, health beliefs, and health goals that patients bring to medical encounters. Current policies for financing long-term care focus on traditional Western medicine.

In designing future policies that incorporate diversity, one must recognize (1) the salience of health practices and beliefs for diverse populations and how they both are and are not complementary to Western medicine; (2) the potential cultural conflict and miscommunication between practitioners and patients regarding options and choices for long-term care; and (3) the possibility that alternative medicine approaches that, for example, manage pain, treat general weakness and failure to thrive, and strengthen immune systems might offer effective models for chronic and long-term care.

Health care, in the context of chronic (incurable but manageable) disease processes, often focuses on symptomatic relief and the ability to arrest or allay disease. Only recently has geriatric medicine clearly focused on interventions that support maximum functioning toward independence in activities of daily living (e.g., management of pain or incontinence) or the interaction among emotional, biological, and physiological responses to medications for chronic conditions like heart disease or diabetes. Long-term care programs that focus on improving or sustaining functional health have made a large impact on care for persons with chronic disease. At the same time, Western medicine might offer a limited view concerning the part health care plays in life quality and the ability to manage conditions toward levels of health in the context of chronic disease.

Conclusions

Three value areas have been used to illustrate ways in which diversity in the United States results in differences in community perceptions of public and private responsibility for the provision of long-term care services. These perspectives, informed by culture, class, life experiences, and family and economic resources, can lead to differing expectations and abilities concerning filial responsibilities to do "what is expected" or "what one was brought up to do" for persons needing long-term care.

This discussion suggests that it would be beneficial to conduct a systematic review of how values and norms underscore social policies today, including those concerning long-term care financing. This chapter does not argue that the existing infrastructure needs to be dismantled. However, it does suggest that the knowledge required to create a more responsive social and economic long-term care infrastructure is still being developed. Explicit discussions of public and private responsibilities as well as expectations regarding community versus individual rights and duties are needed. There may be too many assumptions about what "everyone" presumes is expected from government or from families, and what incentives best support interdependence of the individual and the community.

Evaluations of schemes to promote fair resource distribution grow more complex when diversity is taken into account. Populations may continue to have different opportunities and life chances and therefore varied needs related to socially pooled long-term care resources. Ethnic and cultural beliefs about family and societal roles to support and be supported by kin differ. Finally, differences in personal and community definitions of health, old age, and the use of formal service providers may impose different burdens in sharing costs.

Fundamental next steps to enhancing the responsiveness of policy to increasing population diversity include support of policymaking processes in which multicultural perspectives are incorporated into policy development, program implementation, and program evaluation. Long-term care program initiatives that emphasize consumer choice and support individual autonomy should first understand how the decision-making process varies among ethnic and cultural populations. Greater understanding about care receiver preferences requires explicit discussions that result in consensus concerning the nature of the problem, the interventions that are reasonably available, and the ability to negotiate care arrangements that are appropriate, acceptable, and affordable.

In the context of long-term care, several areas require further exploration to enhance community-based acceptance and success of policy initiatives. First, policymakers must consider how culture and ethnicity affect community perceptions of long-term care insurance products. When economic resources are held by the family unit and not individuals, intergenerational factors (such as investing in the education of the youngest generation, a house to shelter an extended family, or capital for a family business) may take priority over the needs of one family member for home health care, nursing home care, or other long-term care in old age. Alternatively, a family's priorities may be to obtain insurance that will help bear the risk of high-cost care for the eldest family members in order to protect family resources for the younger generation. Assumptions underlying a market of insurance products that emphasizes the value of provident behavior and management of financial risk may have only limited success in communities where family-centered decision-making, rather than individual decision-making, is used.

Second, programs to provide and finance long-term care should be informed by data on how quality of health care services is determined in the context of diversity. The application of universal standards based on individual needs and experiences with service utilization may need reconsideration. A "one-size-fits-all" approach to identifying adequate or high-quality care may not work when care receivers and their family members have differing views of care goals. Individuals seeking relief from pain, reassurance that needed care will be available, or control over the use of extraordinary measures to maintain life may apply different criteria when evaluating the effectiveness of interventions in the context of their willingness to rely on others because of social status, family versus individual-centered decision-making, or different health beliefs. The development of standards for acceptable care that are value-centered need to be broad enough to be inclusive as well as pluralistic to allow for diverse expressions of preferences and needs.

Voucher programs, for example, have grown in popularity because they promise to maximize choice across broad consumer preferences. For certain populations, however, appropriate and acceptable providers may not be available. Providers in a community may not have the capability of assigning direct care staff who are fluent in languages other than English. Food preferences and the use of herbs or alternative medicine may not be understood in ways that support the care objectives of the elder as well as the clinician. While vouchers may appear to exemplify market-driven solutions that support diverse service delivery approaches, both theory and experience demonstrate that only those with purchasing power beyond their health plan fees can attain care that is truly responsive to preferences.

Finally, communities themselves must increase awareness among policymakers regarding the need for long-term care programs to be responsive to multicultural traditions. Through forums, public education programs, and open planning processes, community groups can identify and express the implications their race/ethnicity and culture may have on public and private responsibilities for financing long-term care and maximizing choice. Better recognition of community preferences that stem from core values related to self-reliance, traditional family-based paradigms, and health beliefs will improve long-term care policymaking, program design, and program implementation in ways that will be responsive to older persons in the new century.

References

Batts, V. A. (1989). *Modern racism: New melody for the same old tunes.* Cambridge, MA: VISIONS, Inc.

Bell, C. C. (1994). Race as a variable in research: Being specific and fair. *Hospital and Community Psychiatry, 45*(1), 5.

Capitman, J. A., Hernandez, W., & Yee, D. L. (1990). *Cultural diversity and the aging network: An exploratory study.* National Aging Resource Center for Long-Term Care, Heller School, Brandeis University.

Council on Scientific Affairs. (1991). Hispanic health in the United States. *Journal of the American Medical Association, 265*(2), 248–252.

Diehr, P., Yergan, J., Chu, J., Feigl, P., Glaefke, G., Moe, R., Bergner, M., & Rodenbaugh, J. (1989). Treatment modality and quality differences for black and white breast-cancer patients treated in community hospitals. *Medical Care, 27*(10), 942–958.

Eisenberg, D. M., Kessler, R. C., Foster, C., Norlock, F. E., Calkins, D. R., & Delbanco, T. L. (1993). Unconventional medicine in the United States: Prevalence, costs, and patterns of use. *New England Journal of Medicine, 328*(4), 246–252.

Epstein, A. (1996, December 1). Arizona law on English faces test. *Boston Sunday Globe,* A30.

Frieden, T. R., Fujiwara, P. I., Sashko, R. M., & Hamburg, M. A. (1995). Special article: Tuberculosis in New York City—turning the tide. *New England Journal of Medicine, 333*(4), 229–233.

Furnham, A., & Forey, J. (1994). The attitudes, behaviors and beliefs of patients of conventional vs. complementary (alternative) medicine. *Journal of Clinical Psychology, 50*(3), 458–469.

Greenfield, S., Blanco, D. M., Elashoff, R. M., & Ganz, P. A. (1987). Patterns of care related to age of breast cancer patients. *Journal of the American Medical Association, 257*(20), 2766–2770.

Hamlin, C. (1995). Commentary: Finding a function for public health: Disease theory or political philosophy? *Journal of Health Politics, Policy and Law, 20*(4), 1025–1031.

Hernandez, D. J. (1993). *America's children: Resources from family, government, and the economy.* New York: Russell Sage Foundation.

Hoffman, C., & Rice, D. P. (1996). *Chronic care in America: A 21st century challenge.* Princeton, NJ: The Robert Wood Johnson Foundation.

Kaptchuk, T. J. (1983). *The web that has no weaver: Understanding Chinese medicine.* Chicago, IL: Congdon & Weed.

Leutz, W., Capitman, J., MacAdam, M., & Abrahams, R. (1992). *Care for frail elders: Developing community solutions.* New York: Auburn House.

Miranda, M. R., & Kitano, H. H. L. (Eds.). (1986). *Mental health research and practice in minority communities: Development of culturally sensitive training programs.* Rockville, MD: U.S. Department of Health and Human Services, PHS, ADAMHA, National Institute of Mental Health.

Murray, J., & Shepherd, S. (1993). Alternative or additional medicine? An exploratory study in general practice. *Social Science Medicine, 37*(8), 983–988.

Murray, R. H., & Rubel, A. J. (1992). Sounding board: Physicians and healers—unwitting partners in health care. *New England Journal of Medicine, 326*(1), 61-64.

Reed, E., Cohen, D. J., Barr, M. L., Ho, E., Reemtsma, K., Rose, E. A, Hardy, M., & Suciu-Foca, N. (1992). Effect of recipient gender and race on heart and kidney allograft survival. *Transplantation Proceedings, 24*(6), 2670-2671.

Skolbekken, J. (1995). The risk epidemic in medical journals. *Social Science Medicine, 40*(3), 291-305.

Tesh, S. N. (1995). Miasma and "social factors" in disease causality: Lessons from the nineteenth century. *Journal of Health Politics, Policy and Law, 20*(4), 1001-1024.

U.S. Department of Health and Human Services. (1986). *Health status of the disadvantaged. Chartbook 1986.* Washington, DC: Public Health Service, Bureau of Health Professionals.

U.S. Department of Health and Human Services Public Health Service. (1990). *Healthy People 2000: National health promotion and disease prevention objectives* (PHS 91-50213). U.S. Department of Health and Human Services, Public Health Service, Washington, DC.

U.S. Department of Health and Human Services Public Health Service. (1994). *Healthy People 2000: National health promotion and disease prevention objectives.* Midcourse revisions. U.S. Department of Health and Human Services, Public Health Service, Washington DC.

Wenneker, M. B., & Epstein, A. M. (1989). Racial inequalities in the use of procedures for patients with ischemic heart disease in Massachusetts. *Journal of the American Medical Association, 261*(2), 253-257.

West, C. (1994). *Race matters.* New York: Vintage Books.

Wilson, W. J. (1996). *When work disappears: The world of the new urban poor.* New York: Knopf.

Woloshin, S., Bickell, N. A., Schwartz, L. M., Gany, F., & Welch, G. (1995). Language barriers in medicine in the United States. *Journal of the American Medical Association, 273*(9), 724-728.

Wu, F. H. (1996, December 20). Supreme Court to rule on English-only case. *ASIANWEEK,* 11.

Yip, A. (1996, December 6). Tuberculosis rates up in APA community. *ASIANWEEK,* 8-9.

CHAPTER 4

Justice and Prudential Deliberation in Long-Term Care

NORMAN DANIELS

This chapter argues that long-term care is an issue of moral importance from a philosophical perspective. It explores the principle of distributive justice as a relevant goal for long-term care financing policy. Guiding tenets for fulfilling this goal are discussed.

Controversy about the design and financing of long-term care services often is cast in the familiar economic and political language of policy analysis. Beneath the surface of these policy disputes, however, lurk important issues of distributive justice that are generally not made explicit. Disagreement about these deeper issues is often what makes the policy debate more heated and intractable than it would otherwise be. This chapter makes explicit the moral questions that are often hidden by the language of economic cost and political feasibility.

This chapter discusses the most important among these underlying moral issues. Whose obligation is it to make provision for long-term care — the individual's or society's? To the extent we believe these are individual responsibilities, which individual has the obligation? Is it the responsibility of each of us to secure adequate insurance for our own long-term care needs as they emerge, or is it the family's obligation to provide needed care for frail, elderly parents? Is there a shared obligation between individuals and society? If so, how is this shared obligation divided? Is it society's obligation merely to facilitate the emergence of private markets for long-term care insurance, or should society shoulder the burden of establishing social insurance schemes? And even if there ought to be social insurance schemes, how broad must their benefits be? If society has obligations to provide some form of social insurance, can we design a system that is fair to different birth cohorts?

The purpose of this chapter is to harvest a crop of answers to these questions from an approach explicitly cultivated to address them: the fair equality of opportunity account of justice in health care and the Prudential Lifespan Account of justice among age groups (Daniels 1985, 1988). This approach will be used as a framework for making relevant distinctions about issues of fairness and justice in order to make them explicit in deliberations about the design of long-term care programs.

Background

The aging of the population

As the age profile (the proportion of the population in each age group) in a society changes, social needs change. For example, as society ages, there are proportionally fewer children and young adults to educate and to train for employment. In contrast, there are proportionally more elderly who need employment, income support, and health care, including long-term care. The especially rapid expansion of cohorts over ages seventy-five and eighty-five, a trend that will accelerate by the end of the first quarter of the next century, suggests that unmet needs for long-term care may be the major health care crisis of the next century. Where the change is rapid, concerns arise about the stability of intergenerational transfer schemes, and tension rises among age groups and among birth cohorts.

Changing needs find political expression. The old and the young appear to compete for scarce public funds that meet basic human needs. The shared problems of meeting needs that all will eventually have and of modifying common institutions so that they can distribute goods fairly across age groups and birth cohorts are more likely to be seen as problems of "us" versus "them" (e.g., the young versus the old, children versus the elderly, workers versus retirees, or current retirees versus future retirees). The differences among these different versions of "us" versus "them" are conflated and confused in the resulting appeal for "intergenerational equity."

The trend toward privatization

In addition to the changing age profile of the population, a second trend impacting the long-term care debate is the increased reliance on private markets and resources in lieu of government programs and public resources. The roots of this trend lie in complex economic and political forces such as the growth of multinational corporations and the integration of a world economy; the failure of centralized economies and the resulting uncritical, triumphal touting of the liberating force of capitalism; and the increased support in the past quarter of the century for more conservative political parties and governments in various countries. This increased reliance on private markets is supported by the philosophical rationale of classical liberal views such as libertarianism, which posits a robust set of liberties of the person and imposes strict limits on the role of the state, as well as a vague appeal to utilitarianism, which emphasizes the productive forces of a free market.

The failure of national health insurance reform and the rapid corporatization of the health sector epitomize this trend in the United States toward increased reliance on private markets and resources. Existing public health insurance programs, Medicare and Medicaid, are both under pressure to use private organizations to contain costs and enhance efficiency. In addition, there is extensive discussion of privatizing part or all of the Social Security system. These developments take place in the context of two decades of downsizing government in favor of private-sector solutions to social problems, including education, environmental policy, housing, and job creation.

This privatizing trend carries with it a political and moral message, namely, that the individual is best served by relying on competitive market forces rather than government to achieve well-being. Government's role in the delivery of goods and services that enhance well-being in many dimensions of life is reduced to the much more modest task of making sure that private markets do not fail. The message of privatization is that social obligations are limited and individual responsibility for welfare is primary.

This message is reinforced by the threat that the aging of the population poses to the stability of public solutions to income support and health care across the lifespan. When there is rapid economic growth and a reasonable ratio of workers to retirees and the elderly, there is likely to be support for generous public welfare policies through social insurance schemes. However, support for such programs may be more difficult to achieve when an elderly population must be supported by a relatively small

working population in a period of modest economic growth.[1] The implication of the aging trend is that public resources, which derive primarily
from the working population, will become even scarcer than they are now.
The implication of the privatization trend is that public solutions are inefficient. It is time, proponents argue, to turn to the greater efficiencies
created by market solutions and to "free" the young to invest in their own
futures rather than in consumption by the old.

In the context of the support for privatization, discussions of responsibilities to meet long-term care needs tend to be given an individualistic
answer. Individuals should prepare to meet their own future needs related to retirement income, acute medical services, and long-term care.
The public responsibility is only to make sure tax structures and minimal
regulation create the conditions for individual, largely private schemes to
function efficiently.

Privatizing and the appeal to filial obligations

In the United States, the harshness of the view that it is a private responsibility to provide for one's own long-term care needs is disguised by the
appeal to traditional family values, such as filial obligations. It is suggested
that in the "golden age" of the extended family, the young reciprocated
for all the support their elders had given them, and this is as it should be
now. Expansive public programs should not undermine the valuable institution of the family by providing incentives to abandon traditional forms
of intergenerational support within the family unit.

This appeal to traditional family values distorts the public debate and
the task of policy design in several ways. First, the number of frail elderly is
proportionally much greater today than in earlier centuries. Most families
face the need to provide care to the frail elderly. Second, the magnitude
and distribution of the caregiving burden current generations face is quite
different from that faced by earlier generations. Third, in largely agrarian
societies, which predominated in earlier centuries, the elderly were able
to contribute to productive work in ways that are not possible, or have
not been arranged, in today's economy. Finally, despite appeals to return
to traditional family values, there is no one set of values or patterns of
support families provide. Rather, there is enormous cultural diversity regarding attitudes and obligations to support elderly populations.

1. Focus on the ratio of workers to retirees ignores the ratio of workers to total dependents (children plus retirees)—a ratio that has been more stable during the decline
of the former.

Appeals to traditional family values should not act as an obstacle to defining reasonable social obligations today. Those who want to support families in providing care for their elders, and in this sense support family values, should be wary of any fundamental alliance with those whose primary message is to advocate privatization and individual responsibility rather than societal responsibility.

Theoretical Context

Distributive justice in the context of age groups and birth cohorts

Two distinct problems of distributive justice underlie the questions about intergenerational equity and obligations related to long-term care raised at the beginning of this chapter. First, what is a just or fair distribution of social resources among the different age groups competing for these resources? The Prudential Lifespan Account (Daniels, 1988) involves imagining that we can prudently allocate a lifetime fair share of a particular resource, such as income support or health care, to all stages of our lives. Then, what is viewed as a prudent allocation among stages of a life will guide what is considered as just distribution among age groups. However, an institution that solves the age group problem must also solve the second problem, the problem of equity among birth cohorts. What is fair treatment of different cohorts as they age and pass through transfer and savings schemes that support fair distribution among different age groups?

Calls for intergenerational equity often confuse and conflate the problem of distributive justice related to age groups with that related to birth cohorts. Some confusion is understandable, since the term *intergenerational* is ambiguous. Intergenerational might refer to the perennial struggle between the generations, meaning the conflict between age groups, or it might refer to the generation of the 1960s versus the generation of the 1980s, meaning particular cohorts that were either born or came of age in those periods.

Age groups and birth cohorts are different notions and give rise to distinct problems of distributive justice. Over time, an age group includes a succession of birth cohorts. Age groups do not age, but birth cohorts do. Each birth cohort encounters unique conditions as they pass through life, resulting in important demographic, social, and economic differences among cohorts. In contrast to the notion of birth cohort, the notion of age group distinguishes people by reference to their place in the lifespan, rather than by the years during which they were born or experienced various life stages.

Not only are age groups and birth cohorts conceptually distinct, but they also relate to distinct issues of justice. For example, insisting that different birth cohorts should be treated equitably does not tell us what transfers society ought to guarantee between the young and the old, that is, between age groups. Conversely, worries about age bias and age discrimination are largely concerns about justice among age groups, not birth cohorts.

The Prudential Lifespan Account

What is a just distribution of resources between the young and the old? The key to answering this question lies in the humbling fact that we all age. In contrast, generally we do not change gender or race. The relevance of these simple observations requires some explanation.

If we treat blacks and whites or men and women differently, then we produce an inequality between persons, and such inequalities raise questions about justice. For example, if we hire and fire on the basis of race or gender rather than talents and skills, then we create inequalities that are objectionable on grounds of justice. In contrast, if we treat the old and the young differently, we may or may not produce an inequality between persons. If we treat them differently arbitrarily, then we are treating different persons unequally. However, if we treat the young one way as a matter of policy and the old another way, and we do so over their whole lives, then we treat all persons the same way over their lifespans. No inequality between persons is produced since each person is treated both ways in the course of their lifetime. Thus the simple fact that we age means that age is different from race or gender for purposes of distributive justice.

The Prudential Lifespan Account of justice among age groups builds on the fundamental point that unequal treatment at different stages of life may be exactly what we want from institutions that operate over a lifetime. Since our needs vary at different stages of our lives, we want institutions to be responsive to these changes. For example, in many industrialized countries, people defer income from their working lives to the postwork retirement period through some combination of individual savings and employee or government pension or social security plan. In many such schemes, there are no vested savings, but a direct transfer from the working young to the retired old. Viewed at one moment in time, it appears that young workers are taxed to benefit the old. If the system is stable over the lifespan, and individuals' needs for income vary through the different stages of life, such a system treats people appropriately, and differently, at different ages.

The same point holds for health care. When people reach age sixty-five in the United States, they consume health care resources at far greater the rate (in dollars) than they do prior to age sixty-five. However, young working people pay a combined health care insurance premium (through private premiums, employee contributions, and Social Security taxes) that covers not just their actuarially fair costs, but also the health care costs of the elderly and of children. Age groups are treated differently. The old pay less and get more; the young pay more and get less. If this system continues as we age, others will pay "inflated premiums" that will cover our higher costs when we are older. In effect, the system allows us to defer the use of resources from stages in our lives when we need them less into ones in which we need them more. In general, budgeting these transfers prudently enables us to take from some parts of our lives to make our lives better as a whole.

The unequal treatment of different age groups demonstrates two important lessons. First, treating the young and old differently does not mean that persons are treated unequally over their lifespan. Second, unequal treatment of the young and old may have effects that benefit everyone. These two points provide the central intuition behind the Prudential Lifespan Account of justice among age groups. Prudent allocation among the stages of life is a reasonable guide to what is just between the young and the old.

The lifespan account involves a fundamental shift of perspective. The problem must not be viewed as one of justice between distinct groups in competition with each other, for example, between working adults who pay high premiums and the frail elderly who consume services. Rather, each group represents a life stage, and prudent allocation of resources through the stages of life can result in justice among groups. From the perspective of stable institutions operating over time, unequal treatment of people by age is not different than budgeting over a lifetime. If we are concerned with net benefits within a life, we can appeal to a standard principle of individual rational choice. It is rational and prudent that a person take from one stage of life to give to another to make his or her life better as a whole. If the transfers made by an income support or health care system are prudent, they improve individual well-being. The prudential lifespan scheme results in differential treatment by age, unequal treatment of the young and the old. However, it also results in treating people equally and benefiting them over the span of their entire lives.

To illustrate the idea of the Prudential Lifespan Account, consider the design of a health care insurance policy that operated over the lifespan. Suppose I am willing to spend only a certain amount of my lifetime resources to ensure myself against health care risks. Assuming the insurance benefits associated with the lifetime premium will not meet every conceivable medical need, I would be willing to trade coverage for some needs at certain stages of life for coverage at other stages of life, giving equal consideration to my interests at all points in my life. However, from the perspective of what I consider important at my current age and point in my life, I may underestimate the importance of services I will need much later in life. To compensate for this bias, I should consider all the trade-offs I impose at each stage of my life. For example, the choice of too much acute health care at the end of life is at the expense of other services, such as long-term care services that might improve my quality of life over a considerable period late in life.

Just as individuals set reasonable limits on their lifetime insurance premiums, prudent planners acting on behalf of society are limited by what counts as a "fair share" of health care. This share is not simply a dollar allotment per person, but consists of entitlements to services that are contingent on people having certain medical needs. The planners' problem is to find the distributive principle that allocates this fair share over the whole lifespan. Their goal is a distribution that people in each age group would think is fair because they would all agree it makes their lives as a whole better than alternatives. To ensure that planners avoid biasing the design in favor of their own age group, we shall require that they accept a distribution only if they are willing to live with what it does to them at each stage of their lives. Each stage of their own lives thus stands in as proxy for an age group, and they will age from conception to death in the system of trade-offs to which they agree.[2]

One must specify what principle of distributive justice governs the "lifetime fair share" of health care to understand the Prudential Lifespan Account in the context of health care. The Prudential Lifespan Account is

---

2. Daniels, 1988. Chapter 3 of this work gives a more detailed statement of these and some other qualifications on the concept of "prudent deliberation" appropriate for solving the age group problem. Considerations of prudence require even further restrictions on the knowledge of the deliberators, making them even less like the standard "fully informed consumer" of economic theory. For example, they should judge their well-being by reference to all-purpose goods, like income and opportunity, rather than through the very specific lens of the "plan of life" they happen to have at a given stage of life. Otherwise the design of the lifetime allocation may be biased by a conception of what is good, based on what happens to be held at a given point in life. See also Rawls, 1971, 1993.

quite general, providing a way of thinking about the distribution of many important goods, not just health care. For example, if society were interested in income support at various stages of life, how should such support be distributed over the lifespan? The young and the old seem to be in competition in this example just as much as in the case of health care. The Prudential Lifespan Account asks us to think about how planners who do not know their age would allocate a lifetime fair share of such entitlements to each stage of life. Here, too, the lifetime fair share is not some lump sum in dollars, but a range of contingent entitlements to support. These entitlements are specified relative to what is permitted in the way of economic inequalities between persons.

Prudent planners, operating under the constraints described previously, would have to reason as follows about which such entitlements to support. They cannot expand their lifetime income share by allocating it in certain ways, for example, by setting aside income early in life and investing it heavily in their own human capital or otherwise. Assuming a fixed but fair lifetime budget, such investment strategies are already accommodated within the notion of a lifetime fair income share. These planners must allow for the fact that their preferences or views about what is good in life will change over the lifespan. The prudent course of action would be to allocate their fair share in such a way that the standard of living would remain roughly equal over the lifespan (call this the Standard of Living Preservation Principle). They would want institutions to facilitate income transfers over the lifespan in such a way that individuals have available, at each stage of life, an adequate income to pursue whatever plan of life they may have at that stage of life. Of course, "adequate" is relative to the individual's fair income share, as determined by the acceptable inequalities in the society. This principle has implications for income support in old age.

The generality of the Prudential Lifespan Account is one of its virtues, offering a unified account of how to distribute various goods across the lifespan. Its strengths and weaknesses should be assessed independently, particularly the specific account of justice for health care that is combined with it to address the problem of long-term care (see Daniels, 1989, pp. 677–678, in response to a criticism by Jecker, 1989). Before turning to the account of health care, an important qualification to the Prudential Lifespan Account is necessary.

One objection to the Prudential Lifespan Account is that its application can create some intergroup inequalities. This objection must be taken seriously because the rationale for adopting the prudential model for the age group problem is that we can assume that intralife transfers will be an appropriate model for inter-age group transfers, but if different demographic groups age differently, then the model's appeal for guiding just distribution is weakened substantially. For example, raising the age of eligibility for income support benefits under Social Security, which arguably is a prudent and fair way to address both the age group and birth cohort problems, might leave African Americans, who have lower life expectancy, worse off than whites or Asians. Similarly, a policy of rationing lifesaving medical services by age, which may be permissible under very special conditions of scarcity, might have differential impact by class, race, or gender. Where such effects take place, they may constitute good reasons for not adopting such a rationing policy, or they might provide reasons to link the rationing to facts about group life expectancy. The general point is that the Prudential Lifespan Account presupposes that solutions to the age group problem will not disturb more general requirements of justice (Daniels, 1988).[3] Where the presupposition fails, adjustments must be made.

Fair equality of opportunity and the lifespan allocation of health care

Consider how the Prudential Lifespan Account might be applied to the design of health care systems. A central, unifying purpose of health care is to maintain and restore functioning that is typical or normal for our species (Daniels, 1985). Health care derives its moral importance from the fact that normal functioning has a central effect on the opportunity open to an individual. It helps guarantee individuals a fair chance to enjoy the normal opportunity range for their society. The normal opportunity range for a given society is the array of life plans reasonable persons in it are likely to construct for themselves. An individual's fair share of the normal opportunity range is the array of life plans he or she may reasonably choose in light of personal talents and skills. Disease and disability shrink that share from what is fair; health care protects it. Health care allows individuals to enjoy that portion of the normal range to which their skills and talents would give them access, assuming these are not impaired by special social disadvantages. The suggestion that emerges from this account is that we should use impairment of the normal opportunity range as a fairly crude measure of the relative moral importance of health care needs at the macro level.[4]

3. One further objection to this account is the charge that it presupposes an inadequate way of thinking about equality, namely, the view that we are primarily concerned about equality over complete lives rather than between simultaneous segments of lives (McKerlie, 1989, 1993). This objection has been applied elsewhere (see Daniels, 1993a).

4. The concept of equal opportunity may be interpreted in a much more expansive

Because society has obligations to assure people fair equality of opportunity, we have social obligations to provide health care services that protect and restore normal functioning. This account implies that there should be no financial, geographical, or discriminatory barriers to a level of care that promotes normal functioning, given reasonable or necessary limits on resources. Difficult public policy choices concerning the provision and financing of various services can be judged by their relative impact on the normal opportunity range. Rights to health care are thus relative to the system: entitlements to services can only be specified within a system that works to protect opportunity as well as possible, given limited resources.[5]

Prudent planners solve the age group problem if they can clarify what the right to health care means for each age group. To do this, they must agree to a principle for allocating their lifetime fair share to each stage of life. This means that it is especially important for them to ensure social arrangements that provide individuals the option to enjoy their fair share of the normal range of opportunities open to them at each stage of life. Protection of opportunity at each stage of life is particularly important, since individuals are planning for their whole lives and must keep in mind the importance of being able to revise their views about what is valuable in life as they age.[6] However, impairments of normal functioning caused by disease and disability[7] clearly restrict the portion of the normal opportunity range open to individuals at various stages of their lives. Consequently, health care services should be allocated throughout a life in a way that respects the importance of the age-relative normal opportunity range.

Application to Long-Term Care

Problems in long-term care

Long-term care is clearly a neglected stepchild in the U.S. health care system. Criticisms of the long-term care system focus on the following central issues and problems.

---

way, so that it calls for eliminating any disadvantages that are not our fault. For a defense of a more limited view against these more expansive interpretations, see Daniels, 1996a, Chapters 10 and 11.

5. For a systematic discussion of the implications of this account for the design of health care systems, see Daniels, Light, & Caplan, 1996. They develop a matrix of ten dimensions on which the fairness of health care reform may be assessed.

6. For a discussion of the constraints operating on deliberators, see Daniels, 1988, Chapter 3 and Appendix.

7. To see how the fair equality of opportunity account can explain features of U.S. legislation protecting people with disabilities, see Daniels, 1996b.

- It is very difficult for poor patients, especially Medicaid recipients who need high levels of care, to obtain nursing-home placements.
- The cost of nursing home care, and the eligibility requirements for Medicaid reimbursements, drive spouses into poverty, often reducing their ability to maintain independence.
- There is premature institutionalization of many individuals who could be sustained in less restrictive settings if alternative services were available.
- There are many unmet needs for personal care and social support services for frail elderly people trying to maintain independent living arrangements.
- Care in institutions for the elderly is often not aimed at rehabilitation.
- There are few services aimed at relieving the burden of informal caregivers, such as day care centers or supplementary home services, or adequate tax relief or income support to purchase such services.
- There is no adequate market for private or group insurance against the risk of needing long-term care.

Even in the context of Clinton's comprehensive effort at national health care reform, there was an understanding that the problems of long-term care would not be addressed in a comprehensive way. If the United States lacks the moral clarity and political will to meet current needs, then the aging of society will indeed precipitate a crisis.

A number of factors explain, but do not justify, this neglect of long-term care. Many long-term care services are not medical, but are the kinds of services a wealthy person might buy to improve the quality of life (e.g., assistance with shopping, cleaning, or cooking). Such services do not ordinarily carry the sense of moral importance or urgency that medical services do. Indeed, it is only when long-term care can be "medicalized," because the needs are serious enough to warrant institutionalization and medical supervision, that social obligations are felt and public resources are deployed. There is also a tendency to see the disabilities of the elderly not as the result of specific disease processes but as the "normal" course of aging. This view, which geriatricians have fought hard to discount, explains the weak efforts at rehabilitation and supplements the prejudice against ascribing moral urgency to nonmedical services.

Further, the public provision of such personal and social long-term care services also seems open to special abuse. Eligibility for either public provision of these services or private reimbursement through insurance would have to depend on an acceptable measure of functioning. However, such measures are difficult to construct and hard to use in the absence of careful assessment by interdisciplinary teams of health and social workers.

In addition, there are important obstacles to the provision of private individual and group insurance for these services, including the difficulty of assessing functioning, the problem of adverse selection that might face any insurance schemes, and the problem of protecting benefits from inflation in any long-term scheme adopted early in life.[8] In general, family networks have substituted for insurance. Since families provide so much of the necessary long-term care, there has been great reluctance to provide public substitutes that would shift the costs from families to the government. This reluctance to shift costs is supported by the concern that shifting responsibility might undermine traditional moral values and family structures.

Two issues are central to these explanations of the problems in the U.S. long-term care system. First, there is confusion about the moral importance of long-term care services, that is, about the relative importance of long-term care services and medical services. Second, there is controversy about how to mesh public obligations to provide long-term care with the belief that families are responsible for caring for their elders. The Prudential Lifespan Account of just health care provides a unified view of both these issues.

The moral importance of long-term care

The moral importance of personal *medical* services derives not from their glamour or prestige but from their function: to maintain, restore, or compensate for the loss of normal functioning. In general, this function has special moral importance because of its impact on an individual's share of the normal opportunity range. The Prudential Lifespan Account refines this general point. We must assess the moral importance of medical services by their impact on the age-relative normal opportunity range.

The moral importance of *long-term care* services also derives from their function, which is identical to the function of medical services. Long-term care services maintain, restore, or compensate for the loss of normal functioning, and their importance, for purposes of distributive justice, should be measured by their impact on age-relative normal opportunity range. It does not matter that the services necessary for adequate long-term care are often nonmedical. Personal care, social support services, and rehabilitative services, whether delivered in the home, the community, or the

---

8. For a classic discussion of these issues, see Bishop, 1981.

nursing home, may be needed to compensate for impaired function and disability. The disabilities that require long-term care are generally not life-threatening, and people live for many years with them. However, they have a dramatic impact on an individual's opportunity to carry out otherwise reasonable parts of a plan of life, including continued independence in living arrangements. Since these disabilities affect such a substantial portion of the late stage of life for so many people, it is imprudent to design a system that ignores them and meets only the acute care crises of the elderly. That long-term care is the neglected stepchild of the U.S. health care system is morally indefensible.

Many advocates of increased home care services, including personal care and social support services, have emphasized the importance of independent living. They have sometimes cited a principle calling for care in the "least restrictive environment" (Callahan, & Wallack, 1981; Vogel & Palmer, 1982). Similarly, one can describe the loss of dignity and self-respect that accompanies premature or inappropriate institutionalization. The moral importance of this debate stems from the loss of opportunity range, which has a direct effect on autonomy, dignity, and self-respect. The Prudential Lifespan Account supports the view that institutionalization should be a last resort, and it makes it clear that the arguments for alternatives to institutionalization need not be based only on relative cost. Instead, protecting independence, and thus crucial elements of an individual's range of opportunities, has importance that overrides at least some considerations of cost. Of course, cost must enter the picture, since we want a system that is effective in protecting opportunity in the broad range of cases.

Two qualifications of this account of the moral importance of long-term care are in order. First, it assumes that at least most of the impaired functioning that requires long-term care for the elderly is the result of specific disease processes, which, though more frequent among the elderly, are not normal features of the design of our species. It should be noted, however, that this stance ignores an issue of some controversy in the philosophy of biology (Caplan, 1981). The qualification is important because the assumption plays a role in characterizing the normal opportunity range for the late stages of life. Second, there is the problem of extreme cases. Where disability is so severe that services do nothing to compensate for loss of normal functioning, such as in very advanced stages of Alzheimer's disease, we cannot explain the importance of these services based on their effect on opportunity. This problem is not special to long-term care, for medical services face the same issue in cases of terminal illness. In these contexts, other moral considerations, such as beneficence, may require humane care where principles of distributive justice no longer inform us about the relative importance of treatment (Daniels, 1985). The Prudential Lifespan Account illustrates that there are social obligations to provide an appropriate array of long-term care services, and it clarifies that these obligations are of comparable weight to those governing medical services.

Consider first that there is no significant market for long-term care insurance, despite the fact that the uncertainty facing the onset and costs of disability makes it an obvious candidate for insurance schemes. Specifically, it would be prudent for individuals to buy contingency claims on the joint risks of disability and other facts, such as the absence of family support or the unsuitability of living arrangements. However, prudent deliberators would meet the obligation to assure access to appropriate long-term care services by constructing a public or mixed public-private insurance scheme.

A social insurance scheme would constitute the decision to save health care resources at an appropriate rate, given the age profile and the disability/age profile for the society. Specifically, since the aging of U.S. society means that more people will live long enough to experience partial disabilities in the late stage of life, health care resources must be saved at a greater rate overall. Moreover, the savings must be in the form of contingent claims on the services appropriate to meeting long-term care needs.

If resource constraints limit the degree to which we can expand the health care system, then some difficult choices must be made. Long-term care services are morally important for the same reasons medical services are. Consequently, choices will have to be made that may reduce expenditures for medical services, even those that marginally extend life for the terminally ill, in order to provide for long-term care services that significantly enhance opportunity in the late stages of life. The thrust of the discussion of the moral importance of long-term care is that prudent deliberators might well reduce expenditures on medical resources that have little impact on protecting normal opportunity range, in favor of significantly improving opportunity for those who need long-term care.

Nevertheless, the account sketched here is unable by itself to resolve some of the central problems involving allocation or rationing choices we must make. Some long-term care services might take priority over some acute medical services both because they meet the needs of the sickest patients and because they produce greater benefits. In other cases, however, helping the sickest patients may conflict with producing larger medical benefits elsewhere in the system. This typifies a type of rationing problem that we have no adequate philosophical tools to resolve (Daniels 1993,

1996a). In such cases, we must rely on fair, publicly accountable deliberative procedures (Daniels & Sabin, 1997).

The division of labor between family and society

One central issue facing prudent deliberators is the appropriate division of responsibility for long-term care between private (e.g., family) and public mechanisms. Controversy surrounding this issue is part of the explanation for many inadequacies in the current system. Earlier, it was argued that it would be morally wrong to protect the supply of family care by legally imposing some set of filial obligations for which we can provide no adequate moral justification. The following discussion demonstrates how prudent deliberators might address the problem of family care, simply knowing that most adult children in their society are willing to provide some long-term care to frail parents, out of either love or a feeling of obligation. The important point is that not all choices from the perspective of prudent deliberators are part of a zero-sum game. What is given to one stage of life, to one age group, is not necessarily a loss to another.

Prudent deliberators would want to protect against the contingency that there are no family supports to provide long-term care. They would design the system so that social obligations were met through the appropriate public or private insurance scheme. Given resource limits, they would want to protect the normal opportunity range by providing the least restrictive forms of long-term care possible. But the more common condition is that some family supports would also be available. Then it would be prudent to arrange institutions so that such support would not be unduly burdensome to family members.

Reducing these burdens is important for several reasons. It means that the care is less likely to be discontinued by families. What care is given by families may then be of higher quality (Dunlop, 1980). To the extent that relief services improve the duration and quality of the care provided by families, the elderly are likely to maintain their independence longer and with better quality. Also it will be delivered with less stress on family relationships (Doty, 1986).

Prudent deliberators would consider this issue not only from the perspective of the recipients of such care, but also from the perspective of its providers, for they are designing a system they will live through at each stage of life. As family members providing such care, they would be prudent to design a system that gives relief from the daily routine. Day care facilities for the elderly, social support services to relieve the family, and, to a lesser extent, tax incentives to reduce the stress on family obligations to younger children all would make it easier to provide care for elders out of love or filial duty. When family members who actually provide care are asked what sorts of assistance they most require, they put home medical and personal care assistance, as well as community day care, high on the list (Doty, 1986). Relief services can also have a significant impact on opportunities available to the primary caregiver. This point may be of special importance in a period when more women, who have traditionally been the primary caregivers for elderly parents, are joining the workforce and pursuing careers until late in their own lives. Thus, from the perspective of prudent deliberators, such relief services benefit individuals at each stage of life.

Conclusions

The prudential lifespan perspective has led to conclusions that address many of the criticisms (noted earlier) of the existing system in the United States. The bias of that system in favor of medical services, and in favor of "medicalizing" long-term care through premature institutionalization, is not defensible on grounds of justice. There are social obligations to guarantee access to adequate long-term care services, whether institutional-, community-, or home-based. This will require the government to guarantee a public or mixed public-private insurance market for these services. Home- and community-based services that preserve independence for the partially disabled, regardless of age, including rehabilitation to the extent feasible, are requirements of the prudent—and just—design of a health care system. To the extent that society wants to preserve family provision of many long-term care services, it is both prudent and just, from the perspective of provider and recipient alike, to relieve the burden on families.

These general conclusions leave many other issues about the division of public and private responsibility unaddressed. However, having elucidated some considerations of justice that bear on these issues, this discussion may make it possible for deliberations about policy design, discussed elsewhere in this volume, to consider questions of fairness more explicitly.

Acknowledgment

I have drawn on material from my *Am I My Parents' Keeper? An Essay on Justice between the Young and the Old* (New York: Oxford University Press, 1988), especially from Chapter 6, and from my "Prudential Lifespan Account of Justice Across Generations," reprinted in Daniels, 1996a, Chapter 12. Work on this essay was partially supported by the Retirement Research Foundation.

References

Bishop, C. (1981). A compulsory national long term care insurance program. In J. J. Callahan & S. S. Wallack (Eds.), *Reforming the long-term care system* (pp. 61-93). Lexington, MA: Heath.

Callahan, J., & Wallack, S. S. (Eds.). (1981). *Reforming the long-term care system.* Lexington, MA: Heath.

Caplan, A. (1981). The "unnaturalness" of aging—a sickness unto death? In A. Caplan, H. Engelhardt, & J. McCartney (Eds.), *Concepts of health and disease: Interdisciplinary perspectives* (pp. 725-737). Reading, MA: Addison-Wesley.

Daniels, N. (1985). *Just health care.* New York: Cambridge University Press.

Daniels, N. (1988). *Am I my parents' keeper? An essay on justice between the young and the old.* New York: Oxford University Press.

Daniels, N. (1989). The biomedical model and just health care: A reply to Jecker. *Journal of Medicine and Philosophy, 14*(6), 677-680.

Daniels, N. (1993a). The Prudential Lifespan Account of justice across generations. In L. Cohen (Ed.), *Justice across generations: What does it mean?* (pp. 197-214, 243-248). Washington, DC: American Association of Retired Persons, Public Policy Institute.

Daniels, N. (1993b). Rationing fairly: Programmatic considerations. *Bioethics, 7,* 224-233.

Daniels, N. (1996a). *Justice and justification: Reflective equilibrium in theory and practice.* New York: Cambridge University Press.

Daniels, N. (1996b). Mental disabilities, equal opportunity, and the ADA. In R. Bonnie & J. Monahan (Eds.), *Mental disorder, work disability, and the law* (pp. 282-297). Chicago, IL: University of Chicago.

Daniels, N., Light, D., & Caplan, R. (1996). *Benchmarks of fairness for health care reform.* New York: Oxford University Press.

Daniels, N., & Sabin, J. (1997). Limits to health care: Fair procedures, democratic deliberation, and the legitimacy problem for insurers. *Philosophy and Public Affairs, 26,* 303-356.

Doty, P. (1986). Family care of the elderly. *Milbank Quarterly, 64,* 34-75.

Dunlop, B. (1980). Expanded home-based care for the impaired elderly: Solution or pipe dream? *American Journal of Public Health, 70,* 514-519.

Jecker, N. (1989). Towards a theory of age-group justice. *Journal of Medicine and Philosophy, 14,* 655-676.

McKerlie, D. (1989). Equality between age groups. *Philosophy and Public Affairs, 21,* 275-295.

McKerlie, D. (1993). Justice between neighboring generations. In L. Cohen (Ed.),

Justice across generations: What does it mean? (pp. 215–226). Washington, DC: American Association of Retired Persons, Public Policy Institute.

Rawls, J. (1971). *A theory of justice.* Cambridge, MA: Harvard University Press.

Rawls, J. (1993). *Political liberalism.* New York: Columbia University Press.

Vogel, R., & Palmer, H. (Eds.). (1982). *Long-term care: Perspectives from research and demonstrations.* Washington, DC: Health Care Financing Administration, U.S. Department of Health and Human Services.

PART II

The Public-Private Dilemma in Long-Term Care

Policy Responses

CHAPTER 5

Public-Private Partnerships in Long-Term Care

MARK R. MEINERS

This chapter describes an innovative collaboration between public and private sectors to develop an insurance-based approach to financing long-term care. Principles of a Partnership model are outlined, and the utility of this model for a national program is explored.

Recent public policy debates stimulated by the Clinton administration's health care reform proposals sent two critical messages regarding the financing and organization of health care for the elderly and disabled: long-term care is important but expensive, and neither the public nor the private sector alone is capable of providing adequate funding for that component of the health care delivery system (Meiners, 1996). In order to begin to address major gaps in long-term care, the Clinton team recommended the following: incremental policy that encouraged innovation on the part of the states in the area of home and community care; improvements in means-tested public programs; and support for private-sector responsibility (Clinton administration, 1993). Underlying these proposals is the expectation that states will continue to have a major role in administering and reforming the U.S. long-term care system, and that progress will come about on an incremental basis.

Subsequent to the failure of the Clinton health care plan, concern about the financial prospects of Medicare and Medicaid has served to reinforce the incremental approach to long-term care system improvements. The recent passage of long-term care insurance tax clarification language in the Kassebaum-Kennedy legislation marked a first step. This legislation is intended to make long-term care insurance more visible and acceptable as a way to prepare for the risk of catastrophic long-term care costs. An early indication of the effect of tax-favored status of long-term care insurance is anticipated within the next few years, as the baby boom generation enters its fifties, the age for pre-retirement planning.

However, it is likely that more than just this incremental step is needed to address long-term care financing needs of the population (Freudenheim, 1996). Significant progress on long-term care will require a public-private financing partnership that includes consideration of Medicaid by careful design, not by default. The private market could be helped by government support of experimentation with new systems of care and financing. Government assistance could occur through innovation in the Medicaid program since it is the principal payer for long-term care. A new means-tested program for long-term care that is designed to complement private-market options is one logical way to proceed.

Means-testing for long-term care is the approach that states are most familiar with, since they have experience with this approach through administration of the Medicaid program. However, means-testing is unacceptable to some policy analysts and interest groups, who maintain that this approach leads to poorly funded, inadequate programs because the political constituency is not broad enough to advocate effectively against these trends. Strategies to minimize this risk must be developed, such as structuring a linkage of the means-tested program with long-term care insurance.

This is the approach being used in the Partnership for Long-Term Care program, a multistate initiative to create a model of long-term care financing that relies on both public and private responsibilities (Meiners & McKay, 1989). Supported by the Robert Wood Johnson Foundation (RWJF), the program focuses on the potential role that private insurance might play in filling the need for long-term care within the nation's health care system (Merrill & Somers, 1989; Somers & Merrill, 1991). This chapter discusses the design features of this program and some of the key learning experiences throughout program development and early implementation. The Partnership program is a real-time case study of one approach to balancing public and private responsibilities for financing long-term care.

Background

The concept of public-private partnerships

A public-private partnership may take many forms, depending on how broadly the issue is defined. For example, most long-term care is either provided by family and friends directly or purchased by them. The interrelationship between public and private sources of support can be complicated. However, any realistic public intervention must support, not replace, individuals' willingness to accept personal responsibility for long-term care needs.

Private enterprise can be used to forge a strong public-private collaboration. This happens when high-quality, affordable products that meet long-term care needs as perceived by consumers and their families are developed and marketed. Examples that have recently emerged include the growing number of home and community care options, assisted living communities, health systems that are designed to integrate acute and long-term care, and long-term care insurance. Accordingly, one form of partnership is for the government to support the formulation and promulgation of such options, leaving the payment decision and responsibility up to the individual.

A more aggressive strategy is to reform the financing of long-term care. One approach is to segment the risk, covering some of it through public programs and leaving the rest as the responsibility of individuals. For example, the long-term care risk could be partitioned so that nursing home care is paid publicly and home and community care is paid privately. Another approach would require the individual to assume the initial risk, and the government to bear the long-term catastrophic risk. Currently, Medicare provides selected skilled nursing home and home care benefits while Medicaid offers extensive coverage of nursing home care. This configuration bears a striking resemblance to ideas of segmenting risk, although more by default than by design. The Partnership for Long-Term Care attempts to improve the system, within the limitations of current and future public financing.

The Partnership for Long-Term Care program

To stimulate the long-term care insurance market and to help balance competing pressures between product value and price, four states (California, Connecticut, Indiana, and New York) implemented an innovative long-term care insurance program. The program involves a public-private partnership that protects consumers from depletion of their assets in the financing of long-term care. Under an asset protection model, individuals who purchase a state-certified Partnership insurance policy are allowed to access Medicaid-covered benefits without becoming impoverished.

The states expect to benefit if the long-term care insurance market can be expanded to include those at risk of spending down their resources to the level of impoverishment where Medicaid must pay. Program incentives encourage the elderly and their children to buy insurance policies that will protect them from ever having to spend all of their life savings on home care or nursing home services. The policies may also serve as an alternative to the growing appeal of Medicaid estate planning (as discussed in Chapter 8).

Partnership long-term care insurance policies work in the following way. By buying a Partnership policy, a person qualifies for Medicaid benefits under special Medicaid rules. Once non-Partnership policy benefits run out, individuals must spend virtually all of their savings before they qualify for Medicaid. In contrast, when a Partnership policy's benefits are exhausted, the policyholder is permitted to retain assets equal to the amount his or her insurance paid out (in New York, policyholders can keep all remaining assets). The person is then eligible for coverage under Medicaid without having to entirely deplete previous savings.

Insurers participating in the Partnerships must meet the program certification standards (McCall, Knickman, & Bauer, 1991), which ensure that approved long-term care policies are of high quality. Among the standards required in each state are inflation protection and minimum benefit amounts. Participating insurers are also required to provide the state with information on purchasers of certified products and the utilization of benefits.

Asset protection models

There are two Partnership asset protection models. The model in California, Connecticut, and Indiana provides a dollar of asset protection for each dollar paid out by a state-certified long-term care insurance policy (Mahoney & Wetle, 1992). The program allows for a variety of product designs with benefits ranging from one year of coverage on up. This flexible approach allows persons of different means the option of choosing the amount of protection most in line with their resources and ability to pay.

The impoverishment protection feature of the Partnership programs being implemented by the participating states is designed to be budget-neutral. Impoverishment protection encourages individuals to plan for their long-term care needs by purchasing long-term care insurance protection in an amount commensurate with their assets. Thus, an individual with $25,000 in assets might buy $25,000 in insurance protection while another individual with $150,000 in assets might buy $150,000 in insurance protection. Insurance payments for long-term care services would be considered as equivalent to the spending of assets for the purpose of establishing Medicaid eligibility. Once on Medicaid, individuals would be able to keep control of assets up to the amount that insurance paid; income would still have to be applied toward long-term care expenses.

The opportunity to avoid impoverishment by buying long-term care insurance is an incentive intended to help those who are most at risk of depleting their resources when long-term care is needed. Middle-income elderly ($20,000–$40,000 per year) generally have less assets to protect and are least able to afford currently offered private insurance "lifetime" protection (four years or more) that would minimize the risk of impoverishment. Yet when they need long-term care, the cost of Medicaid (spending down assets and income to the poverty level) can very well be catastrophic. In order to have enough protection to cover the risk of an average length of stay, middle-income elderly in the current market must buy insurance benefits that often substantially exceed their assets. Consequently, the market for this type of insurance is unlikely to extend to this group without the impoverishment protection incentive offered by the Partnership. This incentive makes purchases of one to three years of protection both more meaningful and more affordable to those in the middle-income group, who are most at risk for spending down their resources and requiring Medicaid.

The asset protection model used by New York bases its incentive on time rather than the dollar amount of coverage purchased (Holubinka, 1992). Partnership policies in New York are required to pay three years of nursing home care, six years of home care, or some combination (with two days of home care equaling one day of nursing home care), after which all remaining assets are protected. A high priority of the New York approach is to offer a viable alternative to asset transfers (Nussbaum, 1992). With about 80 percent of its nursing home residents on Medicaid compared to a national average of about 60 percent, New York feels this approach is best suited to keeping people with significant financial means from using Medicaid unnecessarily. Transfer of assets is thought to be quite common in New York and such a growing phenomenon that any strategy which encourages individuals to take financial responsibility for their own care could yield savings to the state.

Program Analysis

Arguments in support of the Partnership

The Partnership states selected the strategy of linking the purchase of long-term care insurance to Medicaid eligibility after considering several alternatives (Meiners, 1988). The Partnership has a number of strengths. The program is fiscally conservative, helps middle-income people avoid impoverishment, serves as an alternative to Medicaid estate planning, promotes better-quality insurance products and consumer protection efforts, enhances public awareness regarding long-term care needs and options, and helps maintain public support for the Medicaid program (Meiners & Goss, 1994).

The Partnership provides a fiscally conservative form of premium subsidy in that only those who buy a policy and use the benefits receive the special protection. Program-related expenditures occur well after program initiation, and savings would be accruing to cover future costs. In contrast, traditional premium subsidies (including tax breaks) entail public expenditures at the time of purchase for all purchasers. Under the Partnership, middle-income people may obtain assistance with catastrophic long-term care expenses without becoming impoverished. Under special arrangements with the state, participating insurance companies can assure policyholders they no longer have to be impoverished to qualify for Medicaid. Assets protected under the Partnership can mean the difference between autonomy and dependence if a policyholder exhausts his or her insurance and still needs assistance.

Policymakers in recent years have devoted significant attention to the practice of Medicaid estate planning. Partnership purchasers have less reason to resort to legal maneuvering to hold on to their savings. The Partnership policies are an alternative to transferring assets to relatives or friends to avoid spending savings on long-term care. Participants can control their funds instead of worrying about how someone else might be handling their money. Policyholders also do not have to be concerned about state and federal government efforts to stop Medicaid estate planning. The states can pursue regulations to minimize Medicaid estate planning with less controversy, knowing people are being given a reasonable alternative.

The Partnerships bring the states into a close working relationship with insurers, providing both the means and the incentive to monitor insurer performance. Partnership policies are subject to a rigorous review beyond that conducted for non-Partnership policies and carry a stamp of approval from the states indicating they have meet rigid state certification requirements. Further, regulatory oversight is strengthened to help consumer protection and confidence. All participating insurers are required to provide the state with extensive data for program monitoring. The data will make possible a variety of special studies, including analysis of underwriting rules, utilization patterns, and insured event criteria.

As part of the program, educational campaigns are increasing public awareness about what long-term care is, risks of needing long-term care, and the limited financing options. The public information campaigns are multifaceted, directed at persons for whom long-term care insurance may be especially beneficial. This component of the Partnership has been successful in each of the states.

Finally, the Partnership program can help mitigate concerns about means-testing—that programs for the poor are poor programs because they lack broad-based political support. By linking the Partnership incentive to Medicaid and by including middle-income persons as potential Medicaid recipients, the constituency for the means-tested program can be enhanced rather than eroded.

Concerns about the Partnership program

In the early stages of program development, arguments against the Partnership were raised primarily by social insurance advocates, who viewed the program as an incremental step that would erode support for more ambitious reform (Meiners, 1993). As the Partnership was implemented, insurers voiced their dissatisfaction with certain aspects of the program design because it deviated from some of the standard approaches used to market this coverage and required extra attention beyond that for non-Partnership products.

As long-term care insurance began to emerge as a viable reform instrument, it was viewed by some as more an obstacle than a help with long-term care reform since it did not provide universal insurance. It was argued that any further growth of the private long-term care insurance market would both relieve public pressure for reform and build opposition to social insurance reform from private-sector advocates whose stake in future long-term care insurance policymaking increased. For advocates of social insurance, Medicaid, as a means-tested program, was viewed as part of the problem crying for a social insurance solution. The linking of long-term care insurance with Medicaid as a way to address financing problems of long-term care was philosophically unacceptable, if not damaging to the cause, for some advocates.

Concerns about the link to Medicaid also resonated with the Partnership insurers and their agents, as well as the program developers. The applicability of the model is limited because many state Medicaid programs do not offer comprehensive home and community benefits or a system of care management that supports the continuity of care desired in such a partnership. States that have not developed strong programs for the poor will have trouble justifying asset protection models. With discussion of block grant programs and cutbacks in federal funding, the future form and substance of Medicaid is uncertain.

This uncertainty surrounding Medicaid reinforces the standard marketing practice of insurance agents selling against Medicaid. A basic message from many insurance agents is to not depend on Medicaid, in fact, to avoid it at all reasonable cost. Compatible with this message has been the emphasis on lifetime coverage to assure avoidance of Medicaid. Over this early period of market development, the standard product has increased from three years (designed to cover the average of two and half years in a nursing home) to lifetime coverage.

These complexities have made getting insurance agents to understand and buy into the Partnership message more difficult than initially anticipated. Though lifetime coverage only assures avoidance of Medicaid if the product is inflation-protected and covers both nursing home and home care, these features are often relegated to secondary consideration in the marketing presentation. The bottom-up message of the Partnership—everyone should have some coverage, trading lifetime coverage for shorter, comprehensive, inflation-protected benefits, and then, if necessary, accessing Medicaid coverage without being impoverished—has been difficult to integrate into mainstream selling practices.

Equally important is the fact that the primary target audience for Partnership policies differs from the market agents have customarily worked with. Selling to the high end of the income and asset spectrum is easier than targeting sales to those most in need of the Partnership products. The problem is compounded by the fact that agent commissions are directly related to the size of the premiums they sell.

An additional factor that may work against Partnership sales is that the Medicaid rules under which the Partnership operates do not waive income rules along with asset rules. As a result, income must be applied to the cost of care once insurance runs out. People expecting to have high income when they exhaust their insurance may not need the extra asset protection because their income will cover the entire bill. This tends to be a greater issue at the high end of the market, but can make the decision to choose Partnership coverage less attractive.

The lack of portability of the asset protection feature has also been cited as a barrier to sales. Since only a few states have Partnership programs and the details of each state's Medicaid program vary, reciprocity agreements that allow asset protection outside the home state have not been established at the time of this writing. While this has no effect on the value of the insurance benefit payment itself, it is a concern for those who feel they might move and depend on the asset protection feature as the primary motivation for choosing a Partnership policy.

The participating insurers have also cited state-by-state differences in Partnership program details as being too costly and time-consuming. Nearly all insurers participating in the Partnership maintained their regular product offerings. The Partnership policy development, approval process, and data reporting is an additional set of responsibilities they are required to carry out in order to participate in the program. Only in the case of the data reporting system have the participating states agreed to do things in a uniform way. In nearly every other aspect, even when states use the same asset protection model, knowledge of differences in program details are required for insurers participating in more than one state.

Another concern raised about the Partnership is that increased Medicaid costs could result because the extra protection offered by the states would be available to those who would have purchased long-term care insurance even without the Partnership incentive. The concern is that the program could not be targeted only to people who would otherwise not have bought long-term care insurance without the Partnership incentive (Nyman, 1994). Because there is an emerging market for long-term care insurance that has significant growth potential, the merits of this targeting problem have been debated (Meiners & Goss, 1994).

A related concern has to do with crowding out segments of the private market that might have emerged if the government-supported asset protection incentive were not offered. For example, this could happen if someone who would have bought lifetime inflation-protected coverage instead buys a shorter, less expensive Partnership policy because of the asset protection.

In summary, there are essentially three perceived drawbacks of the Partnership approach. The first is political in nature, that is, this incremental step takes the wind out of radical, comprehensive reform of long-term care. The second is somewhat process-oriented. Getting both the insurers and agents to truly buy in to the concept and promote it effectively can be challenging. Finally, there are issues of economic efficiency having to do with targeting the incentive and possible crowding out private responsibility for financing care.

Experiences in Partnership Implementation

Most of the arguments for and against the Partnership share common elements viewed from different perspectives. Central to the strategy is the fact that Medicaid is the primary public payer for long-term care, that states are the key decision-makers regarding Medicaid rules and insurance regulation, and that the states must determine that programs are budget-neutral before undertaking efforts to provide incentives for insurance purchase. At the time when the Partnership programs were initiated, two countervailing forces clashed. First, state interest in the Partnership grew well beyond the four states funded by the Robert Wood Johnson Foundation. In fact, twelve states passed enabling legislation to create programs modeled on the RWJF program.

Second, the Omnibus Reconciliation Act of 1993 (OBRA 93), enacted the same year as the RWJF Partnership was implemented, contained language with both indirect and direct impact on the expansion of Partnership programs. Indirectly, the act closed several loopholes in the Medicaid eligibility process, thereby providing further incentives for persons to purchase private insurance for long-term care. The act also makes specific mention of Partnership programs. The statute contains a grandfather clause that recognizes as approved the four initial states, plus a future program in Iowa and a modified program in Massachusetts (protecting only the home from estate recovery). These states were allowed to operate their partnerships as planned since the Health Care Financing Administration had approved their state plan amendments before May 14, 1993.

While states obtaining a state plan amendment after that date are allowed to proceed with Partnership programs, they are also required to recover assets from the estates of all persons receiving services under Medicaid. The result of this language is that the asset protection component of the Partnership is in effect only while the insured is alive. After the policyholder dies, states must recover what Medicaid spent from the estate, including protected assets. With participating insurers already concerned about variability in state-by-state approaches, this has had the effect of stifling the growing interest in replicating the Partnership in other states.

Partnership policy sales

Partnership policy sales at the time of this writing indicate steadily growing interest in public-private long-term care insurance policies. However, the numbers also reveal that the public is still wary about the need for such policies. The following are highlights from Partnership policy sales in four states (California, Connecticut, Indiana, and New York) as of June 30, 1996. At that time, the programs had between two and four years of experience, with Connecticut first (1992) and California last (1994) to implement.

More than 26,000 applications had been received for the purchase of Partnership policies by mid-1996 across the four participating states. From these applications, almost 20,000 Partnership policies were purchased (there is a lag between application and purchase). Of these purchases, there are currently more than 15,000 policies in force in the four states. Three of the four states (California, Connecticut, Indiana) allow the sale of one- and two-year Partnership policies. The proportion of purchasers in these states buying one- and two-year policies remains high (California: 91%, Connecticut: 49%, and Indiana: 40%). The majority of Partnership policy purchasers are first-time buyers. The proportion of first-timers ranges from a high of 95 percent in California to a low of 79 percent in Indiana. A significant proportion of Partnership policy purchasers are under age sixty-five, ranging from a high of 56 percent in Connecticut to a low of 31 percent in California.

Variations on the Partnership theme

Several states decided to proceed with Partnership programs in the aftermath of the OBRA 93 restrictions. Believing that access to Medicaid coverage without impoverishment was a major benefit for citizens, Maryland and Illinois secured state-plan amendments to offer Partnership programs modified to meet the OBRA 93 requirements. Both states modified the programs developed and implemented by their predecessors.

Maryland decided to make state-certified long-term care insurance policies eligible for asset protection rather than have special rules associated with Partnership policies. This approach made the Partnership strategy more visible and eliminated marketing against the Partnership. Though targeting concerns might be exacerbated by this approach, it was also a way to develop widespread knowledge concerning the Partnership incentive among the middle-income people who need the protection most.

One major change implicit in this model was that Maryland did not require inflation protection. In the development of the RWJF Partnership program, inflation protection was a major point of contention with the insurers and the agents, who preferred that inflation protection not be required since the related significant price increase reduces demand. However, all the RWJF Partnership states require inflation protection because they feel it is important to the budget neutrality of the program. It also helps assure the states' promise of protection of assets. Without inflation protection, the growing cost of deductibles and co-pays could impoverish a policyholder before much asset protection can be secured. Maryland planned to deal with the inflation issue through consumer education campaigns, leaving the choice to consumers.

As the Maryland approach has not been implemented, this Partnership strategy has not received a market test. Maryland tabled its program because of concerns about the estate recovery language in OBRA 93. The definition of the estate is broader than currently in use in Maryland, which would have the potential of penalizing insurance purchasers relative to those who had not purchased insurance—quite the opposite of the intent of the program (McKay, 1995).

Illinois, the other state approved after OBRA 93, did not share this concern with Maryland and has implemented its program. Although initially Illinois chose the dollar-for-dollar model, the state recently revised the program, developing a hybrid approach that switches to total asset protection for those who buy $200,000 of protection. The required inflation protection is optional. These changes were made to stimulate sluggish insurer interest. At this writing, it is too soon to tell whether the changes will overcome the perceived problems.

Colorado took yet a different approach in the face of the OBRA 93 estate recovery provisions. The state legislature requires that any insurer certified to sell insurance in Colorado must also actively market a basic and a standard policy that meets specific requirements, using the insurers' normal sources and methods of distribution. The basic plan was to be one that would be affordable to purchasers of moderate income, while the standard plan was to reflect the features most commonly sold in the existing market (middle- or high-income purchasers). No special asset protection provisions were made. The Colorado strategy combines the dissemination of a shopper's guide along with a consumer education campaign and relatively simple comparable product offerings to focus attention on long-term care insurance and help consumers make an educated purchase decision.

Another model of note has been implemented by the California Public Employees Retirement System (CalPERS) in cooperation with the California Partnership program. The CalPERS long-term care insurance program is a group offering for active public employees, retirees, and their dependents designed to achieve lower premiums through group marketing economies. A range of ten options was offered, which included a one-year and a two-year Partnership policy. Through this initiative, California took the lead in encouraging employer-group offerings as a way to mainstream this type of protection at younger ages when it is especially affordable. CalPERS is self-funding and relies on its own investment expertise, thereby freeing itself from a number of regulatory and reserving requirements normally exercised by the State Insurance Department.

In a span of only eighteen months over seventy thousand policies were sold (about 5 percent were Partnership policies). A new open period offering will be launched during 1997 so the self-funded CalPERS program may soon be among the largest group long-term care programs in the country. This initial success has been attributed to three key ingredients (Mahoney, 1995). First, CalPERS' solid reputation for managing health care costs without sacrificing quality of care gave it special credibility with this completely new program. Second, the design of the product was based on elements members had identified as essential and simplicity was emphasized. Third, CalPERS and United Health Care (the private contractor administering the program) made a serious commitment to member education and marketing efforts.

Finally, the Partnership insurance strategy has also captured international attention. Great Britain, faced with long-term care gaps in its public funding systems similar to those in the United States, is in the early stages of debating the details of a national version of the RWJF Partnership program (HM Secretary of State for Health, 1997). It appears the favored scheme is the pound-for-pound, modified to provide a greater incentive (pound and a half or even two pounds of asset protection) and greater assurance that protection of the home will be accomplished for those at the low end of the resource spectrum.

Movement to a National Partnership

The idea of a uniform nationwide public-private partnership approach that uses extra asset protection as an incentive to buy long-term care insurance is not new. It has been suggested by representatives of both political parties. In 1990, then Senators Packwood and Dole took the lead in proposing such an approach, along with a revised Medicaid program designed to be more uniform across the states (Packwood & Dole, 1993). More recently, to complement the Clinton long-term care proposals, Senators Kennedy and Wofford proposed a self-funded public insurance program for nursing home care very much modeled on the RWJF Partnership for Long-Term Care (Kennedy & Wofford, 1994). The voluntary program included a special incentive of asset protection from Medicaid rules of $30,000 to $90,000, depending on the amount of insurance purchased. The proposed program was to be publicly run, with more liberal enrollment rules than private insurance. It would have allowed all individuals to enroll during an open period at each of ten-year intervals, beginning at age thirty-five, regardless of preexisting conditions.

Because state-by-state development is costly and dependence on Medicaid as the basis for the stop-loss protection does not easily allow for reciprocity agreements between states, the idea of uniform national partnership has prompted discussions among the states and insurers who have been most active in the current RWJF Partnership effort. However, consensus on how to implement a national partnership program that would simplify the implementation and operation for states and insurers has been difficult to achieve. Two approaches have emerged from these efforts.

One approach is to determine a set of insurance features that would comprise a Partnership policy approved by all participating states. From this cafeteria of features, insurers could choose the details of their Partnership product and receive timely approval in those states. The set of features and approval process would be independent of what the participating state did with non-Partnership products. The strength of this approach is that it achieves uniformity across the states in all basic Partnership policy features. The weakness is that insurers offering Partnership and non-Partnership policies would still have two separate products with separate filing requirements. One suggestion to further simplify this approach is to have the Partnership product reflect a limited set of options (e.g., a two-year and a four-year policy only) with the features fully standardized.

The second approach is to distinguish a Partnership policy by requiring a limited set of features such as inflation protection and uniform data reporting. The remaining features would be the same as those for non-Partnership policies in the participating states. The approval process would be expedited and paperwork minimized by allowing companies to use their current policy as the base, with the option of including the Partnership requirements if they wanted it to qualify for the special asset protection. Although both approaches require agreement on Partnership features, the second approach requires agreement on a smaller set of features. The second model may also be easier for states to accept, as it fits with the current insurance regulatory environment, where states have considerable control over what gets sold.

None of this addresses the issue of Medicaid as the backup (payer of last resort). The asset insurance model and a more uniform means-tested long-term care program in the states would be mutually complementary. Yet improvements to the means-tested program can only be sustained as affordable and appealing private-market financing options serve to prevent people from using those benefits except as a legitimate last resort.

By linking the Partnership incentive to Medicaid (or a new means-tested long-term care program), the constituency for the means-tested program may be enhanced rather than eroded. As noted earlier, this strategy is intended to help secure middle- and upper-class support for a viable and quality means-tested program by making it part of what they may also need to depend on in the face of otherwise catastrophic long-term care expenses. However, insurance agents often find it easiest to market against Medicaid. This basic conflict has yet to be resolved in the Partnership program.

One approach to this problem would be to separate the asset protection from Medicaid. This could be done by creating a new entitlement under Medicare that would require the purchase of a certified private long-term care insurance policy in exchange for a commitment to protect some level of assets. A less ambitious alternative step in this direction would be to create a new optional benefit in which states could choose to contribute to a backup pool (perhaps with federal matching funds like with Medicaid) with reciprocity arrangements for participating states. The key to either of these approaches is that the stop-loss incentive is removed from its direct link to Medicaid, which would eliminate concerns about variability across states and over time. It could also serve to allow for some combination of income and assets to be protected. The recent movement toward product standardization under the tax qualification requirements of the Kassebaum-Kennedy legislation might serve to facilitate agreements on the qualifying features.

Next steps in program development

A key question in research and program development is identifying the problem that needs to be solved. Even among those actively involved in the development and implementation of the Partnership program, there is disagreement about the nature and scope of the long-term care financing problem. The original goals of the Partnership program centered on helping consumers take more personal responsibility for paying for long-term care by increasing the value and affordability of long-term care insurance. The intervention needed to be at least budget-neutral and work from existing state and federal financial and administrative structures so as to allow for incremental learning and acceptance. Furthermore, the program needed to be an effective vehicle for educating consumers about the probability of needing long-term care, as well as the availability and benefits of quality long-term care insurance coverage for individuals with middle and modest levels of income and assets.

These are ambitious goals, particularly since they did not completely coincide with the goals of some of the key partners, the insurers and the agents. Throughout the development and implementation of the Partnership program, tax clarification was the primary public policy goal of the long-term care insurance industry. It was viewed as a way to show that the government supported the role of private insurance in protecting against this risk. Equally important was that tax clarification signaled that the government was not going to pursue a broad-based new entitlement. However, since these were also reasons for supporting the Partnership program, a cooperative working relationship has emerged, with potential for further development.

As the market matures and the effect of the Kassebaum-Kennedy legislation becomes clear, it is likely that there will be renewed interest in finding ways to reach the broader market. The lessons learned in the Partnership program will be valuable to that renewed interest. At least two possible options fit within the framework of incrementalism. One option is to revise the product design to make it as identical to that offered in the market as possible, given the goals of the program. This would relieve the burden of creating and receiving approval for two separate products. The other option is to develop selective partnering strategies along with distribution channel innovations that emphasize lifetime protection as the top priority in a marketing approach.

Bottom-up marketing would convey that everyone needs some protection against the risk of long-term care and should buy as much as possible, using their resource base as a guide. This message would be targeted to groups of potential purchasers of middle and modest means at risk of impoverishment if they needed long-term care. Prospective purchasers would be coached to make their purchase decision by assessing the level of resources that they would like to have at their disposal while still qualifying for Medicaid's help.

As the next steps unfold, some version of both these strategies may be tried. However, without the repeal of the OBRA 93 restrictions on

Partnership-style asset protection, it may be difficult to stimulate the multistate interest necessary to justify the commitment of resources by insurers and their agents to support these alternative marketing strategies. But there is growing recognition that states need flexibility in dealing with the pressures on the Medicaid system and that private long-term care insurance is a needed alternative to public financing. The National Governors' Association has recently called for elimination of federal barriers to public-private insurance Partnerships like those in the RWJF states and the expansion of authority to all states to implement such programs (National Governors' Association, 1997). Future efforts will also involve investigation of strategies that do not depend on direct links to Medicaid. For example, the growing interest in managed care for both Medicare- and Medicaid-eligible populations has promoted greater recognition of the potential value of integrating acute and long-term care. Minnesota, Colorado, Florida, New York, and Wisconsin, to name a few states, are developing managed care programs for those eligible for both Medicare and Medicaid. These programs have as their goal better, more cost-effective care through the integration of provider systems and the coordination of care. Though the initial focus is on public-pay clients, the delivery system development lessons are equally relevant to long-term care insurance links that might be made with Medicare managed care products as the private-market alternative for those not eligible for Medicaid.

Conclusions

Strategies for enhancing the market for private long-term care insurance abound. The menu of options originally suggested as the impetus for the Partnership program remains relevant today (Meiners, 1988). Options can be categorized into the following four distinct, but related, target categories.

The first category focuses on general public policy interventions. It includes educational campaigns to enhance public awareness, regulatory review to encourage market flexibility while promoting consumer protection, support for improved data development and sharing to minimize uncertainty, and coordination of public cost and care management mechanisms (e.g., preadmission screening, utilization review, case management, benefit coverage, and rate regulation) with those of the private market. The second category focuses on consumers. It includes tax credits or deductions, deductible or co-pay subsidies, and inflation protection in addition to liberalized asset spend-down requirements. The third category focuses on insurers and premium tax relief and public reinsurance. The fourth category focuses on special populations and notes buy-in of Medicaid-eligible and special risk pool subsidies. The dilemma faced in moving forward with long-term care reform is that different approaches— universal social insurance versus means-testing—make compromise difficult (Meiners & McKay, 1990; Mahoney & Meiners, 1994). During the development of the Clinton long-term care plan, there was clear tension between the preference for universal social insurance and the realities of budget constraints. The Clinton plan, on the one hand, supported private action and preparation through tax clarification and national insurance regulations. On the other hand, the plan proposed a home and community care benefit that leaves the impression that government programs will be sufficient to meet individual needs even though the details really suggest a "capped entitlement" to states, a more limited policy. There was considerable concern on the part of the states regarding the proposal's implementation, given their fiscal constraints.

To have effective private financing options, a clear delineation of where the public role ends and personal responsibility begins is required. This is especially the case if individuals are expected to plan for and bear some of the risk of chronic disability. If planning does not occur, more people will be dependent on public support. There is a need to commit to a vision for the future, because long-term care is a risk that will require prefunding if it is to be affordable either privately or publicly. Incremental solutions would seem to make sense both in terms of the cost and the experience necessary for solid progress to be made.

References

Clinton Administration. (1993, September 7). Description of *President's Health Security Act of 1993*. Bureau of National Affairs, Washington, DC.

Freudenheim, M. (1996, November 17). Deductions coming for long-term care: Incentives to buy insurance may not entice many boomers. *New York Times*.

HM Secretary of State for Health. (1997). *A new partnership for care in old age*.

Holubinka, G. (1992). New York Partnership for LTC Insurance. *LTC News & Comment, 3*, 9–10.

Kennedy, E. M., & Wofford, H. (1994). Senate Bill 1833, 103d Cong., 2d Sess.

Mahoney, K. J. (1992). Financing long term care with limited resources. *Journal of Aging and Social Policy, 4*, 35–50.

Mahoney, K. J. (1995, November 6–7). Strategies for making private long-term care insurance more accessible to the middle class: Lessons from the California experience. Prepared for the Florida Commission on Long-Term Care's Legislative Symposium.

Mahoney, K. J., & Meiners, M. R. (1994). Private and social insurance—the feasible option. *Western Journal of Medicine, 160,* 74–76.

Mahoney, K. J., & Wetle, T. (1992). Public-private partnerships: The Connecticut model for financing long-term care. *Journal of the American Geriatrics Society, 40,* 1026–1030.

McCall, N., Knickman, J., & Bauer, E. J. (1991, Spring). Public/private partnerships: A new approach to long-term care. *Health Affairs,* 164–176.

McKay, H. (1995, August 23). *Partnership implementation post OBRA '93.* Partnerships for Long-Term Care memo.

Meiners, M. R. (1988). Enhancing the market for private long-term care insurance. *Business and Health, 5,* 19–22.

Meiners, M. R. (1993). Paying for long term care without breaking the bank. *Journal of American Health Policy, 3,* 44–48.

Meiners, M. R. (1996). The financing and organization of long-term care. In R. H. Binstock, L. E. Cluff, & O. von Mering (Eds.), *The future of long-term care.* Baltimore, MD: Johns Hopkins University Press.

Meiners, M. R., & Goss, S. C. (1994). Passing the "laugh test" for long-term care insurance partnerships. *Health Affairs, 13,* 225–228.

Meiners, M. R., & McKay, H. L. (1989). Developing public-private long-term care insurance partnerships. *Pride Institute Journal, 8.*

Meiners, M. R., & McKay, H. L. (1990). Private versus social long-term care insurance: Beware the comparison. *Generations, 14.*

Merrill, J. C., & Somers, S. A. (1989). Long-term care: The great debate on the wrong issue. *Inquiry, 26,* 317–320.

National Governors' Association. (1997). Executive committee winter meeting recommendations.

Nussbaum, S. (1992). The New York State Partnership for Long-Term Care. *The Bulletin—Official Publication of the New York City Association of Life Underwriters, 72,* 27–36.

Nyman, J. A. (1994). The economic and political feasibility of long-term care insurance partnerships. *Health Affairs, 13,* 220–224.

Packwood, R., & Dole, R. (1993). Senate Bill 1600, 103d Cong., 1st Sess.

Somers, S. A., & Merrill, J. C. (1991). Supporting states' efforts to provide long-term care insurance. *Health Affairs, 10,* 177–179.

CHAPTER 6

Jump Starting the Market

*Public Subsidies for Private
Long-Term Care Insurance*

JOSHUA M. WIENER

*This chapter provides an analysis of policy responses to the
long-term care financing programs that rely on public subsidy
models. Each of three major programs is assessed in terms of
its capacity to address affordability barriers to long-term care
insurance.*

This chapter briefly describes the current limitations of the long-term
care insurance market. The following three approaches to public subsidies
for private long-term care insurance are presented, with advantages and
impediments identified for each: (1) employer tax subsidies, (2) tax deductions or credits, and (3) waiver of some or all of the Medicaid asset
depletion requirements for purchasers of qualified insurance policies. The
chapter concludes with observations about the potential contributions of
these strategies in making long-term care insurance more affordable.

Background

The current U.S. system of financing and delivering long-term care for the
elderly and the younger disabled population is badly broken. At present,
the United States does not have, in either the private or the public sectors,
satisfactory mechanisms for helping people anticipate and pay for long-

term care. In particular, the disabled elderly and their families find, often to their astonishment, that the costs of nursing home and home care are not covered to any significant extent by either Medicare or their private insurance policies. Instead, the disabled elderly must rely on their own resources or, when those have been exhausted, turn to welfare in the form of Medicaid. Moreover, although the vast majority of disabled elderly live in the community, nearly two-thirds of public expenditures for long-term care for the elderly are for nursing home care (Wiener, Illston, & Hanley, 1994).

To address these problems, a small but growing private long-term care insurance market has developed over the past ten years. Although over 95 percent of the elderly have Medicare coverage and about 70 percent have supplemental private insurance policies, insurance against the potentially devastating costs of long-term care is relatively rare (Committee on Ways and Means, 1996). As of the end of 1993, approximately 3.8 million long-term care policies had been sold (although fewer were in force), overwhelmingly marketed to the elderly on an individual rather than group basis (Coronel & Fulton, 1995). Employer contributions toward the cost of long-term care insurance are uncommon.

By far, the greatest impediment is the high cost of good-quality policies. Despite the marked improvement in the financial position of the elderly over the past twenty years, long-term care insurance remains unaffordable for most. The average annual premium for policies covering three years of nursing home and home care with inflation protection in 1995 was over $2,000 a year if purchased at age sixty-eight and over $4,000 a year if purchased at age seventy-five (Lewin-VHI & The Brookings Institution, 1996).

The policies are expensive for two reasons: (1) nine out of ten are sold individually and, therefore, carry high administrative costs; and (2) most policies are bought by older people whose risk of needing long-term care is substantial. Consequently, most studies estimate that only 10 percent to 20 percent of the elderly can afford good-quality private long-term care insurance (Wiener, Illston, & Hanley, 1994; Crown, Capitman, & Leutz, 1992; Rivlin & Wiener, 1988). Other research has found the percentage of the elderly who can afford private insurance to be higher, but these studies have done so by assuming purchase of policies with limited coverage, by assuming the elderly would use their assets as well as income to pay premiums, or by excluding a large proportion of the elderly from the pool of people considered interested in purchasing insurance (Cohen et al., 1992; Cohen et al., 1987). Affordability is not likely to dramatically improve in the future (Wiener, Illston, & Hanley, 1994).

Given the limitations of the current market for private long-term care insurance, public subsidies to promote its purchase are frequently proposed. One approach is to provide employers with a tax subsidy for the purchase of long-term care insurance policies for their employees by allowing them to deduct insurance contributions as a business expense. A second strategy is to provide a tax deduction or credit to individuals for purchase of private long-term care insurance. Tax incentives for employers and individuals were part of the Health Insurance Portability and Accountability Act of 1996 (the Kassebaum-Kennedy bill). A final strategy is to waive some or all of the Medicaid asset depletion requirements for purchasers of qualified private long-term care insurance policies, an approach being tried in several states. The intent of these strategies is to induce more people to purchase policies by lowering premium costs through tax breaks or guaranteeing publicly funded coverage once privately purchased coverage is exhausted. Proponents argue that a key consequence of any of these actions is public endorsement of the importance and desirability of private long-term care insurance.

All of these options will, no doubt, promote the purchase of private long-term care insurance, but to what extent is unclear. Moreover, with the possible exception of easing access to Medicaid by persons who purchase private long-term care insurance, these strategies are not free to the government. All of these options could result in substantial loss of federal revenue, which is spending just as certainly as the direct expenditures of a public insurance program.

Employer-sponsored Market for Long-Term Care Insurance

Advantages and disadvantages

One approach to address the affordability problem is to encourage the purchase of private long-term care insurance at younger ages, especially through employers.

Theoretically, employer-sponsored plans offered to the nonelderly provide several advantages over those purchased individually. First, premiums for younger policyholders can be substantially lower than those for older policyholders because younger policyholders pay premiums over a longer period of time and because earnings on premium reserves have more time to build. For example, the premiums for a forty-two-year-old will be approximately one-quarter to one-third of the premiums for a sixty-seven-year-old (Wiener, Harris, & Hanley, 1990). Computer simulations suggest that purchase of long-term care insurance by the younger population could largely solve the affordability problem of private long-term care insurance, even without employer contributions (Wiener, Illston, & Hanley, 1994).

Although lower premiums are tied to the age of the purchaser and not necessarily to the fact that the policy is employer-sponsored, the non-elderly are easiest to reach through their place of employment. The workplace is where most health, life, and disability insurance is purchased and most retirement savings through pensions are established.

Lower administrative and marketing costs offer another potential source of savings over individual policies. Administrative and marketing costs are high in individual policies because sales have to be made one at a time. Group markets are able to achieve lower costs through economies of scale. Moreover, in group policies, employers bear many of the costs of administering the policy, such as collecting premium payments through payroll deductions. Employers may also elect to assume part of the costs of marketing the plan to their employees. However, informal discussions with insurance actuaries suggest that most assume only a 10 percentage point difference in the anticipated medical loss ratio between individual and group plans.[1] Thus, although the administrative savings of group policies are desirable and not trivial, they will not dramatically lower premiums.

Enrolling people at younger ages through the workplace also reduces the risk of adverse selection and therefore the need for medical underwriting. Disability is relatively rare at younger ages. The less frequent underwriting typical of employer-based policies is an improvement over the universally strict practices used for purchase of individual insurance policies. However, most younger persons with significant disabilities are not in the workforce and would not, therefore, be eligible for these policies.

Finally, advocates of employer-sponsored insurance argue that the quality of policies should improve through the involvement of company benefit managers. Large groups have more market power than individuals to negotiate with insurance carriers for less restrictive policies with richer benefits and lower prices. In general, the quality of policies in the employer market is quite good, especially in providing home care benefits. On the other hand, most employer-sponsored policies have grossly inadequate inflation protection. Under most policies, the insured must purchase

---

1. The loss ratio is the percentage of the premium that is for benefits rather than administrative and other overhead. Many companies assume a loss ratio of 60 percent for individual policies and 70 percent for group policies.

additional coverage from time to time to compensate for inflation, but at the new older age and therefore at a substantially higher premium.[2]

Despite the potential advantages of selling to the nonelderly population through employer groups, the employer-sponsored market for long-term care remains small and may not expand enough to play a significant role in financing long-term care. As of the end of 1994, a total of over 400,000 policies had been sold through 968 employers, although the number of policies in force is lower (Coronel & Caplan, 1996). In a key difference from acute care policies, where most employers pay a large proportion of the cost of insurance, most employer-sponsored long-term care policies are offered on an employee-pay-all basis (Coronel & Caplan, 1996).

Employers are reluctant to offer the policies, and employees are not rushing to purchase them. In particular, employers have been unwilling to contribute to the cost of policies.

Encouraging Employer Contribution through Tax Incentives

Employer sponsorship

Employer contributions could make long-term care insurance more affordable by reducing the amount that employees have to pay out of pocket and might give employees confidence in the product. Until passage of the Kassebaum-Kennedy bill in 1996, private long-term care insurance was not specifically recognized in the federal tax code. Because of its unique characteristics, long-term care insurance did not fit neatly into the existing tax models of health and accident, life, or disability insurance, pensions or private annuities. As a result, the tax status of employer contributions and insurance benefits was unclear, and this lack of clarity no doubt slowed the growth of long-term care insurance, at least to some extent. The Kassebaum-Kennedy bill clarified that contributions toward the cost of group long-term care insurance policies is a tax-deductible expense for employers (like health insurance) and that benefits (within limits) are not considered income for the insured.

2. For example, if a person buys a policy at age forty-two that pays $60 a day in nursing home benefits and if inflation is 33 percent during the next five years, then the insured can buy additional coverage of $20 a day to compensate for the inflation but at the price charged forty-seven-year-olds, not forty-two-year-olds. We estimate that to retain purchasing power, the inflation-adjusted premium at age eighty-two would be approximately ten times what it was at age forty-two. This is because nursing home use is exponential by age.

A persistent problem with tax incentives is the probability that most of the tax expenditures will be for people who would have purchased policies anyway. As a result, tax subsidies can be very costly ways of promoting private insurance. For example, Wiener, Illston, and Hanley (1994) estimate that if the federal government allowed employers to deduct the cost of their contribution to private long-term care insurance, the lost revenue would be $7,900 to $11,300 per year per additional policy sold.

These tax benefits are also not free to the federal government, producing potentially substantial tax losses. Some advocates argue that reductions in government expenditures for Medicaid nursing home and home care will offset the tax loss because some people who will buy private insurance would otherwise be eligible for Medicaid. At least for a long time period, these offsets are unlikely to occur due to an imbalance in timing that guarantees short-term tax losses. The tax loss happens immediately, since the revenue loss is linked to premium payments, while the savings (if any) will not occur until the benefits are used, typically many years into the future. Using a computer simulation model, Wiener, Illston, and Hanley (1994) estimate that it could take twenty-five years before the annual tax loss approximately equals the annual Medicaid savings.

While the uncertain tax status of long-term care insurance has no doubt prevented some employers from offering long-term care insurance policies to their employees, these factors are likely to be overwhelmed by the financial problems facing employer-sponsored acute health insurance benefits for retired employees that supplement the Medicare program. Unlike pensions, virtually all corporations offering postretirement health benefits have financed them on a pay-as-you-go basis rather than prefunding them. Prodded by accounting rules established by the Financial Accounting Standards Board that require companies to disclose their future financial liability for these benefits, corporations are now aware that, collectively, they have an estimated $187 billion to $400 billion in mostly unfunded liabilities (U.S. General Accounting Office, 1989, 1993; Warshawsky, 1992).

As a result, large numbers of employers, concerned about health care costs for both their active employees and retirees, are cutting back on retiree benefits, making retirees pay a greater part of the cost or dropping that coverage altogether. For example, data from Foster Higgins' annual survey of mostly large employers found a drop in retiree health benefits between 1988 and 1992 (Foster Higgins, 1993). In 1988, 55 percent of responding firms offered retiree health benefits to Medicare-eligible retirees; by 1992, only 46 percent of responding firms did so. The percentage of full-time workers in state and local governments with retiree health benefits declined between 1990 and 1992 from 58 percent to 50 percent

(U.S. Department of Labor, 1994, 1991). A recent study of fifty of the largest companies showed that thirty-one reported increases in retiree cost sharing for medical benefits in 1994 (Watson Wyatt Worldwide, 1995). In this environment, it seems unlikely that many additional employers will want to contribute to a new, potentially expensive insurance plan that will primarily benefit retirees twenty years to thirty years after they have left the company. Indeed, employers are trying to distance themselves as much as possible from such benefits.

Limited employee demand

To date, employee demand has been limited and therefore has not played a large role in the decision of companies to add long-term care insurance to their benefit package. The desire to maintain a company's image as a leader in employee benefits and a personal sensitivity by a senior officer or employee benefit manager to the problem have been larger factors. Nonetheless, surveys of large employers suggest the possibility of a large increase in the number of companies offering policies, if not paying for them.

Employees also have been reluctant to purchase insurance. The Health Insurance Association of America estimates that, depending on how the universe of eligibles is defined, only 5.3 percent to 8.8 percent of those offered employer-sponsored long-term care insurance have purchased policies (Coronel, 1993).

Several factors limit employee demand. First, although premiums for policies without inflation adjustment are quite low at younger ages, they cost more than many people are willing to pay voluntarily. Moreover, a high-quality long-term care insurance policy with a level premium, inflation protection, and nonforfeiture benefits purchased at age fifty can cost more than $1,000 a year (Wiener, Harris & Hanley, 1990). In a survey of nonpurchasers of employer-sponsored policies offered by two major insurers, LifePlans, Inc. reported that 82 percent of respondents felt that the fact that "the policy costs too much" was either "very important" or "important" in their decision not to purchase a policy (LifePlans, 1992). Even though economists contend that increased employer contributions for fringe benefits are mostly offset by reduced wages, 90 percent of respondents in this survey said that they would be more willing to purchase a policy if their employer contributed to the cost.

In addition, middle-age workers usually must contend with other, more immediate expenses, such as child care, mortgage payments, and college education for their children. In the LifePlans, Inc. (1992) survey, 80 percent of nonpurchasers stated that "more important things to spend money on at this time" was either "very important" or "important" in their decision not to purchase a policy. The risk of needing long-term care is too distant to galvanize many people into buying insurance.

Finally, selling to the nonelderly population raises difficult considerations of pricing and product design. An actuary pricing a private long-term care insurance product for a forty-five-year-old must predict what is going to happen forty years into the future, when the insured is age eighty-five. To say the least, this is difficult. Ironically, although one of the advantages commonly claimed for private insurance is its flexibility in responding to the needs and wants of consumers, policyholders who buy insurance at younger ages could be locked into the existing model of service delivery decades before they use services. Who knows what the optimal delivery system will be a half century from now?

Encouraging Individual Purchase of Private Insurance through Tax Incentives

Another set of options would improve the affordability of private long-term care insurance by offering direct tax incentives to individuals who purchase policies. For example, the Kassebaum-Kennedy legislation allows individuals to count private long-term care insurance premiums as a health expense.[3] Health care expenses in excess of 7.5 percent of adjusted gross income are tax-deductible. As a result of the ability to deduct part of the cost of private long-term care insurance, the net price of insurance policies will be reduced. Some insurance advocates argue that providing a tax benefit will have a "sentinel" effect, promoting insurance beyond merely reducing the price. A tax incentive, they contend, will signal potential purchasers that the government thinks private long-term care insurance is a worthwhile product.

The type of tax chosen to provide the tax subsidy defines the scope of who can benefit. Allowing taxpayers to deduct all or part of the cost of a private long-term care insurance policy would provide a premium subsidy valued at the marginal tax rate of the household. Since upper-income taxpayers have higher marginal tax rates than lower-income taxpayers, deductions are regressive in nature. That is, they are worth more

---

3. The level of private long-term care insurance that can be included varies by age. For 1997, it was limited to $200 for persons age forty and younger; for persons age seventy and older, it was limited to $2,500.

to upper-income people than to lower-income people. However, for the 72 percent of taxpayers in the 15 percent tax bracket in 1993, this type of tax subsidy reduces the cost of obtaining long-term care insurance by only about one-seventh, probably not enough to motivate very many additional people to purchase policies (Cruciano & Strudler, 1996). The other major drawback is that relatively few taxpayers itemize their deductions. In 1993, only 29 percent of all tax returns included itemized deductions; only 4 percent claimed a deduction for medical expenses (Internal Revenue Service, 1996).

The other broad approach is to provide a tax credit, which is a direct reduction in the amount of tax owed, for purchase of policies. In theory, tax credits need not be as regressive as deductions. However, as a practical matter, moderate- and low-income taxpayers may not have the cash on hand to pay premiums during the year so as to be able to claim a tax credit in the following year. The other problem is that, unless the credit is refundable, it is an ineffective policy for people who do not have a tax liability. This is especially a problem for the elderly, only about half of whom have any federal income tax liability (Committee on Ways and Means, 1996).

As with tax subsidies for employer contributions to private long-term care insurance, the key issue is whether tax incentives are an effective and efficient way to promote the purchase of private long-term care insurance, and thereby, the reform of nursing home and home care financing. For example, estimating the effect of an income-related tax credit for the purchase of private long-term care insurance, Wiener, Illston, and Hanley (1994) calculated the cost per additional policy induced by the tax benefit at between $1,700 and $1,900 per year. Similarly, they estimate that the tax loss per year through 2018 will be at least four times the Medicaid savings.

Public-Private Partnerships

While changing the tax code is the most commonly proposed way of publicly subsidizing private long-term care insurance, the initiatives by Connecticut, Indiana, California, Iowa, and New York take a substantially different approach. Commonly referred to as the Robert Wood Johnson Public-Private Partnerships (for the foundation that promoted this strategy), these states provide easier access to Medicaid for persons who purchase a state-approved private long-term care insurance policy. (See Chapter 5 in this volume for a more detailed description and an alternative perspective.) In essence, these states allow nursing home patients with private long-term care insurance to be Medicaid-eligible with substantially higher levels of assets than is normally allowed.[4] At present, Medicaid only allows unmarried nursing home patients to retain $2,000 in assets (excluding the home). While employer-paid plans and tax incentives seek to reduce the net cost of insurance, this public-private partnership does the reverse by trying to increase the amount of benefits received per dollar spent.

There are two models for linking Medicaid and private insurance.[5] In both cases, Medicaid acts as reinsurance for persons with limited private long-term care insurance. In one model used by Connecticut, California, Indiana, and Iowa, the level of Medicaid-protected assets is tied to the amount that the private insurance policy pays out. For example, if a person buys a policy that pays $100,000 in long-term care benefits, then that individual can keep $100,000 in assets and still be eligible for Medicaid. Consumers are able to purchase insurance equivalent to the amount of assets they wish to preserve, potentially reducing the amount of insurance individuals need to buy.

The other model, used by New York, provides protection of an unlimited amount of assets if an individual purchases a policy that meets state standards, including coverage of at least three years of a combination of nursing home and home care, with a minimum $100 per day indemnity payment. The rationale for not requiring an asset test for Medicaid coverage is that nursing home costs are so high in New York that few individuals can avoid Medicaid over an extended period of time.[6] Thus, New York is targeting a higher-income population with potentially more assets than are the other states.

The key observation supporting the public-private approaches is that long-term care insurance that covers shorter periods of nursing home and

4. Medicaid law allows states great flexibility in determining countable income and assets of medically needy patients—patients with high medical bills in relation to their income. In essence, states using this strategy exclude insurance-related assets from their definition of resources that must be counted in determining Medicaid eligibility. However, the Omnibus Budget Reconciliation Act of 1993 (OBRA 93) severely restricts the ability of additional states to pursue this option by including the insurance-related protected assets in an individual's estate. OBRA 93 requires states to attempt to recover the cost of institutional care from the estates of Medicaid patients. Thus, patients may not be able to pass on these additional funds to their heirs, substantially lessening the appeal of this approach.

5. In both models, nursing home patients must still contribute all of their income toward the cost of care except for a small (usually $30 per month) personal needs allowance.

6. In 1993, the average Medicaid rate was $185 per day, compared with $88 for the United States as a whole (American Health Care Association, 1996).

home care is cheaper and more affordable than policies that cover longer periods of care.[7] The problem with the current system is that if an individual buys a policy that covers, for example, two years of nursing home care and ends up staying in a nursing home five years, then the insured's assets can still be lost. Thus, under these Medicaid initiatives, it is possible to obtain lifetime asset protection without having to buy an insurance policy that pays lifetime benefits. Proponents of this approach contend that the goal is not asset protection per se, but preservation of financial autonomy toward the end of life.

Supporters assert that by encouraging purchase of insurance, Medicaid long-term care expenditures will possibly be reduced or, at least, will not increase. This argument is probably stronger for the approach used by Connecticut, Indiana, Iowa, and California, where there is a dollar-for-dollar correspondence between the amount the insurance pays and the level of Medicaid-protected assets. In New York, the ability to protect potentially large amounts of assets makes this argument weaker, although still possible. To the extent that these systems are budget-neutral, these strategies will be a move toward what economists call Pareto optimality, that is, making some people better off without making anybody worse off. Insurance dollars are simply substituted for private asset dollars.

There are two other potential advantages to this approach. First, since only "approved" policies are eligible for the enhanced asset protection, state regulators can use the initiative as a carrot to induce insurance companies to upgrade the quality of their policies.[8] Second, by giving the elderly the alternative of protecting their assets by purchasing insurance, legal and illegal transfers of assets for the purpose of obtaining Medicaid eligibility may be reduced.

Despite these arguments, there are several concerns about the equity and efficiency of this option. The first concern is whether it is appropriate to use a means-tested welfare program—Medicaid—as a mechanism

7. For an individual who is age sixty-seven, a prototype individual private insurance policy costs $2,337 a year for a policy that covers four years of nursing home and home care, but $1,617 a year for a policy that covers only two years of nursing home and home care (Wiener, Harris, & Hanley, 1990).

8. For example, Connecticut mandates compound inflation adjustment of indemnity benefits. In addition, the state is requiring a type of nonforfeiture benefit that mandates companies to offer a policy with less extensive coverage to individuals who discontinue their premium payments and let their policy lapse. Connecticut has also mandated training for insurance agents selling certified policies and is requiring the distribution of a consumer booklet that compares insurance policies.

to protect the assets of upper-middle and upper-income elderly. Indeed, under this approach, it remains an open question how far down the income distribution insurance purchase will go. Computer simulations by Wiener, Illston, and Hanley (1994) suggest that the vast bulk of private insurance expenditures will be for the relatively well-to-do elderly.

The second concern is whether providing improved asset protection will actually induce substantial numbers of people to purchase long-term care insurance who would not otherwise have bought it. As of December 1995, participation in partnership plans had been disappointing, with only 11,399 policies in force, over half of which were in New York State (Laguna Research Associates, Inc., 1996). While it is difficult to precisely measure people's motivations for buying insurance, one study of purchasers found that only 23 percent of respondents listed protection of assets as the "most important" reason for buying insurance (LifePlans, 1995). Asset protection may have a narrow appeal because most elderly have relatively modest levels of financial wealth (Radner, 1993).

Politically, by emphasizing asset protection, advocates of this strategy lean heavily on a weak reed for public support for long-term care reform. If long-term care reform is primarily about ensuring the intergenerational transfer of wealth, then many people may ask what the public interest in such an initiative is.

Even more fundamentally, many elderly do not want easier access to Medicaid. Indeed, one of the major reasons people buy long-term care insurance is to avoid having to apply for welfare. One survey of insurance purchasers found that 91 percent of respondents reported that avoiding Medicaid was an "important" or "very important" reason for buying a policy (LifePlans, 1995). Medicaid's relatively low reimbursement rates have led to inadequate access and quality of care problems in nursing homes heavily dependent on Medicaid (Nyman, 1988; Institute of Medicine, 1986; Scanlon, 1980). In addition, upper-middle and upper-income elderly will probably find the $30 a month personal needs allowance of the Medicaid program to be inadequate. Therefore, they would use up at least some of their newly protected assets for daily living expenses. Avoiding Medicaid is also the principal argument that insurance agents use to market policies; the partnership plans require a radical revision in an agent's sales pitch. In sum, it is not clear that easier access to Medicaid will be enough of an inducement to get large numbers of additional elderly to purchase private long-term care insurance.

The third concern is whether the public-private partnership will be truly budget-neutral. After all, Medicaid benefits are being offered to people who would otherwise not be eligible. Because most policies probably will be sold to healthy young elderly who are at least ten years to twenty years away from needing nursing home care, even fragmentary evidence as to the effect of the partnership on the public purse will not be available for a decade or two. If additional public expenditures should prove to be required, then one may well ask whether providing asset protection to relatively well-to-do elderly is the best place to put the next long-term care dollar.

It is also important to realize that an indispensable component for assessing the effect on the Medicaid budget is establishing a comparison level of expenditures. In a world with no private long-term care insurance at all, it is likely, although not certain, that the partnership would be budget-neutral. However, there is likely to be continuing modest growth in the number of private long-term care insurance policies sold. Compared to this scenario, if the partnership does not induce substantial numbers of additional insurance purchasers, then the partnership will require larger Medicaid expenditures than would otherwise be needed. This is because under current Medicaid rules purchasers of insurance who would have bought policies without the public-private partnership would have to spend down their assets after their insurance benefits have been exhausted before qualifying for Medicaid—something that they are not required to do under the partnership.

In addition, while supporters argue that the partnership offers persons a more appealing alternative to transferring assets as a way to avoid Medicaid's claim on these resources, it is conceivable that it will actually *increase* the level of premature asset transfer. Current rules prohibit the transfer of assets to other persons at less than fair market value for thirty-six months prior to application for Medicaid eligibility (Burwell & Crown, 1996). Once the partnership has encouraged the elderly to look to Medicaid as a way to protect their assets, some insurance purchasers may only buy the thirty-six months' worth of coverage required to comply with Medicaid rules and then legally transfer the remainder of their financial wealth upon entry into a nursing home. Others may calculate that they can transfer or shelter their assets and obtain Medicaid benefits without purchasing any long-term care insurance policy.

Conclusions

Limitations in the affordability of private long-term care insurance for the elderly and the lack of employer contributions in the group market have led to a range of proposals to provide public subsidies as a way to expand the market. This essay examined three broad options to jump start the private long-term care insurance market.

One strategy is to clarify the tax code in ways that encourage employers to contribute to the cost of private long-term care insurance for their employees. This strategy is contained in the Kassebaum-Kennedy law. However, even with tax incentives, most large corporations face a large unfunded liability for retiree acute care benefits and are unlikely to want to contribute to yet another benefit for retirees.

Another option would improve the affordability of private long-term care insurance by offering tax deductions or credits to individuals who purchase policies. Again, this strategy is contained in the Kassebaum-Kennedy law. This approach is likely to be highly inefficient, with most of the benefits going to persons who would have bought the policies without the subsidy. Moreover, at most levels of subsidy, this strategy is not likely to be able to reduce the price enough to significantly improve affordability for the elderly.

A final option would provide easier access to Medicaid for people who purchased approved private long-term care insurance policies. People who do so would be able to retain a higher level of assets than is normally permitted and still be Medicaid-eligible. This approach can provide a lifetime level of asset protection without requiring people to buy expensive policies with unlimited coverage. It is not clear, however, whether many people want easier access to Medicaid, which is, after all a welfare program, even if it allows greater asset protection. Moreover, the strong emphasis in this strategy on asset protection makes the appropriateness of government efforts to protect inheritances open to question.

In sum, common sense dictates that private insurance is more likely to be affordable with these types of public subsidies than without them. But such approaches are likely to be only modestly effective in improving the affordability of private long-term care insurance compared to the unsubsidized options; most people are unlikely to ever have private long-term care insurance. Two approaches described here (employer tax subsidies and tax deductions or credits for individual purchasers) will result in significant tax losses to the federal government, and the third (waiver of Medicaid asset depletion requirements for purchasers of qualified policies) might increase Medicaid spending. Thus, policymakers must decide whether they wish to put additional spending into direct funding of services or whether they want to put it into promoting private insurance.

References

American Health Care Association. (1996). *Facts and trends: The nursing facility sourcebook, 1996.* Washington, DC: American Health Care Association.

Burwell, B., & Crown, W. (1996). Medicaid eligibility policy and asset transfers: Does any of this make sense? *Generations, 20,* 78–83.

Cohen, M. A., Kumar, N., McGuire, T., & Wallack, S. S. (1992). Financing long-term care: A practical mix of public and private. *Journal of Health Politics, Policy and Law, 17,* 403–423.

Cohen, M. A., Tell, E. J., Greenberg, J. N., & Wallack, S. S. (1987). The financial capacity of the elderly to insure for long-term care. *Gerontologist, 27,* 494–502.

Committee on Ways and Means. (1996). *Overview of entitlement programs: Background material and data on programs within the jurisdiction of the Committee on Ways and Means, 1996.* U.S. House of Representatives. Washington, DC: U.S. Government Printing Office.

Coronel, S. (1993). *Long-term care insurance in 1991.* Washington, DC: Health Insurance Association of America.

Coronel, S., & Caplan, C. (1996). *Long-term care insurance in 1994.* Washington, DC: Health Insurance Association of America.

Coronel, S., & Fulton, D. (1995). *Long-term care insurance in 1993.* Washington, DC: Health Insurance Association of America.

Crown, W. H., Capitman, J., & Leutz, W. N. (1992). Economic rationality, the affordability of private long-term care insurance, and the role of public policy. *Gerontologist, 32,* 478–485.

Cruciano, T. M., & Strudler, M. (1996). Individual tax returns and tax shares, 1993. *SOI Bulletin, 16,* 7–35.

Employee Benefits Research Institute. (1989). Issues and trends in retiree health insurance benefits. *EBRI Issue Brief* (No. 89).

Foster Higgins, Inc. (1993). *Health Care Benefits Survey, 1992, Report 2: Retiree health care.* New York: Foster Higgins.

Institute of Medicine. (1986). *Improving the quality of care in nursing homes.* Washington, DC: National Academy Press.

Internal Revenue Service. (1996). Selected historical and other data. *SOI Bulletin, 16,* 126–128.

Laguna Research Associates. (1996). *Partnership for long-term care: National evaluation summary statistics as of December 31, 1995.* San Francisco, CA: Laguna Research Associates.

Lewin-VHI, Inc., & The Brookings Institution. (1996). *Key issues for long-term care insurance: Ensuring quality products, increasing access to coverage, and enabling consumer choice.* Fairfax, VA: Lewin-VHI.

LifePlans, Inc. (1992). *Who buys long-term care insurance.* Washington, DC: Health Insurance Association of America.

LifePlans, Inc. (1995). *Who buys long-term care insurance: 1994–95 Profiles and inno-*

vations in a dynamic market. Washington, DC: Health Insurance Association of America.

Nyman, J. A. (1988). The effects of competition on nursing home expenditures under prospective payment. *Health Services Research, 23,* 555–574.

Radner, D. B. (1993). An assessment of the economic status of the aged. *Studies in Income Distribution* (No. 16). Washington, DC: Social Security Administration.

Rivlin, A., & Wiener, J. M. (1988). *Caring for the disabled elderly: Who will pay?* Washington, DC: The Brookings Institution.

Scanlon, W. J. (1980). A theory of the nursing home market. *Inquiry, 17,* 25–41.

U.S. Department of Labor. (1994, 1991). *Employee benefits in state and local governments, 1990 and 1992.* Washington, DC: U.S. Government Printing Office.

U.S. General Accounting Office. (1989). *Employee benefits: Companies' retiree health liabilities large, advance funding costly* (GAO/HRD-89-52). Washington, DC: U.S. General Accounting Office.

U.S. General Accounting Office. (1993). *Retiree health plans: Health benefits not secure under employer-based system* (GAO/HRD-93-125). Washington, DC: U.S. General Accounting Office.

Warshawsky, M. J. (1992). *The uncertain promise of retiree health benefits: An evaluation of corporate obligations.* Washington, DC: AEI Press.

Watson Wyatt Worldwide. (1995). *Top 50: A survey of retiree benefits provided by plans covering salaried employees of 50 large U.S. companies as of January 1, 1995.* New York: Watson Wyatt Worldwide.

Wiener, J. M., Harris, K. M., & Hanley, R. J. (1990). *Premium pricing of prototype private long-term care insurance policies.* Washington, DC: The Brookings Institution.

Wiener, J. M., Illston, L. H., & Hanley, R. J. (1994). *Sharing the burden: Strategies for public and private long-term care insurance.* Washington, DC: The Brookings Institution.

CHAPTER 7

Empowering the Community

Public Initiatives in Consumer-directed Services

KEVIN J. MAHONEY,
LORI SIMON-RUSINOWITZ,
MARK R. MEINERS,
HUNTER L. MCKAY,
KATHLEEN C. J. TREAT

Acknowledging the growing interest in care models that provide consumer involvement in organizing services, this chapter describes policy responses designed to support such approaches. The conceptualization, implementation, and evaluation of two public programs are presented. The central role of informal care in delivering long-term care is discussed.

There have been numerous public policy initiatives to support informal caregiving, including family leave, tax incentives for family caregiving and the purchase of long-term care insurance, respite care benefits, and even family responsibility laws. This chapter focuses on two recent initiatives that use public funds to cultivate informal resources or, at least, integrate informal care with formal care. The first, the cash and counseling program, is attempting to make Medicaid more supportive of informal care and in keeping with individual preferences; the second, service credit banking, augments the availability of informal care by employing a more formal structure to support access to and utilization of informal services. This chapter describes these efforts, discusses how they blend public and private resources, and, finally, reflects on how the changing, malleable boundaries between formal and informal care affect the development of a rational overall approach for financing and delivering community care for persons with disabilities who require long-term care.

Background

Nowhere is the division of public and private responsibility for providing and financing long-term care so uncertain and variable as in the case of community-based care. Certainly, in the United States, private responsibilities are dominant. More than two-thirds of persons over age sixty-five who require assistance with any activity of daily living (ADL) or instrumental activity of daily living (IADL) receive only informal care, that is, unpaid care provided privately by family, friends, and neighbors (Jackson, 1992). Twenty-four percent receive formal (paid) as well as informal help, and a meager 9 percent of the disabled elderly receive care from formal sources alone (Jackson, 1992). Even in the case of formal care, a sizable portion is financed through a variety of private sources, ranging from out-of-pocket to private long-term care insurance.

This is not to say that the public role is unimportant. The major public programs, Medicaid and Medicare, are dominant players in both home care and home health care, accounting for between three-fifths and three-quarters of total expenditures for formal home care (National Association for Home Care, 1992, 1994). Other major public sources of funding include the Social Services block grant, the Older Americans Act, the Veterans Administration, and various state general revenue programs, as described in Chapter 1. Home care now represents about 6.5 percent of total Medicaid spending. All states cover home health services in their Medicaid programs. In addition, twenty-eight states and the District of Columbia have opted to cover personal care services, which are less medical in nature but must be furnished under a physician's supervision. In 1993, Medicaid expenditures for home- and community-based services totaled $6.7 billion, representing 15.3 percent of its long-term care outlays. Furthermore, the role of the public sector is growing. All states now have one or more home- and community-based care waivers, under which spending totaled $2.8 billion in 1993 (Mental Health Policy Forum, 1996). Exponential and rapid increases in Medicare expenditures for home health care have generated a debate over whether the Medicare home health benefit is becoming a long-term care benefit. From 1988 to 1994, aggregate payments for home health care under Part A increased by 550 percent and average payments per person rose 229 percent (Mental Health Policy Forum, 1996).

The recent growth in public-sector payments for home care is fueled by several factors: loosening of federal regulations, demographic trends, and quicker, sicker discharges from hospitals. These factors will result in steady pressure to increase formal care as the ranks of the elderly grow and as more and more women enter the paid workforce. The trend already seems clear. Between the 1982 and the 1989 National Long-Term Care Surveys (Jackson, 1992), there was some reduction in the percentage of elderly receiving informal help only and a modest increase in the use of formal services. Even in this relatively brief seven-year period, caregivers appear to be slightly older, in slightly better health, with better financial status, more apt to be female, more apt to be working, and more likely to be caring for more severely disabled elders. Aging baby boomers may stretch the public long-term care system to the limit. Some even question the ability of the public sector to continue its current key role in financing long-term care.

These demographic changes, pressures on the public program, and growing dissatisfaction with the current delivery system have led to the development of several innovative alternative programs. Two such innovations are the cash and counseling program and the service credit program.

Cash and Counseling Program

Program description

As the costs of various types of publicly funded long-term care have continued to rise, policymakers and others have sought new ways to control costs while maintaining or increasing customer satisfaction. Concurrently, there is increasing interest among the aging and disability communities in models of consumer-directed health care (Kapp, 1996; Simon-Rusinowitz & Hofland, 1993; Ansello & Eustis, 1992; Mahoney, Estes, & Heumann, 1986). Among them is "cash and counseling," where Medicaid home care recipients can choose between traditional care manager-prescribed, agency-delivered care or its cash equivalent. If the consumer chooses the latter, cash allowances (coupled with a range of information services) are paid directly to persons with disabilities—enabling them to purchase the services, assistive devices, or home modifications they believe would best meet their needs. If the consumer desires, these funds can even be used to pay friends and relatives to provide needed care. Cash allowances exemplify a model of consumer-directed care that emanated from the disability rights and independent living movements (DeJong, Batavia, & McKnew, 1992). Consumer direction emphasizes maximum choice and autonomy for persons with disabilities who need long-term care. As defined in the Health Security Act of 1994, consumer-directed personal assistance services means that, to the extent possible, an individual with disabilities (and the individual's family) selects the services needed and the person who provides them. The person receiving services also manages and trains the provider (H.R. 3600, 1994).

In principle, cash allowances maximize consumer choice and promote efficiency since consumers who shop for the most cost-effective providers may be able to purchase more services (Kapp, 1996). For example, imagine that a formal provider from a home health agency can deliver services for no less than three hours per visit, yet the individual only needs an hour or two at a time. With a direct cash payment and counseling about options, that individual may develop a flexible care arrangement through a combination of other supports, such as formal services to complement care from a daughter and a neighbor.

Experience in state home care programs where consumers are allowed to select independent providers suggests that many will choose family and friends. In California's In-Home Supportive Services Program, 91 percent of the providers are nonagency and 55 percent are friends living at the same address or family members; in Michigan's Home Help Program, 95 percent to 98 percent of the providers are nonagency and approximately 45 percent are family members and friends (Schwalberg & Wiker, 1995). However, it is unclear whether contracting with family or friends would necessarily prove to be the most common approach. Contrary to the California and Michigan experiences, preliminary findings from focus group research (conducted as part of the cash and counseling demonstration and evaluation in New York and Florida) indicate general resistance among consumers and surrogate decision-makers to the idea of hiring family members as home care providers.

In the winter of 1996–97, four states (Arkansas, Florida, New Jersey, and New York) received grants of up to $500,000 from the Robert Wood Johnson Foundation for the implementation of cash and counseling programs for the delivery of personal assistance services (PAS). This initiative seeks to provide more autonomy to consumers of long-term care services while controlling health care costs. This is accomplished through empowering persons with disabilities to purchase the assistance they require and desire in performing their activities of daily living. The evaluation of this program is being co-sponsored with the U.S. Department of Health and Human Services, Office of the Assistant Secretary for Planning and Evaluation (DHHS/ASPE).

Program design

The major program design, experimental characteristics, and evaluation characteristics of these cash and counseling programs are summarized below.

1. There are highly variable definitions of eligible populations among the programs. States include both elderly and younger adults with disabilities in the demonstration. Florida also covers developmentally disabled children. Both new and current clients participate.

2. The demonstrations must run for a minimum time frame (at least twenty-four months) to allow for adequate participant enrollment and experience.

3. Maximum flexibility as to the use of cash payments is encouraged. Restrictions on disabled beneficiaries' use of cash benefits are the minimum possible, consistent with law and regulations governing the federal Health Care Financing Administration's (HCFA) authority to grant Medicaid 1115 research and demonstration waivers, as well as requirements for other means-tested programs such as Social Security supplemental income (SSI) and food stamps.

4. Integration with existing programs is permissible. For example, Arkansas, New Jersey, and New York are offering a cash alternative to their Medicaid personal care option. Florida and New Jersey are cashing out some portion of their (more broad-based) Medicaid home- and community-based care waivers; Florida is also folding certain state-funded home care programs into the demonstration.

5. The amount of the cash payment was not set prior to the selection of these states. The formula for establishing the amount of the cash payment, the period the payment must cover (e.g., a month), and the frequency for reviewing the adequacy of this payment will be established in conjunction with the chosen states prior to program implementation in the spring of 1998. As a general rule, these states are planning to follow current assessment and care planning practices, establish the value of the individualized care plan, and then offer the consumer a cash allowance in line with what he or she would have received under the traditional program.

6. States are developing impartial approaches for informing potential participants of their opportunity to take part in this demonstration. This is especially important in Arkansas, New Jersey, and certain programs in Florida, where home care providers serve as the gatekeepers for traditional services.

7. The availability of counseling services is integral to a consumer-directed approach and to this demonstration. At a minimum, counseling involves helping consumers decide whether to choose the cash option and how they might best spend the money available to them. Consumers should decide whether to have total control over the "who, what, where, when, and how" of PAS or to consult with, collaborate with, or delegate certain aspects of decision-making and ongoing management to someone else.

8. In addition to these basic services, the states will offer a range of optional supportive services. Such services include, but are not limited to, developing a list of available workers; screening workers; training the consumer and worker; backup or emergency services; assistance with tax forms and insurance paperwork; and monitoring functions as desired by the consumer. A variety of agencies may be available to provide counseling, including Area Agencies on Aging; Centers for Independent Living; consumer organizations serving older people or persons with disabilities; and case management organizations committed to consumer-directed services. Minimum criteria regarding counseling services are being established by the demonstration states.

Program evaluation

The evaluation has two major components: a classical experimental design using randomized treatment and control groups, and a process evaluation to study program implementation. Evaluation of the demonstrations is a central component. States agree to support a rigorous experimental design with randomized control and treatment groups for those who are willing to receive cash. Consumers in the experimental group (or their surrogate decision-makers) receive cash payments in lieu of traditional agency-delivered services. Demonstration participants who receive PAS benefits in the form of the experimental intervention (i.e., cash) are, in general, precluded from receiving any additional personal assistance services via Medicaid. The experimental demonstration programs may (but need not) be implemented statewide; however, participating states are required to provide sufficient program participants to meet minimum sample size requirements.

The demonstration and associated evaluation will address research questions pertaining to differential outcomes with respect to cost, quality, and client satisfaction between traditional PAS services and alternative choice modalities. The research will not include an evaluation of the effectiveness of various counseling services per se. The evaluator will examine a broad range of questions, however. The preeminent research questions are: (1) Do treatment group members use significantly different types and amounts of services than control group members receiving traditional PAS? (2) Are the programmatic and administrative costs for treatment group members significantly different than the programmatic and administrative costs for control group members receiving traditional PAS? (3) Do treatment group members experience a different level of consumer satisfaction and quality of care (including adverse health and functional outcomes) than control group members receiving traditional PAS? (4) What counseling services are offered to clients receiving cash payments? Which clients take advantage of additional supports offered, such as counseling, provider training, and provider payrolling? What is the client's assessment of the value of the counseling services?

In addition to a careful study of client characteristics and behaviors, the impact of the demonstration on formal and informal caregivers will be examined. This series of research questions includes: (1) What is the impact of the cash payment option on informal caregivers? Do the number of hours or types of care they provide change? Are paid hours substituted for unpaid hours? Is there any effect on burnout or stress? (2) What is the impact of the cash payment option on formal caregivers? Are there payment problems? Are workers paid a fair wage? Do formal agency providers lose market share? (3) Did the experimental intervention affect the supply of formal service providers and the cost of services?

There is no doubt that the interplay of family norms and values with employment and entitlement rules and requirements will present challenges to cash and counseling participants and sponsors alike. Some consumers will probably prefer to utilize family and friends to assist with tasks as personal as those involving basic ADLs. Some will view the opportunity to pay family members as a way to provide some recompense (i.e., to even out the exchange) for all the assistance the family is providing. Others will not find the ability to hire family and friends an attraction, as they prefer to keep the various parts of their lives separate and would rather not impinge on family to provide care. An example of this difference in norms and values came to light during focus groups that took place in New York prior to the implementation of the cash and counseling demonstration. One young quadriplegic, when asked if he would like to hire a family member as his personal care assistant, said, "No," and then described a past experience where his brother came to help him dress each morning. The brother, as the story goes, came when he got around to it. The young person with disabilities found it hard to schedule medical appointments and impossible to hold employment. The personal care recipient/consumer drew the conclusion, "My brother felt he was doing me a favor; I viewed it as a job."

Observations to date

While the evaluation will assist policymakers in understanding when and how often consumers with disabilities choose to pay family and friends to provide care, there are a number of insights that can be offered at this juncture in the program's evolution. First, the ability to hire family is an important departure from traditional public policy, representing a major breakthrough for Medicaid. In general, family members have been discriminated against in terms of hiring home care workers for relatives on public programs. Recent examples of such traditional approaches abound; a particularly striking one can be found in Kansas. Regulations adopted in that state in November 1996 prohibit payment to family members for home- and community-based services (HCBS) except in situations where: (1) the consumer's residence is documented in writing by three HCBS provider agencies to be so remote or rural that HCBS are otherwise completely unavailable; (2) the consumer's health, safety, or well-being would be jeopardized and is so documented in writing by two health care professionals, including the attending physician; (3) due to advancement of chronic disease, the consumer's means of communication can only be understood by the spouse or parent of a minor child and is so documented in writing by the attending physician; or (4) there is written documentation from three HCBS providers that delivery of HCBS services to the consumer poses serious health or safety issues for the provider, thereby rendering HCBS otherwise unavailable.

Second, the fear that allowing payment to family members will lessen the amount of informal caregiving is an assumption to be challenged and empirically tested. Recent research shows that hiring family and neighbors to fill personal care assistant positions can have beneficial effects. In their evaluation of California's In-Home Supportive Services Program, Barnes and Sutherland (1995) found that providers unfamiliar to the consumer were paid substantially more than relative providers in all three contract counties. This result is positive as long as family members were not taken advantage of. The provider-client relationship was found to be the dominant variable influencing consumer evaluations of provider reliability. Barnes and Sutherland note that family members and friends are more reliable than strangers, regardless of client functional level, context of care needs, or provider characteristics. Finally, although clients rate the reliability and work quality of their relatives and friends higher than that of strangers, the survey staff found the level of personal care and household maintenance lower for friends than strangers.

Third, there is an uneasiness—even among state policymakers—in stipulating that indigent consumers who use public dollars to hire family members as personal care assistants should shoulder all the responsibilities of being an employer. Similarly, there is some uneasiness when such payments (wages) disqualify the family member who receives the pay from receiving other public entitlements. The best example of this ambivalence was found when the state of Florida attempted to introduce the cash and counseling approach into its Developmental Services for Children and Young Adults With Developmental Disabilities Program. In the end, the state somewhat reluctantly decided that payments to family members for services provided to the consumer would have to be considered income even if that lessened the incentive to choose the cash and counseling option.

Service Credit Banking

Program description

Another innovative program is service credit banking. The concept of service credits is not new; it integrates elements of traditional volunteerism, barter, and co-op exchanges. Service credit volunteers earn a credit for every hour of service they provide. People receiving services pay for them with credits they have earned or that have been donated to them by the program or other volunteers. Volunteers can thus help themselves by helping others.

In recent years, many new programs have been implemented. The oldest known program still in operation is Work Exchange in Milwaukee, Wisconsin, which has been awarding a form of service credits to volunteers since 1974. In the mid-1980s, Edgar Cahn, a law professor, refined and began to actively promote the concept of "time dollars," a term he coined for service credits. He has written extensively on the subject and continues to work on creating a national network of service credit programs. The Robert Wood Johnson Foundation provided grant funding in 1987 for six sites to implement service credit programs. The programs focused on expanding the array of home-based services available in the community by using elderly neighbors as an untapped resource. Elderly volunteers were recruited and trained to help other elders remain in their homes for as long as possible. The University of Maryland Center on Aging acted as the office for technical assistance and direction. The six sites (Boston, New York City, Washington, D.C., Miami, St. Louis, and San Francisco) had several accomplishments during the three-year grant period. The total number of participants increased from 1,167 after one year of operation to 4,391 at the end of the third year. The number of hours of service grew from approximately 37,000 hours in the first year to more than 143,000 after three years. Today there are roughly seventy-five service credit programs operating in thirty states and the District of Columbia.

The services offered by service credit programs are related to the needs in a particular community. Helping people get to church may be a defined need in one community, while translation services may be required somewhere else. The community in which the volunteers are situated determines which services are important and therefore provided as part of the program. Service credit programs thus mold the focus of volunteering. Traditionally, volunteering was associated with an institution such as a hospital. Service credit programs are focused on the services that have been specifically requested by someone in need. This forces a closer tie between the perceived need within a community and the services offered by the program.

Program evaluation

Frequently, when people hear about service credits they assume that people are volunteering solely to earn service credits. In general, this does not seem to have been the case. People report volunteering for the same reasons they have always volunteered—the basic desire to help others and to be of assistance to the community. However, the credits do appear to be a factor in a person's initial decision to volunteer and to continue as a volunteer. Volunteers appreciate their volunteer time being treated as a valuable commodity. Additionally, many programs have found that the credits attract people who do not ordinarily volunteer or who might be volunteering for the first time, especially men. Most programs have also found that retention rates are higher in service credit programs than in more traditional volunteer programs. This may result from a volunteer's sense of truly being invested in the program.

Although service credit programs depend almost entirely on volunteers to provide services, operating funds are still needed for staff to recruit volunteers and recipients, and to manage the program, office space, equipment, and supplies. Some programs around the country have closed because they could not find this funding to maintain or expand their operations. Because service credits imply a promise of future services, a long-term source of operating funds is a necessity. Public sources have played a major part in launching service credit programs around the country, (e.g., federal Administration on Aging, Connecticut, Florida, Michigan, Missouri, New Jersey, North Dakota, Oklahoma, Texas, and South Dakota), but they are less likely to be a source for maintaining operations. The formal professional assistance that states and the federal government provide is not supplanted by service credit models. Rather, such programs complement formal care by encouraging people to provide for their own needs while helping others. Consequently, government resources may be directed toward individuals who have advanced levels of need but no other sources of care.

Policy Considerations

The two models described above illustrate how the boundaries between private and public (and now between informal and formal) are cloudy and becoming cloudier. Still, it is clear that with scarce resources both are needed. That, indeed, is the first point this chapter makes. Informal resources predominate. It would be hard to imagine the cost and value changes that would accompany any attempt to replace informal caregivers with formal caregivers. On the other hand, there are limits on what the informal (and private resources in general) can do.

Some believe the division of labor between informal and formal sectors should be based on which does the better job at the function in question. According to this school of thought, the informal sector may be better adapted to perform the nonuniform aspects of care (for instance, those that are "simple, idiosyncratic, unpredictable, or require contingencies"), leaving to the formal sector those aspects of care that "require expert knowledge and large-scale resources" (Stone et al., 1987, p. 617). Others believe that, at least at present, use of the formal system occurs only after care needs become more than the family and ancillary helpers can handle alone (Soldo & Manton, 1985).

If there is to be a role for both the informal and the formal sectors in long-term care delivery, and the public and private sectors in long-term care financing, effective coordination and integration are imperative. The coordination itself can be left to the informal sector, but it is more and more typical to find instances where the formal program takes on this responsibility. One example occurs in the California Partnership for Long-Term Care (the partnership between private long-term care insurance and Medicaid described in Chapter 6). Here the care management provider agency has the explicit responsibility to authorize the expenditure of the private insurance funds only when there are unmet needs. Also, the care management provider is charged with the duty of developing a transition plan to help the consumer transfer from private insurance to Medicaid after the insurance benefits are exhausted.

There is disagreement over how far the federal government, or government in general, should go to provide home- and community-based care. Based on an analysis of national polling figures, Meiners and McKay (1990) reported that the U.S. public viewed long-term care for the aged and disabled as an important problem, though not the top priority: "Programs focused on helping the most needy were preferred by 60% of the respondents. Thirty-five percent preferred a government program for all, but a quarter of that group were not willing to pay their share of the new taxes that were estimated as necessary to cover the cost" (p. 35). The results of a February 1993 Gallup poll conducted for the American Health Care Association are even more striking. Of those surveyed, 76 percent felt the government should pay for nursing home care only for those who cannot afford it (Mahoney & Meiners, 1994).

In the current economic climate, it is vital that public programs support and even work to increase private resources. However, when public programs work to increase the private role in long-term care, a tension or ambivalence frequently results. The informal and formal sectors operate under different norms and are often guided by different motivations. The entrance of the public sector generally means accountability requirements, record-keeping, and subtle efforts to shape the way services are provided. In addition, public programs are continuously being scrutinized to see if they reduce the amount of care delivered privately. When public dollars are used to provide incentives encouraging certain private behaviors, critics can reasonably ask whether such incentives were needed (or, more precisely, how many people would have taken the desired steps without the added cost of the incentives).

Although the cash and counseling program offers new freedom to hire family or friends and enhances consumer choice, it also adds responsibilities, such as withholding taxes. The moment one pays informal providers, they cease to be informal providers—at least for the period or the tasks for which they receive pay. Furthermore, paying (i.e., employing) a family member could result in that family member becoming ineligible for certain public benefits. This might have negative implications for the attractiveness of the program to potential participants.

In the service credit banking project, a new motivation was introduced for volunteering, but some wondered if it led to additional volunteers or adulterated the altruism that is normally the motivation behind volunteering. Record-keeping became a necessity. Public programs were willing to help get service credit efforts started, but were reluctant to provide ongoing assistance.

The uneasiness that sometimes accompanies public efforts to increase certain private behaviors seems to be heightened when public funds are used to integrate (or blend) the informal system (which by its very nature is private) into the formal. A fascinating example comes from the New Jersey cash and counseling site, where family members could perform certain paramedical tasks, such as suctioning or giving injections, as long as they performed these functions without pay. The moment they were paid, they entered a gray zone where they potentially needed to receive sixty hours of training and become certified "homemakers." From issues of liability to questions concerning the need to protect the public, family members traditionally have been viewed as different. This may require rethinking under new programs such as those described here.

Conclusions

In summary, when the public sector sets out to increase informal (private) caregiving, policymakers should keep the goals of expanding the overall pool of available resources and increasing the quality of care clearly before them.

Whereas the tension over the boundaries between public and private (and formal and informal) can inspire creativity, it makes planning difficult. People are often reluctant to take on responsibilities they are not sure are theirs to bear. Over time, it will be desirable to further clarify exactly what public programs will, and will not, cover. While policymakers have long acknowledged the importance of informal care, little progress has been made in developing delivery and financing systems that utilize the full strength of both public and private sectors. As government budgets rise and fall and as family demographics continue to shift, the coordination of these two critical components of the system may have to be continually reinvented.

References

Ansello, E. F., & Eustis, N. N. (1992). A common stake? Investigating the emerging intersection of aging and disabilities. *Generations, 16,* 5–8.

Barnes, C., & Sutherland, S. (1995). *Context of care, provider characteristics, and quality of care in the IHSS program: Implications for provider standards.* Interim report to the California Department of Social Services, Institute for Social Research, California State University, Sacramento.

DeJong, G., Batavia, A. I., & McKnew, L. (1992). The independent living model of personal assistance in national long-term care policy. *Generations, 16,* 89–95.

H.R. 3600, 103rd Cong., 2d Sess. (1994); S1757, 103rd Cong., 2nd Sess. (1994), Health Security Act (as cited in Kapp, M. [1996]. Enhancing autonomy and choice in selecting and directing long-term care services. *The Elder Law Journal, 4,* 55–97.

Jackson, B. (SysteMetrics). (1992). *Family caregiving: Still going strong?* Prepared for The Changing Face of Informal Caregiving Conference sponsored by the U.S. Department of Health and Human Services, Office of the Assistant Secretary for Planning and Evaluation, Berkeley Springs, WV.

Kapp, M. (1996). Enhancing autonomy and choice in selecting and directing long-term care services. *The Elder Law Journal, 4,* 55–97.

Mahoney, C. W., Estes, C. L., & Heumann, J. E. (Eds.). (1986). *Toward a unified agenda: Proceedings of a National Conference on Disability and Aging.* San Francisco: University of California and World Institute on Disability.

Mahoney, K. J., & Meiners, M. (1994). Private and social insurance—the feasible option. *Western Journal of Medicine, 160,* 74–76.

Meiners, M., & McKay, H. (1990). Private versus social long-term care insurance: Beware the comparison. *Generations, 14,* 32–36.

Mental Health Policy Forum. (1996). Issue Brief No. 694.

National Association for Home Care. (1992, 1994, 1996). As cited in the National Health Policy Forum Issue Brief No. 694: *Medicare coverage for home health care: Reining in a benefit out of control.* George Washington University.

Overview of Service Credit Programs. (1997). Center on Aging, University of Maryland College Park web site.

Schwalberg, R., & Wiker, G. (1995). *A background paper on payment for family caregivers of the elderly and disabled.* Prepared for the American Association of Retired Persons by Health Systems Research, Inc., Washington, DC.

Simon-Rusinowitz, L., & Hofland, B. F. (1993). Adopting a disability approach to home care services for older adults. *Gerontologist, 33*, 159–167.

Soldo, B. J., & Manton, K. J. (1985). Health status and service needs of the oldest old: Current patterns and future trends. *Milbank Memorial Fund Quarterly/Health and Society, 63*, 286–319.

State of Kansas Regulations. Adopted (1996). 30-5-307.

Stone, R., Cafferata, G. L., & Sangl, J. (1987). Caregivers of the frail elderly: A national profile. *Gerontologist, 27*, 616–626.

Welch, H. G., Wennberg, D. E., & Welch, W. P. (1996). The use of Medicare home health care services. *New England Journal of Medicine, 335*, 328.

CHAPTER 8

Access to Public Resources

Regulating Asset Transfers for Long-Term Care

LESLIE C. WALKER
BRIAN BURWELL

This chapter conceives of federal and state legislation related to Medicaid estate planning as a "program" intended to regulate access to public financing for nursing home care. The dynamic between individual behaviors and public policy in this context is used to illustrate the divergent perceptions regarding individual and societal obligations to provide long-term care.

Medicaid estate planning—the practice of transferring or protecting assets to qualify an individual for Medicaid benefits for long-term care—illustrates the complexity of integrating public and private roles in this arena. This chapter explicates and analyzes the existing regulations concerning Medicaid financing of long-term care, with a particular focus on tensions related to Medicaid estate planning. The chapter is organized into four sections. The first provides an overview of Medicaid estate planning, a description of mechanisms employed to qualify for Medicaid coverage for long-term care, and a summary of current information on the magnitude and prevalence of Medicaid estate planning. The second section reviews federal legislation developed in this area since 1980, highlighting its incremental and fragmented nature. The third section covers a broad range of legal, sociodemographic, economic, and administrative factors that influence Medicaid estate planning. The concluding section offers observations about the interplay between public policy and individual behaviors with regard to financing long-term care.

Background

Definition of Medicaid estate planning

Medicaid is a means-tested, state-administered health insurance program that by its nature requires individuals to be impoverished in order to qualify for benefits. Individuals applying for Medicaid coverage for health care services such as nursing home care must be determined to be "poor" in accordance with state-specific program criteria, including income and asset tests. Medicaid estate planning comprises a range of legal and financial mechanisms that facilitate compliance with financial eligibility requirements for Medicaid coverage for long-term care. Such activities shelter or divert an individual's assets with the intention of excluding such assets in the determination of eligibility for Medicaid.

Mechanisms of Medicaid estate planning

The practice of Medicaid estate planning is highly diverse and varies in prevalence across states. One of the most common approaches is the conversion of countable assets to exempt assets. Countable assets are those that the state considers as part of the individual's total available assets when determining eligibility for benefits. Exempt assets are those, such as the individual's primary residence, that are excluded from calculations. In most states, equity in a primary residence is not considered an asset and is never claimed by the Medicaid program to cover an individual's cost of care, even after death. Assets excluded from Medicaid consideration include limited liquid assets, life insurance with defined face value, limited burial funds and space, an automobile (within limits), and a home, if it is the applicant's, spouse's, or certain other family member's principal place of residence. Assets belonging to a spouse or parent may affect eligibility status, as they may be included in computations of resources available to the applicant. For the purpose of determining Medicaid eligibility, assets are generally considered to "belong" to an applicant (or spouse, with jointly held assets) if that individual has the unrestricted right to liquidation or disposal of such assets. Conversion of assets may be accomplished through the expenditure of countable assets on items that are exempt. For example, home improvements, mortgage payoffs, or purchases of personal property may be used to convert the asset from being a countable asset to being an exempt asset.

A second approach to Medicaid estate planning involves the use of spousal impoverishment rules. The Medicare Catastrophic Coverage Act (MCCA) of 1988 (Pub. L. No. 100-360) established Medicaid spousal impoverishment rules that allow the spouse of an individual living in a nursing home who remains in the community (the "community spouse") to retain one half of countable assets, within minimum and maximum allowable amounts. In addition, the community spouse may retain a certain amount of income necessary to live in the community, again subject to minimum and maximum limits. Medicaid programs are required to offer to perform financial assessments at the point of nursing home admission to ensure married couples are aware of spousal protections available under the law. Some observers believe this provision of the MCCA has stimulated married couples to seek legal advice when nursing home placement is imminent, and has therefore increased the level of Medicaid estate planning.

A third general strategy in Medicaid estate planning is the transfer of assets into trusts, annuities, and other protected investments deemed unavailable to the individual in need of care. A Medicaid qualifying trust is a financial tool that allows individuals to retain control of assets and maintain certain income streams while excluding the trust assets from being considered as countable. Specific trust strategies include the creation of irrevocable and nondiscretionary trusts, where the trustee does not have any discretionary authority over income distribution, and the beneficiary cannot access trust principal. Convertible trusts are activated by a "trigger," such as nursing home admission. Such instruments may be fully discretionary and revocable while the individual is in the community, yet convert to nondiscretionary and irrevocable status upon admission to a nursing home. Regardless of a particular trust's stipulations, some attorneys create a fail-safe provision that destroys the trust upon invasion. The fail-safe provision results in the self-destruction of the trust and the transfer of all trust principal to someone other than the beneficiary or the spouse, should the trust fail to be considered as an exempt asset by the Medicaid agency.

A fourth approach in Medicaid estate planning is the transfer of assets to joint accounts and property in joint tenancy (referred to as "commingling of funds"). For example, a father might create a joint account with his daughter as he begins to need assistance in managing his finances, as well as to avoid probate of the account upon his death. Other less commonly used Medicaid estate planning strategies include using loopholes in penalty language, paying family members for providing informal care, purchasing expensive term life insurance policies, and claiming undue hardship (for example, see Bickel, 1994; Schlesinger, Scheiner, & Schneider, 1993; Macy, 1994; McEowen & Harl, 1991).

Prevalence and magnitude of Medicaid estate planning

Despite the vigorous debate and keen interest in understanding Medicaid estate planning and its impact on Medicaid expenditures, few empirical studies have been conducted that quantify the magnitude of this activity. The following summary of research suggests that the evidence is mixed and that major questions remain unanswered. What is Medicaid estate planning actually "costing" the Medicaid program? What are the most cost-effective, prudent, and appropriate public policies to address Medicaid estate planning?

The majority of empirical research on Medicaid estate planning has been supported by the General Accounting Office and Office of the Inspector General. A 1989 study by the Office of Inspector General regarding the transfer of assets in the Washington State Medicaid program attempted to measure how much is transferred prior to application for nursing home admission. Findings indicated that persons denied and subsequently approved for Medicaid over a one-year period in Washington State had $27.5 million in assets at the time of denial, of which 81 percent was expended through some form of transfer and 8 percent was spent on long-term care. A 1988 study conducted by the Office of the Inspector General surveyed all fifty state Medicaid programs regarding policies, transfer of assets practices, liens, and estate recovery. The study found very weak enforcement of asset transfer restrictions; only two states had implemented lien programs. The report estimated that $589 million annually was passed on to heirs of Medicaid recipients instead of being directed to the Medicaid program.

In 1989, the General Accounting Office published a study on estate recovery programs among two hundred randomly selected nursing home cases in Oregon and seven other states. Findings indicated that Oregon collected approximately ten dollars for every dollar spent administering the program from estates. The report estimated $85 million in six states passed on to heirs.

A second General Accounting Office study was published in 1993. A review of 403 Medicaid applications in Massachusetts was conducted to determine whether assets had been converted from countable to exempt or transferred. The study found 54 percent of Medicaid applicants had converted assets (typically into a burial account) and 13 percent transferred assets within thirty months of filing the application, with an average diverted asset amount of approximately $46,000 per person.

A research project consisting of case studies in four purposefully selected states (Massachusetts, California, New York, and Florida) assessed the magnitude and nature of Medicaid estate planning (Burwell & Crown, 1995). Although there was variation across the states, most eligibility workers reported that 5–10 percent of single applicants and 20–25 percent of married applicants intentionally diverted assets prior to applying for Medicaid. A three-phase study was conducted in Connecticut, a state commonly perceived as having a high prevalence of Medicaid estate planning due to sociodemographic characteristics, increased age of residents, access to elder law attorneys, the generosity of the state's Medicaid program, and the high quality of nursing home care (Walker, Gruman, & Robison, 1996). Respondent groups of Medicaid eligibility workers, elder law attorneys, and certified financial planners differed significantly in terms of their perceptions of trends in asset transfers, the nature and value of transfers, and the "typical" client who engages in Medicaid estate planning. Medicaid workers reported that 46 percent of applicants who transfer assets have less than $1,000 per month in income, and that 52 percent transfer less than $50,000 (which pays for less than eight months in a Connecticut nursing home). Estimates of the average value of transferred assets were significantly different among the respondent groups. Financial planners estimated the highest value (51.9 percent reported an average transfer of over $200,000); 47.5 percent of elder law attorneys estimated transfers between $100,000 and $199,999; the Medicaid workers estimated the lowest values (47.1 percent reported transfers of $25,000 to $49,999).

On the whole, empirical evidence regarding Medicaid estate planning prevalence is inconclusive and varies in terms of approaches and findings. The methodologic challenges are substantial, and include measuring intention (was the transfer for the explicit purpose of qualifying for Medicaid?), defining the unit of analysis (what constitutes an asset that could have been considered available?), and controlling for co-founders (state-specific statutes and regulations, the reliance on self-reported financial data). No study has actually quantified the magnitude of activity or determined the cost-effectiveness of Medicaid estate planning enforcement programs. Although observers agree this activity is occurring at some level, there are no compelling data about its scope.

Legislative Responses to Medicaid Estate Planning

A number of highly complex and interrelated federal and state legislative responses to Medicaid estate planning practices have occurred since 1980. Collectively, these policies may be conceptualized as a "program" designed to regulate access to public financing for nursing home care. The following discussion outlines the evolution in federal laws pertaining to estate planning and illustrates the substantial attention devoted to this issue by federal policymakers and state program administrators.

Several major pieces of legislation have been enacted since 1980 related to the consideration of personal assets in the context of Medicaid eligibility. These federal initiatives have been variably implemented by the states, and the degree to which they have influenced behavior of applicants is not well understood. Each law attempted to define which assets are deemed available to pay for care as well as to define penalties and enforcement protocols for improper transfers. While some of the statutes built on prior legislation, others represented responses to unique issues, such as the spousal impoverishment protections described below.

A federal statute enacted in 1980 (Pub. L. No. 96-611) precluded persons who transferred assets within twenty-four months of applying to Medicaid from becoming eligible for Medicaid benefits. With the Tax Equity and Fiscal Responsibility Act (TEFRA) of 1982, Congress expanded provisions by allowing states to deny Medicaid to individuals who transferred excluded assets (such as a personal residence) as well as countable assets. TEFRA authorized states to restrict asset transfers within two years of Medicaid eligibility, place liens on properties of living recipients, and recover assets from properties of deceased persons. The law was intended to ensure that resources (such as home equity) available to individuals living in nursing homes and not needed for the support of a spouse or dependent children would be used to defray the cost of nursing home care. Yet because the law was permissive rather than mandatory for states, implementation of its new authorities was highly inconsistent.

Prior to 1986, individuals were permitted to place assets in trusts that restricted access, therefore making them unavailable for Medicaid purposes. Such trusts became known as Medicaid qualifying trusts (MQTs), a vehicle by which assets could be retained in estates and ultimately passed on to heirs. The Consolidated Omnibus Budget Reconciliation Act of 1986 (Pub. L. No. 99-272) sought to reduce the use of MQTs by redefining access. Pursuant to this statute, funds in a MQT were required to be counted as available in amounts equal to the maximum payments that could be made from the trust if the individual exercised maximum discretion under its terms.

One of the most controversial pieces of legislation relating to aging health policy, the Medicare Catastrophic Coverage Act of 1988, contained provisions regarding asset transfers. MCCA required all states to adopt transfer of asset restrictions, and extended the look-back penalty period from twenty-four months to thirty months. The look-back requires a determination whether an improper asset transfer occurred, followed by denial of eligibility for a federally specified time period. All assets owned by either or both spouses were defined as available to the institutionalized spouse, with a certain minimum amount protected for the community spouse. Before this statute, states could choose to impose penalties within very broad federal parameters; the law refined rules on asset transfer to target institutionalized persons applying for Medicaid. The Omnibus Budget Reconciliation Act of 1989 (OBRA 89) made technical corrections to MCCA by closing loopholes for unlimited transfers by community spouses.

Enacted in 1990, OBRA's Boren-Long amendments denied SSI eligibility to persons who transferred countable assets for less than fair market value. At their option, states could also deny Medicaid to such persons (eligibility could be denied up to twenty-four months, depending on the amount transferred).

The Omnibus Budget Reconciliation Act of 1993 (OBRA 93) included a number of major changes to federal Medicaid statutes impacting asset transfers, trusts, and jointly held assets. In terms of asset transfers, the look-back period was extended from thirty months to thirty-six months, and the previously existing thirty-month cap on penalty periods was eliminated. Much of the law addressed the use of trusts in Medicaid estate planning. Major changes included the establishment of a sixty-month look-back for certain types of trusts, the treatment of trusts created by third parties or courts in the same manner as if they were established by an individual (if the trust funds came from the individual), and the consideration of trust corpus and income as available to the individual unless specifically prohibited by its terms. Finally, transfers of jointly held assets were defined as prohibited transfers. In 1996, the Kassebaum-Kennedy bill became law, criminalizing certain types of asset transfers and sending a clear message from Congress as to a public policy stance regarding Medicaid estate planning.

Although there has been a steady progression of federal policy responses to Medicaid estate planning since 1980, such initiatives have been incremental, inconsistent, and fragmented. In addition to federal legislation, the respective states may have independently created laws or regulations in this arena as well, making the policy picture even more complicated. This web of policy responses is directed at shaping individual behaviors and perceptions regarding the use of Medicaid resources to finance long-term care for individuals with means.

Factors Affecting the Prevalence of Medicaid Estate Planning

A variety of factors may influence an individual's participation in Medicaid planning activities. An improved understanding of these issues is essential to the design of rational and effective policies to address Medicaid estate planning (to the extent it is a problem) through legislation, regulation, and administrative practices. The wide variation in the level and nature of Medicaid estate planning activities across states may be attributed to the legal, socioeconomic, and health service variables described below (Burwell, 1991).

Financial eligibility for Medicaid long-term care coverage

Federal and state Medicaid eligibility policies have a strong influence on Medicaid estate planning. Such policies establish the level of impoverishment that an individual (or married couple) must meet before long-term care costs are shared broadly by all members of society, as opposed to being the sole responsibility of the individual or the individual's family. In brief, policies operationalize the concept of need, attempting to define public and private responsibilities for long-term care.

One important aspect of Medicaid eligibility policy that influences Medicaid planning behavior is the complexity of financial eligibility rules. Although there are both income and asset criteria for financial eligibility, definitions for income and assets are complicated. Some types of income are counted, while other types of income (e.g., business income) are not. Some assets are counted (e.g., liquid assets), while other assets are not (e.g., private residences, "unavailable" assets). Thus, financial need is defined not only by the absolute level of wealth an individual holds when applying for Medicaid, but also the form in which that wealth is held. Medicaid planners may suggest to clients that Congress intended to permit sheltering of assets to qualify for Medicaid through the enactment of these eligibility rules. Others argue, however, that legislators are unaware of the complexity of Medicaid eligibility rules, and that special interests have been successful in building loopholes into the system through relatively arcane eligibility provisions.

Other attributes of Medicaid eligibility policy affect Medicaid estate planning behaviors as well. On the surface, Medicaid eligibility policy for long-term care coverage is quite restrictive. An individual applicant may qualify for Medicaid only after contributing all of his or her income except for a small personal needs allowance (which was as low as $35 per month in 1997) and after spending down his or her assets to $2,000 or less. Consequently, Medicaid rules leave unmarried nursing home residents with little or no wealth to bequest to their children upon death or to draw upon themselves. For many middle-class elderly persons who have worked all of their lives to accumulate a modest amount of wealth to pass to heirs, the prospect of losing all of their assets and dying impoverished is devastating. Such restrictiveness is therefore often portrayed by Medicaid planners as being inherently unfair. These policies may therefore serve as justification for applicants to use loopholes in eligibility rules in order to protect the strongly valued right to leave an inheritance to heirs.

Medicare coverage policy

Another aspect of public policy that may be perceived as unjust is that Medicare provides protection from the catastrophic costs of acute care episodes, but little or no protection from the catastrophic costs of chronic illnesses that require long-term care services. Why should the fact that one person happens to have an acute illness and another a chronic illness mean that one should have total insurance coverage while the other is forced into poverty? The lack of Medicare or other broad, non-means-tested coverage for long-term care is another public policy factor that may increase Medicaid estate planning activity.

Cost and quality of nursing home care

Markets in which the costs of nursing home care are the highest (e.g., New York, Connecticut, Massachusetts) tend to increase Medicaid estate planning activity. Extremely high costs of long-term care may foster public perceptions that it is fundamentally inappropriate to expect individuals to be solely responsible for the entire expense of a nursing home stay.

An important consideration in Medicaid planning is the potential difference in quality of Medicaid-purchased nursing home care compared to the quality of privately purchased care. The greater the differential in quality, the less likely an individual is to perceive Medicaid-financed care as a valued good. This factor presents policymakers with a dilemma. On the one hand, they do not want to be accused of purchasing a product for public assistance clients that is inferior to that which is available to privately paying clients. On the other hand, the closer the quality of Medicaid-financed care is to the quality of privately financed care, the more likely that individuals will perceive no negative effects of "getting on Medicaid." This issue also affects the behaviors of the children of Medicaid applicants who have an interest in preserving assets through Medicaid estate planning, but also must consider the potential consequences of obtaining lower-quality Medicaid-financed care for their parents.

Income and asset verification procedures

The diligence with which local Medicaid eligibility offices verify the financial information reported by individuals on their Medicaid applications also affects Medicaid planning behaviors. The nature of questions that states ask Medicaid applicants on their eligibility forms about financial holdings may influence an applicant's view of the process. As the assets and property of older Medicaid applicants have become more complex, states have made fairly substantial changes in their Medicaid application forms to elicit more detailed information about applicants' sources of income and assets.

One verification process that all states participate in is the income and eligibility verification systems (IEVS) program, in which states send Social Security numbers of public assistance applicants to the federal government for data matching with sources such as IRS records. Applicants are therefore aware that the state will perform some independent verification of information provided on their Medicaid applications.

Otherwise, there is considerable variability across states in the degree to which local eligibility offices attempt to verify the financial information reported by Medicaid applicants. Most local offices are understaffed and underresourced, so that eligibility workers have little time to reference independent sources. Consequently, other than the IVES income verification procedure, most offices depend entirely on the information contained in the application and associated documentation. A few states have been innovative in contacting local banks for accounts that may have not been reported on applications, checking databases on real estate transactions to identify property that might have been sold or transferred, and cross-matching Medicaid applications with state income tax records. The degree to which Medicaid applicants are aware that the information reported on applications about current financial circumstances and recent asset transfers will be independently verified may reduce Medicaid estate planning.

The aggressiveness of estate recovery programs

In addition to estate recovery policies, the aggressiveness with which states actually pursue recoveries also impacts Medicaid planning behaviors. In the actual implementation of estate recovery policies, states can choose to take an extremely aggressive position and pursue all recoveries regardless of how small they might be and limit "hardship" exemptions to only the most extreme cases. On the other hand, states can be more lenient in their application of estate recovery program policies, and permit more assets in the estates of deceased recipients to pass on to heirs. The aggressiveness of states in pursuing estate recoveries is often used by the Medicaid estate planning industry to influence perceptions, suggesting that it is morally acceptable to participate in Medicaid estate planning activities.

Challenges and Unanticipated Consequences

Transfer of asset rules

The difficulty in defining improper transfers of assets also contributes to Medicaid estate planning activity. Federal regulations pertaining to asset transfers and Medicaid eligibility rely on a key concept: the notion of intent. Only transfers that are made with the intent of obtaining eligibility for Medicaid are subject to penalty. However, the determination of intent is not easily operationalized, and states have had difficulty differentiating intentional transfers from other types of transfers in the implementation of these rules. Often states make relatively arbitrary cutoffs between small and large transfers of wealth, and assume that large transfers are made for the purpose of establishing Medicaid eligibility, unless the applicant can prove otherwise. For example, if a grandfather claims he felt unusually generous one Christmas and decided to give his grandson a $50,000 Christmas check that year, the state might question the ingenuousness of his generosity, particularly under circumstances of failing health.

Some states do not explicitly advise Medicaid applicants that only intentional transfers are subject to penalties, thereby implying that all transfers of assets over the prior three years are subject to penalties. This failure of states to be explicit about applying transfer of asset penalties only to intentional transfers may deter people who have made transfers not intentionally linked to eligibility from even applying for Medicaid, for fear of incurring penalties.

The severity of the penalty also plays a role in Medicaid planning activity. Until recently, improper transfers resulted in a delay in Medicaid eligibility proportional to the amount of the transfer. The larger the transfer, the longer the applicant would be required to pay long-term care costs before the penalty period expired and eligibility for Medicaid became effective. The Kassebaum-Kennedy health reform bill enacted in 1996 criminalized asset transfers as a misdemeanor punishable by a fine of up to $10,000 and imprisonment up to one year. The obvious intent of the legislation is not so much to prosecute frail older people for improper asset transfers, but to create a stronger deterrent to individuals who are contemplating Medicaid estate planning activity. However, the law is also an example of what many believe is an inappropriate and overly extreme public policy effort to alter Medicaid estate planning behavior. Some argue the law will actually deter many people from applying for assistance from Medicaid for their long-term care costs, even if eligible. Due to the negative public reaction to this law, it appears at the time of this writing that this specific provision of the Kassebaum-Kennedy bill is likely to be repealed.

Eligibility worker training

Regardless of the laws, regulations, and rules written by federal and state policymakers addressing Medicaid planning issues, the reality is that states must rely primarily on the ability of individual Medicaid eligibility workers to process long-term care applications and investigate Medicaid planning activities accurately and thoroughly. As the measurement of need for public assistance with long-term care costs has become increasingly complex, the expertise of the people who are measuring that need has grown more sophisticated. Reflecting the experience of eligibility workers, one staffer remarked, "To be a long-term care eligibility worker these days, you need an MBA from Harvard and a law degree from Yale" (Walker, Gruman, & Robison, 1996, p. 23).

Acknowledging contributions of informal caregivers

From a policy perspective, recognizing the contributions of family caregivers who provide the majority of long-term care services in this country is important (Stone et al., 1987). Accordingly, there are a number of

Medicaid program provisions that take into account the caregiving behaviors of family members. For example, Medicaid eligibility rules do not allow Medicaid applicants to retrospectively compensate family members for caregiving efforts (i.e., applicants cannot, immediately prior to application, transfer $15,000 to family members for care provided during the preapplication period). However, states do recognize formal contractual agreements between applicants and family caregivers that specify compensation arrangements for services provided on a prospective basis.

The problem with this policy is that by and large the only individuals who have exercised this option are those who have actively sought out Medicaid planning expertise and been advised accordingly. Further, although states may recognize transfers from applicants to family caregivers under written agreements as "proper" transfers, there is virtually no way for states to be assured that care was actually provided as specified in the contract. Meanwhile, the vast majority of family caregivers remain unaware of this planning option and receive no compensation for their caregiving efforts when they eventually apply for Medicaid assistance.

The end result is that policymakers' efforts to recognize family caregivers may simply create new opportunities for Medicaid planning that are pursued only by those who are most invested in shifting responsibility for long-term care from private to public resources. Yet the discontinuation of policies that appropriately compensate family caregiving efforts may be politically unfeasible, stimulating public cynicism about a system that appears to ignore the major contributions of informal caregivers.

Estate recovery policies

Estate recovery policies reflect our societal beliefs about the right of the government to retroactively recover costs paid on behalf of Medicaid long-term care recipients. Such policies are also consonant with beliefs about the right of Medicaid recipients to pass on at least some level of wealth to heirs, within certain limits. These policies in turn impact Medicaid planning behavior intended to preserve inheritances for children and to protect community spouses.

Federal and state estate recovery policies acknowledge certain circumstances under which Medicaid recipients should be allowed to pass on assets to heirs, rather than have them subject to estate recovery programs. The most notable example is that states are not permitted to seek recoveries from home equity assets if there is a surviving spouse, disabled child, or sibling who has provided informal care for the Medicaid recipient for at least two years. Federal Medicaid law also recognizes the notion of hardship, and requires states to establish rules to determine whether estate recovery efforts would place undue hardship on heirs and to then exempt such cases from estate recovery.

Since the motivation to bequeath at least some wealth to children is a major motivating factor behind Medicaid planning behavior, some argue that policymakers should be more lenient in allowing Medicaid recipients to pass some modest level of wealth to heirs (e.g., $10,000). The argument is that if Medicaid established a minimum exclusion level for estate recovery efforts, then people would be less inclined to pursue Medicaid planning efforts prior to joining the program. The counterargument is that establishing a minimum exclusion level for estate recovery programs would have no effect on Medicaid planning behavior and would simply shift more long-term care financing responsibilities from the private sector to the public sector.

The maturity of the Medicaid estate planning industry

As Medicaid planning is highly complex, the vast majority of Medicaid planning occurs with the assistance of professional Medicaid planners. One way to conceptualize the Medicaid estate planning industry is as a supply of knowledge. Medicaid planning activities depend to a large extent on the supply of knowledge in any market area that Medicaid applicants can access. Although the Medicaid planning industry has grown dramatically in recent years, particularly in urban and suburban areas with high socioeconomic levels, there are still many areas of the country where Medicaid applicants do not have access to this kind of expertise.

The perceived prevalence of Medicaid estate planning

The prevalence of Medicaid planning activity is, to some degree, self-perpetuating. Perceptions of a high prevalence of activity may encourage behaviors that might not otherwise occur. For example, one eligibility worker in Massachusetts reported that persons who paid for their own nursing home care through private resources were often viewed as "fools" by co-residents, who had successfully managed to obtain Medicaid eligibility. Also, in New York, where there is a relatively high level of Medicaid planning activity, there was common acceptance of Medicaid planning as something that "everyone did" without moral predicament (Burwell, 1991).

The purpose of the above discussion is to illustrate that there are myriad policy and program factors that influence whether persons facing long-term care needs choose to participate in Medicaid planning behaviors. Understanding the role of these factors in individual decisions to engage in Medicaid estate planning will allow policymakers to address Medicaid planning as a "policy problem" in a more rational and comprehensive manner. Further, there are often unanticipated consequences of social policy, such as those described above. Such developments pose a new set of challenges to policymakers.

Conclusions

This chapter has discussed the implications of long-term care financing policy that relies primarily on a means-tested program requiring impoverishment to access benefits. Formal public policy and actual practices regarding Medicaid financing of long-term care are inconsistent. Although the current Medicaid program uses a means-tested approach to resource distribution, there is a recognition of and implicit condoning of a parallel system that may facilitate broader access to Medicaid benefits for long-term care coverage. Mistaken public perceptions that Social Security and Medicare provide a comprehensive safety net for older disabled citizens (including long-term care) are beginning to erode. It is also of note that, unlike universal public payment for acute care services, public payment for long-term care is intended to be restricted to those unable to pay for such care themselves. With greater awareness of the limitations of these social programs, Medicaid estate planning may evolve as a way to fulfill individuals' expectations regarding public commitment to the provision of long-term care (Dobris, 1989). In fact, liberalization of the Medicaid program has been identified as an important component of health reform initiatives (Wiener, Illston, & Hanley, 1994).

In summary, this chapter has examined the practice of Medicaid estate planning and regulatory responses to this phenomenon. The interplay between individual behaviors and public policy in the context of Medicaid estate planning is illustrative of the diffuse and divergent perceptions regarding societal and individual obligations to provide long-term care. Attempts to develop public policy that shapes behaviors and attitudes toward such obligations have been fraught with challenges and unanticipated consequences. The limits of policy echo an important theme supported in earlier chapters in this volume: the development of effective, politically acceptable policies for financing long-term care is impeded by varying perceptions of "public" and "private" responsibilities. Careful reassessment of the relevance of this traditional framework is essential in order to move forward in the design of a successful model for financing long-term care.

Acknowledgements

Research for this chapter was supported in part by the Robert Wood Johnson Foundation and state of Connecticut. We would like to acknowledge the helpful comments of Terrie Wetle, Ph.D., Cynthia Gruman, Ph.D., and Julie Robison, Ph.D., on earlier versions of this essay.

References

Bickel, D. (1994). Medicaid eligibility planning after the 1993 OBRA amendments. *The Practical Lawyer, 40*, 21–32.

Burwell, B. (1991). *Middle-class welfare: Medicaid estate planning for long term care coverage.* Lexington, MA: SysteMetrics/McGraw-Hill.

Burwell, B., & Crown, W. (1995). *Medicaid estate planning in the aftermath of OBRA '93.* Cambridge, MA: Medstat Group.

Dobris, J. (1989). Medicaid asset planning by the elderly: A policy view of expectations, entitlement, and inheritance. *Real Property, Probate, and Trust Journal, 24*, 3–31.

General Accounting Office. (1989). *Recoveries from nursing home residents' estates could offset program costs* (GAO/HRD-89-56).

General Accounting Office. (1993). *Medicaid estate planning* (GAO/HRD-93-29R).

Macy, P. (1994). Medicaid planning after OBRA-93: Placing the home in a revocable trust. *Massachusetts Law Review*, 2–15.

McEowen, R., & Harl, N. (1991). Estate planning for elderly and disabled: Organizing the estate to qualify for federal medical extended care assistance. *Indiana Law Review, 24*, 1379–1427.

Moses, S. (1990). The fallacy of impoverishment. *Gerontologist, 30*, 21–25.

Office of the Inspector General. (1988). *Medicaid estate recoveries* (HHS OAI-09-86-00078).

Office of the Inspector General. (1989). *Transfer of assets: A case study in Washington State.*

Schlesinger, S., Scheiner, B., & Schneider, L. (1993). Medicaid planning ideas: What works and what doesn't. *Estate Planning*, 331–339.

Stone, R., Cafferata, G., & Sangl, J. (1987). Caregivers of the frail elderly: A national profile. *Gerontologist, 27*, 616–626.

Walker, L., Gruman, C., & Robison, J. (1996). *Medicaid estate planning for nursing home care in Connecticut: Policies, practices and perceptions.* Prepared for the Office of Policy and Management, Connecticut Partnership for Long-Term Care.

Wiener, J., Illston, L. H., & Hanley, R. (1994). *Sharing the burden: Strategies for public and private long term care insurance.* Washington, DC: The Brookings Institution.

Integrating Theory and Practice in Long-Term Care

LESLIE C. WALKER
ELIZABETH H. BRADLEY

This chapter synthesizes common themes from the theoretical perspective presented in Part I of the volume and uses these themes to analyze critical aspects of the programmatic innovations described in Part II. The chapter argues that the notions of "public" and "private" in the context of long-term care financing warrant careful assessment. Conducting the discourse with new constructs may facilitate progress toward more innovative and successful long-term care financing policy.

Much academic and policy literature on long-term care financing has been framed using the traditional distinctions between public and private programs and responsibilities. In this edited volume, we have examined differing perspectives regarding individual and societal obligations to finance long-term care. The policy struggle that characterizes debates regarding long-term care financing illustrates the collective uncertainty in the United States about where the boundary between public and private roles lies. In fact, there is a question as to whether such a boundary can and should exist amid the evolving models of health reform. A central premise of this book is that the distinction between public and private sectors and responsibilities may be less clear than previously understood. Both theoretical and program-based perspectives demonstrate that successful long-term care policy may require programs that are neither predominantly public nor private but rather recast the two realms, their responsibilities, and their perceived authorities.

Efforts to reform long-term care financing are occurring at a more rapid pace than ever, creating a pivotal juncture in federal and state policymaking. Formulating policy using the traditional framework of distinct public and private sectors and responsibilities is problematic for at least two reasons. First, such bivalent thinking may not be relevant to much of the public. As Schlesinger suggests in Chapter 1, new paradigms that do not frame issues solely in terms of public and private constructs may better capture political reasoning about long-term care by both the public and policymakers. Second, effective long-term care policies must substantively integrate, rather than distinguish, public and private realms. The program chapters describing initiatives to test fuller integration (the Partnership models, cash and counseling) support this notion.

In addition to motivating discussion of specific long-term care financing programs, this text provides theoretical approaches with which to analyze such programs in terms of their political, economic, social, and philosophical implications. This volume presents what is defined broadly as political theory (Chapter 1), economic theory (Chapter 2), social theory (Chapter 3), and theories of distributive justice (Chapter 4). Each of these four chapters offers a distinct perspective on the relative merits of public and private sectors, the nature of public and private interventions, and the usefulness of these terms for defining policy and market options for financing long-term care. Importantly, the chapters are written by authors of differing disciplines and diverse opinions regarding appropriate levels of governmental, market, community, and individual action. Despite this diversity, several common themes emerge from the theory discussion that provide a useful backdrop for better understanding the programs described in the rest of the book. These themes include: (1) variable interpretations of the terms *public* and *private;* (2) substantial theoretical support for the notion that responsibility for long-term care financing should not rest solely with the individual or family; and (3) incongruent policy objectives that may impede the development of efficient and equitable financing mechanisms.

The Theory: Common Themes

Defining public *and* private

Implicit in the theory chapters is the ambiguity of the words *public* and *private*. With the exception of public goods, which have a formal definition within economics as described by Bradley, the terms *public* and *private* are imbued with a variety of meanings. This lack of clarity concerning fundamental concepts can result in considerable confusion, as policy options may be variously cast as supporting public or private institutions or sectors. Public or private may refer to several dimensions of a policy or program, including its financing mechanisms, the care providers, the nature of the services provided, decision-making authorities concerning resource allocation, and access to services. As Schlesinger describes, policies defined as private in one dimension may be defined as public in another. Further, within a given dimension, terms are also ambiguous. For instance, although public generally refers to governmental involvement, the level of government (federal, state, or local) depends on varying interpretations of public. Similarly, private may refer to any nongovernmental institutions or agencies, or to family or individuals themselves. Daniels interprets "privatization" as greater reliance on private markets, a trend reflecting underlying philosophical approaches consistent with libertarianism and utilitarianism. Thus, although these terms appear to simplify policy options through dichotomous categorization, closer analysis reveals that such terms may mask important factors that differentiate programs and explain their level of support among policymakers and the general population.

Data that suggest that the traditional public-private paradigm may be less useful than previously understood are consistent with the concepts of diversity provided in Yee's chapter. Yee illustrates how race/ethnicity and culture influence community perceptions of public and private responsibilities in long-term care financing. Underpinning the notions of public and private are more fundamental concepts of individualism, self-reliance, filial responsibility, community obligation, and social rights. Yee demonstrates how the interpretation of such concepts varies substantially among cultural and racial/ethnic groups. Expectations of self-reliance and the appeal of rugged individualism may be a central tenet in the lives of some, yet may not be so important among other cultures or races/ethnicities. Norms that may be assumed by policymakers to be widely understood and accepted among the general population may not be shared by significant subpopulations of that larger group. Yee calls for a process that incorporates the varying perspectives of diverse populations. Such inclusion efforts may help reframe the traditional formulations of long-term care policy to reflect a larger and more representative spectrum of options.

Allocating responsibility for long-term care

The notion that long-term care is not solely an individual or family responsibility is a premise that is shared across the disciplines represented in the theory section of this volume. This conclusion is supported by arguments for political feasibility, economic efficiency, inclusion of diverse perspectives, and moral justice.

Economic analyses of the market for long-term care insurance reveal that several of the conditions necessary to ensure that the pursuit of individual self-interest maximizes social welfare are not met. As Bradley notes, the extent of asymmetric and imperfect information, as well as the existence of externalities and public goods associated with long-term care, suggest that there may be substantial market failures in the market for long-term care insurance. Such failures suggest a role for government or other collective action to enhance the economic efficiency of this market (assuming such action can be implemented).

From the perspective of cultural diversity, Yee asserts that, for some groups, the concepts of individualism and personal autonomy are far less compelling than for others. Although the dominant view in the general population is to value individual rights over solidarity and community-driven policies, this may be less relevant among diverse subpopulations. Traditional values of self-reliance and individual responsibility for health and welfare may be particularly problematic, as a result of either the incompatibility of such embedded values with diverse cultural norms, inadequate personal resources, or both.

As with the discussions of economic efficiency and social diversity, the discussion of justice also promotes the role of collective or governmental action in allocating long-term care resources. Daniels argues that a just society has a moral obligation to assure people equality of opportunity. He further maintains that long-term care, like health care more generally, is a critical component of individuals' enjoyment of the normal opportunity range for their society. In other words, depriving individuals of long-term care can prohibit them from normal functioning, which in turn prevents them from experiencing the normal opportunity range in their society. This, Daniels argues, is morally unacceptable. He observes that just allocation of long-term care resources may be ensured by "prudent planners" who can determine the distributive principle that allocates the fair share of long-term care resources over a lifetime. Because such planning requires some degree of redistribution to ensure equality of opportunity, the system depends on collective or governmental planning, not merely individual-based resource allocation.

Empirical data suggest that approaches in which a collective entity has responsibility for allocating long-term care resources are well supported by the public and policy elites. In Schlesinger's research, the community obligation policy metaphor was the most widely endorsed. More than 78 percent of the general population and almost 70 percent of the policy elites supported this paradigm. Interestingly, however, there was less support for the societal right metaphor, as might be advocated by Daniels' approach to allocating resources. This finding suggests agreement with the belief that long-term care is a shared responsibility (i.e., is more than merely an individual or family responsibility), yet some discomfort with assigning such responsibility to the society at large. *Community* connotes collective responsibility, but a local sharing of that collective responsibility.

Underlying objectives of long-term care financing policy

An important theme emerging from the theory section of this book is that there are multiple, sometimes competing, policy objectives that are embraced differentially by various theoretical disciplines and program approaches. Such diversity of objectives is expected given the highly complex nature of long-term care organization and financing. Explicit recognition of this diversity may facilitate more effective analysis and more realistic acceptance of chosen policy initiatives. Satisfying these often disparate objectives is not a trivial task. Successful policy proposals will make clear the extent to which these objectives are met.

Four distinct policy objectives are implicit in the theory section: political feasibility, economic efficiency, responsiveness to diverse communities, and distributive justice. The chapter on policy metaphors is based on the premise that the way in which the public and policy elites think about long-term care issues is fundamental to determining which initiatives will be offered and accepted. This view is consistent with the practical reality that effective policy requires substantial political support. While political feasibility is generally associated with incremental policy, authors in this volume suggest alternative approaches to achieving political feasibility. Schlesinger proposes a new framing of proposals using a set of policy metaphors, rather than the standard public-private or liberal-conservative dichotomies. Yee suggests more extensive consideration of community perspectives through inclusion of racially/ethnically and culturally diverse groups in policymaking.

Quite independent from issues of political feasibility, a second objective of policy is economic efficiency, that is, the degree to which policy initiatives can make individuals (or constituencies) better off without making others worse off. The objective of economic efficiency is often used to justify governmental intervention in private markets. One complexity of economic efficiency as an objective is that policies may be *potentially* economically efficient. This means that although policy may increase the social welfare of a population, it may also reduce the welfare of certain individuals. Such policies do not meet the strict definition of economic efficiency because they make some individuals worse off. However, they are considered *potentially* efficient because, with additional policies, social welfare improvements can be redistributed to ensure that no one is made worse off.

A third objective of long-term care policy is responsiveness to community diversity. This objective requires understanding the perceptions and the valuing of various program and policy outcomes by different racial/ ethnic and cultural groups. Accordingly, community values must be taken into account in the development, design, and implementation of long-term care financing policy. Because many racial/ethnic and cultural groups may not be politically or economically powerful, the objective of community responsiveness is conceptually distinct from political feasibility. Further, because this objective involves process as opposed to just outcome, it is distinct from the objective of economic efficiency.

The final policy objective addressed in the theory chapters is distributional justice, meaning the fair distribution of benefits. Daniels' model for allocating resources, the Prudential Lifespan Account, suggests that the objective of distributional justice is fulfilled when birth cohorts are treated equally over their lifetimes. This view of justice allows for unequal treatment at different ages and stages of life as long as individuals are treated equally over their lifespans. In Daniels' view, prudent allocation of scarce resources through the stages of life can result in justice among groups. While the scheme results in differential treatment by age, it ultimately treats people equally and benefits them over the span of their entire lives.

It is important to understand that different policy initiatives reflect differential weighting of these objectives. Some policies may be more consistent with certain of the objectives than other policies. The following section describes the application of theory to the programs detailed in this text.

The Programs: Integrating Theory and Practice

Policy objectives and program design

As described earlier, the theory chapters suggest four broad policy objectives that may be derived from the respective theoretical frameworks: political feasibility, economic efficiency, responsiveness to diverse communities, and distributive justice. Each of the long-term care financing programs discussed in the final chapters reflects these policy objectives to varying degrees. Analysis of these programs illustrates a fundamental premise of this volume. The framing of programs as "public" or "private," or as supporting government-based or market-based solutions, masks important subtleties inherent in their design and public acceptance.

In his chapter on the Partnership for Long-Term Care, Meiners underscores the importance of political feasibility in designing long-term care financing models. This objective is particularly well illustrated by the conceptualization and implementation of the Partnership initiative, which required careful attention to the needs and motivations of both the private (insurance companies and individual purchasers) and public (Medicaid programs) sectors. The notion of political feasibility was central to the establishment of a partnership that was incremental in design, building on existing public and private systems. Although advocates for comprehensive health care reform have criticized the Partnership's incremental approach, others have suggested that a framework of incrementalism (due in part to its political feasibility) is the most effective means to future development of long-term care financing models. The budget neutrality requirements for Partnership programs reflect a desire among policymakers to achieve economic efficiency objectives for public expenditures through the Medicaid program.

Wiener's discussion of public subsidies for private long-term care insurance speaks most directly to the objective of economic efficiency. In his analysis of the relative strengths and weaknesses of various tax incentives for long-term care insurance, Wiener questions the economic efficiency of these models. He observes that tax subsidies may result in potentially large losses in federal tax revenues, perhaps greater than would be saved from public expenditures through the Medicaid program. Although it is still early in the Partnership's implementation, Wiener and others suggest that this program may ultimately prove not to be budget-neutral for Medicaid.

The cash and counseling program described by Mahoney and colleagues can be viewed as addressing policy objectives of political feasibility, economic efficiency, and social diversity. Mahoney notes the growing interest among aging and disability community advocates in models of "consumer-directed care." The cash and counseling program is responsive to this political trend, providing home care clients an opportunity to design and purchase the community-based long-term care services they determine to be most appropriate. Further, there are two aspects of the program that enhance the economic efficiency of the market for home care services: (1) providing choice of direct cash payments as an alternative to defined benefits, and (2) providing consumer information through counseling. Because cash may be valued more highly by consumers than home care services of the equivalent cash value, offering the choice of cash versus service may increase some individuals' utility without reducing others'. Thus, economic efficiency may be enhanced. In addition, the counseling associated with the program may obviate existing information deficiencies, again potentially improving the economic efficiency of the market for home services. The sensitivity of the program to individual preferences regarding both the nature of services and type of provider indicates that the model acknowledges the significance of social diversity. For clients whose kinship network rests at the center of the care plan, this program allows for payment of kin and retention of the kinship network as the system of care delivery.

The service credit program is most directly supportive of the policy objectives of social diversity and distributional justice, and also seeks a degree of economic efficiency. As described by Mahoney and colleagues, the program is especially sensitive to the needs defined by the local community; services offered are a reflection of those perceived as uniquely important from the community's perspective. Further, the notion of contributing volunteer services in the present in order to receive assistance in the future is consistent with the distributional justice precepts defined by Daniels. A prudent planner might be quite attracted to a program that allows for current contributions in return for future benefits. Economic efficiency is another goal of the service bureau programs, in that they are designed to rely on equivalent valuing of services by users.

Finally, the regulatory responses to Medicaid estate planning discussed by Walker and Burwell address three of the policy objectives to some degree: political feasibility, economic efficiency, and distributional justice. The fragmented and inconsistent legislation enacted since 1980 represents political compromise among constituencies with very different perspectives regarding the magnitude and prevalence of Medicaid estate planning, in which assets are either transferred or otherwise protected in order to qualify for Medicaid benefits. The degree to which Medicaid estate planning regulations are economically efficient is unknown, as there has been no comprehensive study of relative costs and benefits of these regulations. However, policymakers and Medicaid program administrators believe assets recovered through such rules exceed the administrative costs of managing the enforcement programs. Governmental efforts to regulate Medicaid estate planning implicitly address societal concerns regarding distributional justice. As described by Walker and Burwell, Medicaid estate planning legislation helps codify the degree to which public funds are accessible to those who have private resources to purchase long-term care. Accordingly, the regulations define in law what society will tolerate as a just distribution of public resources.

Dimensions of the public-private distinction

In addition to addressing differing policy objectives, the programs also vary with regard to models of financing, service delivery, and decision-making authority. The template provided in table C.1 characterizes each of the programs more fully. Building on the concepts described by Schlesinger, five program dimensions may be considered in assessing public and private elements: financing of services, provision of services, nature of services, decision-making authority, and access to services. Although there are both public and private aspects of most social programs, these dimensions assist in examining the primary focus of a given model. The following discussion considers the highlighted programs in terms of these five elements.

The public-private partnerships for long-term care insurance are financed by both individuals (through premiums paid for long-term care insurance policies) and the state (through the Medicaid program when policyholders become eligible for benefits). Services are provided through traditional community- and institution-based delivery systems by formal (paid) caregivers. Decision-making is shared by the individual (who has the authority to choose to purchase a policy or not); the insurer (who determines eligibility for purchase and benefits); and the state (which establishes rules regarding policy standards and access to Medicaid). Access to long-term care insurance has been debated in the literature (Wiener, Hanley, & Illston, 1992; Cohen, Kumar, & Wallack, 1992; Meiners & McKay, 1990). Most commentators agree that these policies are appropriate for a targeted group of relatively young, middle-income individuals. Yet, as Wiener indicates, high premiums place private long-term care insurance out of the reach of many.

Table C.1

Program	Objective Addressed	Financing	Decision-making Authority
Long-Term Care Partnership	Political feasibility Economic efficiency	Individual and state	Individual and state
Tax Incentives	Economic efficiency Political feasibility	Individual and employer	Individual and employer
Cash and Counseling	Political feasibility Economic efficiency Social diversity	State	Individual and family
Service Bureau	Distributional justice Social diversity Economic efficiency	Individual, family, community	Individual and community
Medicaid Estate Planning	Distributional justice Economic diversity Political feasibility	Individual and state	Individual and employer

A program of tax incentives for long-term care insurance is financed by the government, individuals, and sometimes employers. Tax-based models are public subsidies that are publicly financed. Individuals share financial responsibility through the payment of premiums and co-payments or deductibles, and, to the extent that employers are encouraged to contribute toward the purchase of policies for employees, such programs may also be supported by employers. In this insurance-based model, as with the long-term care insurance partnerships, long-term care services are traditional in nature and provided by paid, formal caregivers. Decision-making authorities are shared by policyholders and insurers. Again, evidence suggests that access to long-term care insurance is limited to a targeted segment of the population.

The cash and counseling program is primarily financed by the states through selected Medicaid programs. To the extent individuals "trade in" other public benefits to enter the program, they also bear financial responsibility. In contrast to the approaches described above, decision-making authority rests solely with individual clients. Consistent with the model's design, the nature of services provided is idiosyncratic; that is, services are defined by each client and accordingly are highly variable. Services may be provided by family members, other caregivers, or formal care providers. Decision-making authority explicitly rests with the individual care recipient. As described by Mahoney and colleagues, the program is linked to existing Medicaid home care programs. This approach ties eligibility for entry into the cash and counseling program to Medicaid, thereby making access available to persons of greater income ranges than private insurance approaches.

While the service credit banking program requires some administrative funding, it is primarily "financed" by individuals, families, and the community. Like the cash and counseling program, services are highly individualized and idiosyncratic. Decisions regarding services are made by individuals and the community. Where service credit programs exist, access is nearly universal, since the program requires only donation of time for participation.

Finally, Medicaid financing of long-term care requires that costs are shared by individuals and the state. Services are provided within the formal care system and are primarily institution-based (because Medicaid estate planning typically occurs in the context of seeking nursing home care). Decision-making in this arena is mixed, with both individuals and the state playing a role in the Medicaid application process. The issue of access to Medicaid funds for long-term care is complex, as discussed in the chapter in this volume by Walker and Burwell. Theoretically, those eligible for Medicaid coverage are impoverished, and therefore access is limited to those who satisfy the means tests. For most individuals, this requires a period of private payment until resources are exhausted (spend-down). The evolution of Medicaid estate planning and accordant policy responses suggest, however, that access to the program may be broader than intended. Policymakers may not intend for total family impoverishment to occur, as is reflected in the spousal protection and homestead regulations.

Implications of Theory for Future Long-Term Care Policy

In its best use, theory provides an abstract framework of general principles that explain or shed light on a variety of specific situations, or in this context, long-term care policies and programs. In addition, theory can, to some extent, predict future policy and program actions. What does the backdrop of theory presented in this volume reveal that can enhance the way we think about future long-term care financing strategies?

The theoretical discussions demonstrate that the recognition and negotiation of divergent policy objectives will be fundamental to the future long-term care debate. Incongruent policy objectives pose central questions in the conceiving of program structures and approaches. Such conflicts are inherent in a pluralistic society; however, explicit and comprehensive discussion of divergent policy objectives can improve collective understanding of policy options and the degree to which they fulfill social and individual expectations of adequate reform. Trade-offs among the objectives of political feasibility, economic efficiency, responsiveness to social diversity, and distributional justice occur in development of most social policy. Masking or oversimplifying such trade-offs is unlikely to lead to optimal policy reform. In contrast, analysis of these fundamental trade-offs should be made explicit in every stage of policy development and implementation. Such an approach, although laborious and complex, can define which policy objectives are represented by specific programs, as well as the degree to which alternative objectives have been compromised. At the least, such explicit recognition allows for more informed decision-making on the part of policymakers. At best, the recognition and negotiation of policy objectives may lead to innovative approaches that reveal an intersection of seemingly disparate goals, or, in economic terms, optimalization among the policy objectives.

In addition to tensions related to underlying policy objectives, the theory suggests substantial conflict arises due to varying notions of decision-making held by individuals, their families, and the community. One perspective, typically associated with the discipline of economics, views the locus of decision-making to be the autonomous individual maximizing his or her utility, which may or may not include others' utilities. In contrast, other perspectives view decision-making as a more complex web of interactions among individuals, families, the community, and the larger culture. Through this lens, the individual and his or her own decisions may not be as easily separated from the family or community as theorized by more simplistic decision-making models. Because influencing personal and family decisions concerning health care choices and filial obligations is an inherent part of long-term care financing policy, differing notions concerning the locus and process of decision-making on the part of individuals, families, and communities is likely to generate considerable tension in program design. The theoretical perspectives of the text demonstrate that divergence of these perspectives is unavoidable and suggests that an interdisciplinary approach to policy development is necessary. The diverse characterizations of the roles and responsibilities of individuals, families, and communities must be incorporated into long-term care policy development. If explored and negotiated, such diversity can provide the opportunity for more reasonable and effective policy process and program implementation.

The program chapters represent a range of policy responses to such tensions, from relatively straightforward models such as tax subsidies for long-term care insurance to innovative conceptualizations of new programs. Importantly, some of the innovative program initiatives have been successful in responding to the needs of proscribed subgroups of the population. For example, the cash and counseling program addresses the needs of individuals who value autonomy and personal control over the care they receive. The Partnership long-term care insurance programs provide reasonable alternatives for those with appropriate assets to protect. Such programs represent demonstrations that are quite innovative, yet remain somewhat limited in scope and impact at this point in their development. Their success is consistent with many innovations in their early stages of implementation, and they illustrate the potential for compromise among diverse perspectives and stakeholders, as well as competing policy objectives. What has not been demonstrated is whether such programs, propelled in the early stages by the enthusiasm and commitment of their original creators, can be replicated nationally or sustained over time. Furthermore, as they become more widely known and successful, opponents who emphasize competing policy perspectives may limit program growth and replication via new laws and regulations.

The challenges of forging compromise and sustaining such programmatic innovations on the national level will be central to broader efforts to develop long-term care financing policies. As financing models increase in both scope and magnitude, various stakeholders may emerge to challenge prospective change. Although important as a natural system of checks and balances, the involvement of invested constituencies adds a layer of complexity to the process. Further, the impact of cultural diversity on perceptions of responsibility is amplified substantially as programs expand in scope. Incremental programs designed in specific communities can be sensitive to these issues; however, such sensitivity to individual and community preferences is difficult to reproduce on a national scale. Finally, the notion of collective responsibility grows more complicated as programs broaden beyond local geography. Although supported by theorists in their conceptualizations of long-term care systems, translating collective responsibility into action can be controversial, especially as norms of such responsibility may not be shared. Does *collective* mean government action? What level of government? As a related challenge, perceptions and beliefs about the role of community must be further understood. In particular, are there characteristics of community that resonate with both policymakers and the public? Can these elements be effectively incorporated into long-term care financing and delivery programs? Is the "blurring of the line" between public and private sectors a reflection of evolving notions of community, and how will this trend affect the design and implementation of long-term care systems?

Conclusions

Public policy may be interpreted as an expression of values at two levels: the individual/family and society. Individuals and families may hold certain values with regard to long-term care that determine their choices regarding individual responsibilities. Societal values are translated into policy that, theoretically, represents collective views about public responsibilities. When these two frameworks are congruent, there is strong potential for a program to be successful. For example, in the cash and counseling program individuals may value personal choice and authority in determining needed services. Society may broadly value notions of autonomy, independence, and personal responsibility. On the other hand, the cash and counseling program may engender tension among policymakers who are not comfortable with the concept of paying family members to provide care the family member would have otherwise provided anyway, or with the possibility that clients may make "bad" choices. Where there is discordance, tensions will arise. For example, a policy to provide tax incentives for long-term care insurance will fail if individuals do not perceive a value to insurance or a responsibility to share the financial burden of care through the payment of premiums. These formidable challenges are not unique to long-term care, but are endemic to most social policy and reach to the center of discourse on major social policy, such as health care, welfare, and housing.

Despite the demonstrable value of theory in distilling guiding principles, policymakers often fail to consider and apply such precepts in the design of social programs. The relevance of the constructs *public* and *private* in the context of long-term care financing warrant careful assessment. Since these concepts continue to frame discussions in this area, it is essential to understand whether they continue to identify meaningful distinctions. Despite political cachet, efforts to create a public-private boundary may be both inappropriate and ineffective in developing long-term care policy. Conducting the discourse with new constructs may facilitate progress toward a more innovative and successful conception of financing long-term care.

The reader has now explored a central health policy issue from a variety of theoretical and programmatic perspectives. There is no doubt that long-term care delivery and financing will continue to pose major challenges to policymakers in the coming decades. This book has interpreted and applied theory to illuminate important facets of existing long-term care financing programs and identified challenges that have impeded major progress in this area. At this juncture, we must ask ourselves several critical questions: As a society, do we ultimately seek to live in a caring nation where our most frail and vulnerable citizens are respected and well cared for? If so, how much are we willing to contribute as individuals? How open are we to confronting the challenges? If we agree responsibilities are to be shared among individuals, families, and society, how is this notion operationalized? A frank assessment of our collective commitment to this issue is imperative for thoughtful consideration of policy options for the organization, delivery, and financing of long-term care.

References

Cohen, M. N., Kumar, N., & Wallack S. (1992). Who buys long-term care insurance? *Health Affairs, 11*(1), 208–223.

Meiners, M., & McKay, H. (1990). Private vs. social long-term care insurance: Beware the comparison. *Generations,* 32–36.

Wiener, J., Hanley, R., & Illston, L. H. (1992). Financing long-term care: How much public? How much private? *Journal of Health Policy, Politics and Law, 17*(3), 426–438.

Index

Abrahams, R., 11
Abrams, B., 69
Achenbaum, W., 32
activities of daily living (ADLs), 2–3, 5; geriatric medicine and, 88; informal care and, 151, 154
acute care, 4, 11–14, 106, 138, 139
Adams, E. K., 10
ADLs. *See* activities of daily living
Adreoni, J., 69
adult day care centers, 12, 104, 108–9
adverse selection, 65, 69–70
affordability issues, 134–37
age discrimination, 98
age groups: distributive justice and, 97–98; employee-sponsored plans and, 136–37; long-term care insurance and, 145–46; long-term care needs and, 2, 4; prudent planners and, 103
age profiles, 94–95
aging of society, 94–95, 105, 107
Akerlof, G., 64
alternative medicine, 87–88, 90
Alzheimer's disease, 3, 106
American Association of Homes for the Aging, 4
American Association of Retired Persons (AARP), 9
American Health Care Association, 143, 161
Ansak, M., 12
Ansello, E. F., 152

Area Agencies on Aging, 34, 155
Arizona Long-Term Care System (ALTCS), 13
Arkansas, cash and counseling program in, 153, 155
asset depletion, 10, 118, 136; waivers of, 134
asset protection, 10, 124, 126, 127, 166–68; Medicaid and, 10, 144–45; models of, 118–20; portability of, 123; reciprocity and, 123, 128
asset transfers, 146, 167; New York and, 119–20; penalties and, 175–76; restrictions on, 171
assets, countable, 166–67
assisted-living communities, 4, 117
asymmetric information, 64–67, 69–70, 184
autonomy, 81, 89, 106, 184

baby boomers, 1, 4, 5, 15–16, 152
Barnes, C., 157–58
Batavia, A. I., 153
Batts, V. A., 81
Bauer, E. J., 118
Beauchamp, D., 38
Becker, G., 73
Bell, C. C., 77
Bell, D., 66
Bengtson, V. L., 7
Bickel, D., 168
Binstock, R. H., 14, 16

Bishop, C., 105
Bogardus, S., 71
Bosk, C., 27
Bradley, E., 68, 71, 183, 184
Breslau, N., 3
Brody, E. M., 7
The Brookings Institution, 135
Brown, R. S., 13
Burner, S. T., 14
Burton, L., 7
Burwell, B. O., 10, 146, 169, 172, 178,
    188–89, 191

Cafferata, G. L., 7, 160, 176
California: estate planning and, 169; In-
    Home Supportive Services Program
    of, 153, 157; long-term care insurance
    in, 117, 118, 125, 126–27, 142–44, 161;
    On Lok model in, 12–13
Callahan, J., 106
Callahan, J. J., Jr., 8
Campbell, J., 27
Campbell, R., 27
capitation, 11, 12, 13, 15, 132
Capitman, J. A., 8, 78, 135
Caplan, A., 37, 106
Caplan, C., 138
Caplan, R., 103
caregivers, 6; age of, 152; burdens of,
    96; in family, 7, 177; informal, 80;
    primary, 3, 109; relief schemes for,
    108–9; respite for, 12
Carmines, E., 26, 28, 31
cash and counseling program, 150,
    152–58, 162, 188, 190, 193
Cassel, C. K., 5
Census Bureau, U.S., 4, 6
Centers for Independent Living, 155
Chapman, P., 26
Chellis, R. D., 8
Chen, Y., 33
chronic illness: elderly people and, 13;
    health care and, 1, 88; public versus
    private, 34
Clinton, Bill, 15; health care reform
    proposal of, 14, 56, 104, 115, 128, 132;

Health Security Act (1993), 34, 115,
    153
Clotfelter, C., 69
Cluff, L. E., 16
Cohen, J. W., 15
Cohen, M. A., 8, 66, 135
Cohen, M. N., 189
Coleman, B., 33
Colorado, long-term care insurance in,
    126
colorblind policies, 78–79
communities: of color, 81; cultural di-
    versity and, 77–90; decision-making
    and, 73; public versus private respon-
    sibility, 77–90, 185; volunteers in,
    158–60
community-based care, 5, 6, 7; innova-
    tion in, 115; language barriers and,
    90; managed care programs and, 13;
    options for, 117; public initiatives
    and, 150–63; state Medicaid and, 15
community residences, 4
Congress, U.S., 14, 153; asset shel-
    tering and, 10; Budget Office of,
    5–6, 31; Committee on Ways and
    Means (1996), 135, 142; Medicare
    and Medicaid expenditures and, 14–
    15; Pepper commission, 28; policy
    metaphors survey results, 44–51,
    57; S/HMOs and, 12; specialists in
    health policy and, 28, 29, 40; ways
    and means committee (1996), 135. See
    also legislation
Connecticut: estate planning and, 169;
    long-term care insurance in, 117, 118,
    125, 142–44
consumer-directed care, 152–53
continuing care retirement communi-
    ties (CCRCs), 4, 8
Corder, L. S., 5, 12
Coronel, S., 135, 138, 140
cost-shifting, 9, 13
Council on Scientific Affairs, 82
counseling services, 155
Courtney, M, 33
Crawford, S. L., 7

crowding out hypothesis, 68–69
Crown, W. H., 8, 10, 135, 146, 169
Cruciano, T. M., 142
Crystal, S., 32
cultural factors, 77–78, 96

Daniels, N., 94, 95, 100, 101, 102, 103,
    107, 108, 110, 183, 184–85, 186, 188
Davis, J., 42
decision-making, 28–30; collective, 68;
    interaction and, 73, 189; models for,
    65–67, 70, 73; private care and, 33
deductibles, 8, 126, 131
DeJong, G., 153
Delli Carpini, M., 28, 35, 53
Diehr, P., 82
disabilities: developmental, 1, 13; of
    elderly population, 13, 104, 135, 153;
    risk and, 5; service requirements and,
    2–3; veterans and, 9, 11, 151
disability insurance, 137
disabled population, 115, 151
distributive justice, 73, 97, 107
Dobris, J., 179
Dole, R., 127
domiciliary care, 11
Doty, P., 108, 109
dual eligibility, Medicare and Medicaid
    and, 12
Dunlop, B., 108

Eckert, S. K., 6
economic structures, 30, 77
economic theory, 62–74
Edelman, M., 36
Edelman, P., 7
Edigi, M., 66, 67
education, 126, 130, 131; long-term plan-
    ning and, 71, 126, 130; public health
    campaigns and, 82
Edwards, W., 65, 66
efficiency: allocative, 63; privatiza-
    tion and, 96; technical, 63; welfare
    economics and, 63–64, 74
Eisenberg, D. M., 87
employers: benefit plans of, 16; long-

term care requirements for, 34; tax
    incentives and, 134, 138–41
employment benefit survey, 42
Eng, C., 12
Epstein, A. M., 82
Epstein, T. R., 79
equity: intergenerational, 97; welfare
    economics and, 63–64, 73–74
Ernst & Young, 4
estate planning, 29, 118, 165, 166–69;
    Medicaid and, 10, 188–89
estate recovery programs, 126, 175,
    177–78
Estes, C. L., 152
ethnic factors, 77–78
Eustis, N. N., 152
expected utility theory, 65–67
externalities: social welfare and, 62,
    67–69; welfare economics and, 63, 64

fairness, 97, 100, 103, 109, 185
families: as black box, 73; blended, 7,
    80; cash and counseling programs
    and, 153; as substitutions for insur-
    ance, 105; and traditional values, 97,
    105
family caregivers, 32, 157, 177; elderly
    population and, 6–7, 80; prudent de-
    liberation and, 108–9; public-private
    partnerships and, 117
family issues, 7; consumer-directed
    care and, 153; decision-making and,
    73, 192; disabled individuals and,
    3; elderly parents and, 93–94; frail
    elderly and, 96; insurance and, 105;
    long-term care and, 182; out-of-
    pocket expenditures and, 5, 6; paren-
    tal care and, 32, 80; responsibility
    and, 32, 85–87, 150; stress and, 108–9
Feldstein, P., 68, 72
Ferejohn, J., 27
filial responsibility, 7, 85–87; privati-
    zation and, 96–97; relief and, 108–9.
    See also family issues
Financial Accounting Standards Board,
    139

financing, 182; for long-term health care, 115; objectives of, 185–86; private versus public, 181–82

Florida: cash and counseling program in, 153, 154, 155, 158; estate planning and, 169

Forey, J., 87

Foster Higgins, Inc., 139

Fraser, I., 33

Freudenheim, M., 116

Frieden, T. R., 82

Friedland, R., 8

Friedlob, A., 12

Fries, J. F., 5

Fulton, D., 135

Furnham, A., 87

future outlook: of age profile, 94; of delivery systems, 141; interaction of individual, family, community, 73; for long-term care, 4–5, 6, 14–17, 55–58, 191–94; public resources and, 96; for social support, 69

Gamson, W., 27, 36

Garber, A., 69, 70

General Accounting Office (GAO), 168; employee benefits and, 139; long-term care funding and, 2, 4, 6, 8

geriatric medicine, 12, 88, 104

Glaser, J., 31

Glendon, M., 38

Golant, S., 4

Goss, S. C., 120, 123

government assistance: appropriate role for, 26; financing and, 5–6; means-testing and, 116; private care and, 33; public awareness of, 26, 70; public goods problem and, 68; social welfare and, 72

Graber, D., 27

Gray, B., 68

Grayson, P. J., 8

Greenberg, J., 11

Greenfield, S., 82

Griffin, R., 31

group insurance policies, 137

Gruman, C., 10, 71, 169, 176

Guralnik, J. M., 5

Hacker, J., 38, 55

Hamilton, J., 4

Hamlin, C., 82

Hanley, R. J., 6, 8, 135, 137, 139, 140, 142, 144, 145, 179, 189

hardship exemptions, 175

Harl, N., 168

Harrington, C., 12

Harris, K. M., 6, 137, 140, 144

Hawes, C., 4

Health and Human Services, Department of (DHHS), 82; Healthy People 2000, 81

Health Care Financing Administration (HCFA), 14, 124, 154

health care reform: failure of, 95; long-term care and, 181–82; Prudential Lifespan Account concept and, 102–3

Health Insurance Association of America, 140

health maintenance organizations (HMOs), 11, 12

health service research, 77, 82

Hernandez, D. J., 80

Hernandez, W., 78

Heumann, J. E., 152

Hilgartner, S., 27

Hittle, D. F., 13

HMOs, 11, 12

Hoffman, C., 80

Hofland, B. F., 152

Hogarth, R., 66

Holahan, J., 15

Holubinka, G., 119

home health care, 117; cash allowances and, 153; communities and, 151–52; costs of, 135, 143–44; employee group policies and, 137; homemakers and, 4, 162; independent living and, 106; innovation in, 115; Medicaid and, 9–11; nonprofit agencies and, 33; part-time, 11; quality of, 29; risk-based Medicaid managed care programs and, 13; state Medicaid and, 15; supplementary services for, 104; for veterans, 11, 151

Horney, M., 73

Horvath, J., 12

hospitals, 4, 152; media attention to, 29; medical versus long-term care, 16; Medicare and, 13

Hudson, R. B., 9

Hughes, S., 7

IADLs. *See* instrumental activities of daily living

Illinois, long-term care insurance in, 125, 126

Illston, L. H., 6, 8, 9, 11, 12, 135, 137, 139, 142, 145, 179, 189

impairments: duality and, 34; as measure of need, 102; morality and, 105–6

imperfect information: private insurance and, 69–71, 184; social welfare and, 62, 64–67

impoverishment protection, 118–19, 167, 173

income and eligibility verification system, 174

income levels, 6, 8, 140–41; asset protection and, 125, 145; impoverishment protection and, 119, 173; Medicaid and, 143; out-of-pocket payments and, 14

income waivers, 122–23

Indiana, long-term care insurance in, 117, 118, 125, 142–44

individual rational choice, 99

individual responsibility, 81, 96; decision-making and, 73; versus family rights, 81; versus societal responsibility, 93, 97

inflation protection, 8, 105, 126, 128, 131; employee group policies and, 137–38, 140

informal care, 80, 104, 150–61

Inspector General, asset transfer and, 168

Institute of Medicine, 145

institutionalization: alternatives to, 106; premature, 104, 106, 109

institutions, 2. *See also* nursing home care

instrumental activities of daily living (IADLs), 2–3; informal care and, 151; Medicaid and, 9

insurance: inflated premiums, 99; lemons principle and, 64–65; for long-term care, 8, 107, 116–19, 124–27, 135–47, 161; mandatory universal, 69–70; partnership programs and, 115–32; premiums, 99

insurance, private, 5; imperfect information and, 69–71; Medicaid and, 10; middle-income population and, 14; public subsidies for, 134–47; role of, 7–8

insurance, public, 14, 56, 104, 115, 128–30

insurance agents, 145; inflation protection and, 126; partnership programs and, 122, 129

intergenerational equity, 29, 80, 85–87, 94, 97, 145; social welfare and, 71–72

Internal Revenue Service, 142, 174

Iowa, long-term care insurance in, 124, 142–44

Iyengar, S., 27, 30, 42

Jackson, B., 151, 152

Jacobs, L., 27

Jecker, N., 101

Jeung, M., 71

Jones, B., 27, 29, 35

justice: distribution of, 93–110; distributive, 73, 97, 107; in health care, 17

Kahneman, D., 66

Kane, R. A., 4, 33

Kane, R. L., 12, 33

Kansas, home- and community-based services in, 157

Kapp, M., 152, 153

Kaptchuk, T. J., 87
Kassebaum-Kennedy bill. *See* legisla-
    tion: Health Insurance Portability
    and Accountability Act
Kassner, E., 15
Katz, S., 2
Kaye, L. W., 4, 12
Keeter, S., 28, 35, 53
Kennedy, E. M., 128
Kingma, B., 69
Kitano, H. H. L., 77
Knickman, J., 118
Koontz, T., 33
Kuklinski, J., 26, 28, 31
Kumar, N., 189
Kutza, E., 33
Kyzivat, L., 71

Labor, Department of, 140
Laguna Research Associates, 145
Lau, R., 29, 35, 37
legislation: Balanced Budget Act (1997),
    15; Consolidated Omnibus Bud-
    get Reconciliation Act (1986), 170;
    for elder care, 32; family respon-
    sibility and, 150; Health Insurance
    Portability and Accountability Act
    (1996), 116, 128–30, 136, 138, 147, 171,
    176; Health Security Act, 34, 153;
    Medicaid estate planning and, 170–
    72; Medicare Catastrophic Coverage
    Act (1988), 167, 171; Older Americans
    Act, 9, 34, 39, 151; Omnibus Bud-
    get Reconciliation Act (1989), 171;
    Omnibus Reconciliation Act (1993),
    124–26, 143, 171; Tax Equity and
    Fiscal Responsibility Act (1982), 170
Leutz, W. N., 8, 11, 33, 78, 135
Levit, K. R., 5, 9, 10, 11
Lewin-VHI, Inc., 4, 135
Liebig, P. S., 15
life care at home (LCAH), 8
LifePlans, Inc., 140, 145
lifespan allocations, 8, 98–103, 119, 123
Light, D., 38, 103
Lipsky, M., 36
Liu, K., 7

Longman, P., 32
long-term care, 28; allocation of re-
    sponsibility for, 184–85; buyers
    and sellers of, 64, 67, 69; chronic
    disease and, 88; costs of, 5–11; cross-
    disciplinary efforts and, 62; design
    of, 93; dichotomy and, 30–31; future
    theory implications for, 191–94; need
    and settings for, 2–5; organization of,
    1–17; theory and practice, 181–95
long-term care, financing of, 1–17,
    93, 142–47, 181–82, 185–86; divi-
    sion of, 151; multistate initiative for,
    116; social welfare and, 62. *See also*
    vouchers, for long-term care
long-term care insurance, 8, 107, 116–19,
    124–27, 135–47, 161
long-term care surveys, 45–51, 57, 152
Lux, L. J., 4

Macy, P., 168
Mahoney, C. W., 152, 187–88, 191
Mahoney, K. J., 118, 127, 132, 161
managed care, 2, 11–14
Manning, W., 72
Manton, K. G., 5, 12
Manton, K. J., 161
Manton, K. M., 7
March, J., 66
market forces: long-term care insur-
    ance and, 107; private care and, 33;
    resource allocation and, 63
Marmor, T., 33, 68
Marris, R., 66, 67
Maryland, long-term care insurance in,
    125–26
Maryland, University of, Center on
    Aging at, 158
Massachusetts: estate planning and,
    168–69; long-term care insurance in,
    124
Mayer, W., 27
McCall, N., 118
McElroy, M., 73
McEowen, R., 168
McKay, H. L., 116, 126, 132, 161, 189
McKerlie, D., 102

McKinlay, J. B., 7
McKnew, L., 153
Mechanic, D., 13
Medicaid, 1, 9, 95; cash and counseling program and, 152; eligibility for, 9, 14, 124, 143, 147, 171, 172–73; estate planning and, 10, 165–80, 188–89; family caregivers and, 157–58; home health agencies and, 37; impoverishment protection and, 119; income verification and, 174–75; incremental improvements and, 115–16; informal care and, 150, 151; means testing and, 14, 115, 116, 122, 129, 144; nursing home care and, 9–11, 13, 37, 104, 117, 143–44; partnership programs and, 122–23, 129, 142–46; versus private insurance, 69, 139; qualifying trusts and, 170; risk-based managed care and, 12–13; waiver programs and, 9, 154
medicalization, 9, 37, 104, 109
Medicare, 9, 95; HMOs and, 11; home care and, 151; home health agencies and, 37; increase in use of, 1; incremental approach to improvements and, 115–16; long-term care coverage and, 41; nursing home care and, 10–11, 37, 117; reforms survey results and, 44–51
Meiners, M. R., 10, 115, 116, 120, 121, 123, 131, 132, 161, 189
Mendelson, D. N., 5
Mental Health Policy Forum, 151–52
Merrill, J. C., 116
Michigan, Home Health Program of, 153
Miller, N., 12
Minnesota, Long-term Care Options Project (LTCOP), 13
Miranda, M. R., 77
Modigliani, A., 36
Monk, A., 4
moral hazard, 70
moral issues, 93–110, 105, 178–79
Moran, W., 33
multicultural issues, 81, 82, 85, 90

Murray, J., 87
Murray, R. H., 87

National Academy for State Health Policy, 12
National Academy on Aging, 7
National Association for Home Care, 151
National Governors' Association, 131
Nelson, L., 13
Neuman, W., 31, 54, 57
Newcomer, R., 11, 12
New Jersey, cash and counseling program in, 153, 155, 162
New Mexico, fee-for-service system in, 13
New York state: asset tests in, 143; cash and counseling program in, 153, 156; estate planning and, 169; long-term care insurance in, 117, 119, 125, 142–45
nonprofit organizations, 33, 34, 68
nursing home care, 2, 4, 13; costs of, 6, 14, 104, 135, 143, 161; length of stay in, 144; Medicaid and, 9–11, 13, 37, 104, 117, 143–44; nonprofit agencies and, 33; poverty and, 104; private insurance and, 8; state innovation and, 118; statistics, 135; for veterans, 11
Nussbaum, S., 119
Nyman, J. A., 123, 145

Olshansky, S. J., 5
On Lok model (San Francisco), 12–13
Oregon, estate planning and, 168
Organization for Economic Cooperation and Development, 31
out-of-pocket expenses, 5, 6; employer coverage and, 138; increase in, 15

PACE, 12
Packwood, R., 127
Page, B., 27
Palmer, H., 106
Parsons, W., 27
Partnership for Long-Term Care, 116, 117–31, 187, 193
Pauly, M., 55, 69

Pear, R., 15
perfect information, 64
personal care needs, 4, 104–5, 141, 153–58
policy metaphors, 35–39, 44–51
political reasoning, 28; versus government involvement, 25–58; reform and, 53, 54–55
Poole, D., 33
poverty, 9, 30, 82, 104; Medicaid and, 10, 118
premiums: for employer-sponsored plans, 136–38, 140; inflated, 99; for long-term care insurance, 135; for private insurance, 8; tax benefits and, 132
Preston, S., 12
private responsibility, 32–33, 183–84
private sector, 5, 95, 117; economic theory and, 73; elderly population and, 135; responsibility of, 115
privatization trends, 95–96, 183
Program for All-inclusive Care for the Elderly (PACE), 12
prudent deliberation, 93–110, 184, 188
Prudential Lifespan Account, 98–102, 105, 106–7
public opinion: effect on government of, 27; on long-term care, 161; surveys, 40
public policy, 29; catastrophic illness and, 173; choices and, 103; health care reform and, 115, 121; informal caregiving and, 150; interventions, 131; responsibility issues and, 51–53; welfare economics and, 73
public-private partnerships, 107, 115–32, 142–46
public-private responsibility, 151, 179, 181–82, 189–91; cultural diversity and, 77–90
public responsibility, 32–33, 183–84
Pynoos, J., 4

quality of care, 4, 29, 90; Medicaid and, 15

racial factors: inequality and, 98; Prudential Lifespan Account concept and, 102; public versus private responsibility and, 77–78, 183
Radner, D. B., 145
Raiffa, H., 66
Rawls, J., 100
Reed, E., 82
Reeves, J., 27
Regnier, V., 4
Rein, M., 27, 36
resource allocation, 89, 107; government rule-making and, 33; welfare economics and, 63, 71
respite care, 3, 9
retirement benefits, 139–40
Rice, D. P., 80
risk, 104; education of elderly and, 82; future social support and, 69; lemons principle and, 64–65; means testing and, 116; segmentation of, 117; as social construct, 82
Rivlin, A. M., 8, 31, 135
Robert Wood Johnson Foundation, 10, 116, 124, 126, 142, 153, 159. *See also* Partnership for Long-Term Care
Robison, J., 169, 176
Rosenthal, C., 7
Rosow, I., 3
Rubel, A. J., 87
Rudberg, M. A., 5

Sabin, J., 108
Sandel, M., 26
Sangl, J., 7, 160, 176
Savage, L., 65
Scanlon, W. J., 145
Scheiner, B., 168
Scheingold, S., 38
Schlenker, R. E., 13
Schlesinger, M., 33, 35, 37, 68, 182, 183, 185, 189
Schlesinger, S., 168
Schmitz, M., 69
Schneider, E. L., 5
Schneider, L., 168

Schön, D., 27, 36
Schwalberg, R., 153
Schwartz, W. B, 5
service credit banking, 151, 158–60, 162, 188, 190–91
Shapiro, R., 27
Shaugnessy, P. W., 13
Shepherd, S., 87
Sherwood, S., 8
Shield, R. R., 13
S/HMOs, 11–13, 45–51
Silow-Carroll, S., 38
Simon, H., 66, 67
Simon-Rusinowitz, L., 152
Sirrocco, A., 4
skilled nursing care, 9–11, 37, 104, 117. See also nursing home care
Skitka, L., 42
Skocpol, T., 55
Skolbekken, J., 82
Slovic, P., 66
Smith, S. Rathgeb, 36
Smith, T., 42
Smithey, R., 33, 68
Smyth, K., 6
Sniderman, P., 31
social/health maintenance organizations (S/HMOs), 11–13, 45–51
social insurance, 95, 107; partnership programs and, 121–22
social policy, 79, 97, 103, 109; community standards and, 81; cultural diversity and, 77; dichotomy and, 31; metaphorical reasoning and, 36–37
Social Security, 95, 154
social welfare: individual responsibility and, 95; self-interest and, 62–74
Soldo, B. J., 161
Somers, S. A., 8, 116
Spector, W. D., 15, 16
spending down, and Medicaid, 10, 14, 118, 131, 146
Stallard, E., 5, 12
Standard of Living Preservation Principle, 101
Starr, P., 38

states: home care progams in, 153; insurance innovation and, 115, 117–18, 124–27; insurance regulation and, 10, 126, 144; Medicaid and, 9, 10, 15, 28, 122, 128, 168; public-private partnerships and, 131; reciprocity agreements between, 123, 128; service credit banking in, 159–60
Steiner, G., 32
Stimson, J., 27
Stone, D., 27, 35, 36, 38, 63
Stone, R., 7, 160, 176
Strudler, M., 142
Struyk, R. J., 4
Sutherland, S., 157–58

tax incentives, 131, 132, 134, 190; employers and, 138–41; individuals and, 141–42
Technology Assessment, Office of, 3
Tell, E. J., 8
Temkin-Greener, H., 8
Tennstedt, S. L., 7
Tesh, S. N., 82
Tetlock, P., 42
"third-sector" organizations, 33
Tversky, A., 66

United Health Care (Calif.), 127
utilitarianism, 95
utility theory, 65–67

Verbrugge, L. M., 5
Veterans Affairs, Department of (DVA), 9, 11, 151
Vogel, R., 106
vouchers, for long-term care, 90; survey on, 42, 44–51, 57

waiting periods, for private insurance benefits, 8
Waldo, D. R., 14
Walker, L., 10, 71, 169, 176, 188–89, 191
Wallack, S. S., 8, 106, 189
Ware, J. E., 13

Washington state, estate planning and, 168
Watson Wyatt Worldwide, 140
Weisbrod, B., 68
Weissert, W. G., 6
welfare economics, 62–64, 69, 71–74, 95
welfare reform, 34
wellness programs, 3–4
Wenneker, M. B., 82
West, C., 77
Wetle, T., 118
Wiener, J. M., 6, 8, 9, 11, 13, 14, 15, 31, 33, 135, 137, 139, 140, 142, 144, 145, 179, 186, 189
Wiker, G., 153
Wildfire, J. B., 4

Wilkinson, A. M., 11
Williams, T. F., 8
Wilson, K. B., 4
Wilson, W. J., 77
Wisconsin, service credit banking in, 158
Wofford, H., 38, 128
Woloshin, S., 77
Wu, F. H., 79

Yabate, S., 4
Yee, D. L., 78, 183, 184
Yip, A., 82

Zaller, J., 27, 31
Zashin, E., 26
Zawadski, R. T., 12